# FIELDING'S
# BERMUDA

# The Buzz About Fielding...

## Fielding Worldwide

"The new Fielding guidebook style mirrors the style of the company's new publisher: irreverent, urbane, adventuresome and in search of the unique travel experience."

**—San Diego Union Tribune**

"Individualistic, entertaining, comprehensive."

**—Consumers Digest**

"Guidebooks straight from the hip."

**—Cincinnati Enquirer**

"Guidebooks with attitude."

**—Dallas Morning News**

"Full of author's tips and asides, the books seem more personal and more credible than many similarly encyclopedic tomes."

**—Los Angeles Times**

"At Fielding Worldwide, adventurous might well be the order of the day."

**—Des Moines Register**

"Biting travel guides give readers a fresh look."

**—Houston Chronicle**

"For over 30 years Fielding guides have been the standard of modern travel books."

**—Observer Times**

"These guidebooks have attitude."

**—Tampa Tribune**

"Guidebooks not afraid to show honesty."

**—Deseret News, Salt Lake City**

## Fielding's Las Vegas Agenda

"A concise but detailed look at the capital of glitter and gambling."

**—Atlanta Journal Constitution**

## Fielding's Los Angeles Agenda

"...contains much more than the standard travel guide. The lists of theatres, sports arenas and attractions are worth the book's price by itself."

**—Baton Rouge Advocate**

## Fielding's New York Agenda

"Loaded with advice... puts the whole of the Big Apple in hand."

**—Bon Appetit**

## Fielding's Guide to Worldwide Cruises

"...Lots of tips and inside information on each ship ... valuable beginner's information on the cruise life and choosing a cruise. Very detailed."

**—Los Angeles Times**

"... insightful, always independent, frequently witty and occasionally irreverent personal reviews..."

**—Cruise and Vacation Views**

"... Whereas the term 'expert' is thrown about with abandon when it comes to travel writing, these two are the real deal. Harry and Shirley are cruise *experts*.'"

**—Salt Lake City Tribune**

"You can trust them [Fielding] to tell the truth. It's fun—and very informative."

**—New Orleans Times-Picayune**

"... If you have space for only one cruise guidebook in your library, it should be this one."

**—Cruise Travel Magazine**

## Cruise Insider

"One of the best, most compact, yet interesting books about cruising today is the fact-filled *Cruise Insider*."

**—John Clayton's Travel With a Difference**

## Fielding's The World's Most Dangerous Places

"Rarely does a travel guide turn out to be as irresistible as a John Grisham novel. But *The World's Most Dangerous Places*, a 1000-page tome for the truly adventurous traveler, manages to do just that."

**—Arkansas Democrat-Gazette**

"A travel guide that could be a real lifesaver. Practical tips for those seeking the road less traveled."

**—Time Magazine**

"The greatest derring do of this year's memoirs."

—*Publishers Weekly*

"Reads like a first-run adventure movie."

—*Travel Books Worldwide*

"One of the oddest and most fascinating travel books to appear in a long time."

—*The New York Times*

"…publishing terra incognito…a primer on how to get in and out of potentially lethal places."

—*U.S. News and World Report*

"Tired of the same old beach vacation?…this book may be just the antidote."

—*USA Today*

"Guide to hot spots will keep travelers glued to their armchairs."

—*The Vancouver Sun*

## Fielding's Borneo

"One of a kind…a guide that reads like an adventure story."

—*San Diego Union*

## Fielding's Budget Europe

"This is a guide to great times, great buys and discovery in 18 countries."

-*Monroe News-Star*

"…meticulous detail…incisive commentary."

—*Travel Europe*

## Fielding's Caribbean

"If you have trouble deciding which regional guidebook to reach for, you can't go wrong with *Fielding's Caribbean*."

—*Washington Times*

"Opinionated, clearly written and probably the only guide that any visitor to the Caribbean really needs."

—*The New York Times*

## Fielding's Europe

"Synonymous with the dissemination of travel information for five decades."

—*Traveller's Bookcase*

"The definitive Europe… shame on you if you don't read it before you leave."

—*Travel Europe*

## Fielding's Far East

"This well respected guide is thoroughly updated and checked out."

—*The Reader Review*

## Fielding's France

"Winner of the annual 'Award of Excellence' [with Michelin and Dorling Kindersley]."

—*FrancePresse*

## Fielding's Freewheelin' USA

"…an informative, thorough and entertaining 400-page guide to the sometimes maligned world of recreational vehicle travel."

—*Travel Weekly*

"…very comprehensive… lots more fun than most guides of this sort…"

—*Los Angeles Times*

## Fielding's Italy

"A good investment…contains excellent tips on driving, touring, cities, etc."

—*Travel Savvy*

## Fielding's Mexico

"Among the very best."

—*Library Journal*

## Fielding's Spain and Portugal

"Our best sources of information were fellow tour-goers and *Fielding's Spain and Portugal*."

—*The New York Times*

## Vacation Places Rated

"…can best be described as a thinking person's guide if used to its fullest."

—*Chicago Tribune*

"Tells how 13,500 veteran vacationers rate destinations for satisfaction and how well a destination delivers on what is promised."

—*USA Today*

## Fielding's Vietnam

"Fielding has the answer to every conceivable question."

—*Destination Vietnam*

"An important book about an important country."

—*NPR Business Radio*

# Fielding Titles

Fielding's Alaska Cruises and the Inside Passage
Fielding's Asia's Top Dive Sites
Fielding's Amazon
Fielding's Australia
Fielding's Bahamas
Fielding's Baja
Fielding's Bermuda
Fielding's Borneo
Fielding's Budget Europe
Fielding's Caribbean
Fielding's Caribbean Cruises
Fielding's Disney World and Orlando
Fielding's Diving Indonesia
Fielding's Eastern Caribbean
Fielding's England
Fielding's Europe
Fielding's European Cruises
Fielding's Far East
Fielding's France
Fielding's Freewheelin' USA
Fielding's Kenya
Fielding's Hawaii
Fielding's Italy
Fielding's Las Vegas Agenda
Fielding's London Agenda
Fielding's Los Angeles
Fielding's Malaysia and Singapore
Fielding's Mexico
Fielding's New Orleans Agenda
Fielding's New York Agenda
Fielding's New Zealand
Fielding's Paradors, Pousadas and Charming Villages
        of Spain and Portugal
Fielding's Paris Agenda
Fielding's Portugal
Fielding's Rome Agenda
Fielding's San Diego Agenda
Fielding's Southeast Asia
Fielding's Southern Vietnam on Two Wheels
Fielding's Spain
Fielding's Surfing Indonesia
Fielding's Sydney Agenda
Fielding's Thailand, Cambodia, Laos & Myanmar
Fielding's Vacation Places Rated
Fielding's Vietnam
Fielding's Western Caribbean
Fielding's The World's Most Dangerous Places
Fielding's Worldwide Cruises

# FIELDING'S
# BERMUDA

By
Joyce Wiswell

Cruise Section
By
Shirley Slater & Harry Basch

Fielding Worldwide, Inc.
308 South Catalina Avenue
Redondo Beach, California  90277 U.S.A.

Fielding's Bermuda

Published by Fielding Worldwide, Inc.

Text Copyright ©1997 FWI

Icons & Illustrations Copyright ©1997 FWI

Photo Copyrights ©1997 to Individual Photographers

Some maps ©MAGELLAN Geographix, Santa Barbara, California, Telephone (800) 929-4MAP, www.magellangeo.com

## FIELDING WORLDWIDE INC.

| | |
|---|---|
| PUBLISHER AND CEO | **Robert Young Pelton** |
| GENERAL MANAGER | **John Guillebeaux** |
| MARKETING DIRECTOR | **Paul T. Snapp** |
| OPERATIONS DIRECTOR | **George Posanke** |
| ELEC. PUBLISHING DIRECTOR | **Larry E. Hart** |
| PUBLIC RELATIONS DIRECTOR | **Beverly Riess** |
| ACCOUNT SERVICES MANAGER | **Christy Harp** |
| PROJECT MANAGER | **Chris Snyder** |

### EDITORS

**Kathy Knoles**                    **Linda Charlton**

**Reed Parsell**

### PRODUCTION

**Martin Mancha**                    **Alfredo Mercado**

**Ramses Reynoso**                    **Craig South**

| | |
|---|---|
| COVER DESIGNED BY | **Digital Artists, Inc.** |
| COVER PHOTOGRAPHERS—Front | **Martin Barraud/Tony Stone Images** |
| Back | **Bermuda Department of Tourism** |
| INSIDE PHOTOS | **Bermuda Department of Tourism** |
| AUTHOR'S PHOTO | **Kim Reierson** |
| ILLUSTRATED 3-D MAPS | **Paul Carbo** |

Inquiries should be addressed to: Fielding Worldwide, Inc., 308 South Catalina Ave., Redondo Beach, California 90277 U.S.A., Telephone (310) 372-4474, Facsimile (310) 376-8064, 8:30 a.m.–5:30 p.m. Pacific Standard Time.
Website: http://www.fieldingtravel.com
e-mail: fielding@fieldingtravel.com

### ISBN 1-56952-107-7

Printed in the United States of America

# Letter from the Publisher

In 1946, Temple Fielding began the first of what would be a remarkable new series of well-written, highly personalized guidebooks for independent travelers. Temple's opinionated, witty, and oft-imitated books have now guided travelers for almost a half-century. More important to some was Fielding's humorous and direct method of steering travelers away from the dull and the insipid. Today, Fielding Travel Guides are still written by experienced travelers for experienced travelers. Our authors carry on Fielding's reputation for creating travel experiences that deliver insight with a sense of discovery and style.

Joyce Wiswell presents a unique perspective on Bermuda. She has tackled the daunting task of giving the reader a balanced overview of the island as well as highlighting the outstanding attractions. You'll find the famous, as well as the often overlooked, all rated and reviewed in our easy-to-use agenda format.

The concept of independent travel has never been bigger. Our policy of *brutal honesty* and a highly personal point of view has never changed; it just seems the travel world has caught up with us.

RYP

Robert Young Pelton
Publisher and CEO
Fielding Worldwide, Inc.

# DEDICATION

To my mother, Elaine, and in loving memory of my father, Glenn.

# ACKNOWLEDGMENTS

Many thanks to those who helped with my travel and research in Bermuda, especially Charles Webbe of the Bermuda Department of Tourism, Peter Firth of the Southampton Princess and Muriel Richardson of Rosedon—good ambassadors all.

# ABOUT THE AUTHOR

**Joyce Wiswell**

Joyce Wiswell has been writing about travel for more than 15 years. Various writing assignments have taken her to nearly every state in the union, as well as China, Hong Kong, the Philippines, Thailand, Europe, and, of course, throughout the Caribbean. Her work has appeared in numerous magazines and newspapers. Wiswell is also the author of *Fielding's Las Vegas Agenda*, *Fielding's Western Caribbean* and *Fielding's Caribbean*.

A native of New Jersey, she is a magna cum laude graduate of Connecticut's Quinnipiac College. After paying her dues as a magazine writer and editor in New York City for eight years, she fled for life in California, where she lives happily in Santa Barbara. When not traveling, she putters in the garden and pampers her cats, and worries unduly about both when on the road.

# Fielding Rating Icons

The Fielding Rating Icons are highly personal and awarded to help the besieged traveler choose from among the dizzying array of activities, attractions, hotels, restaurants and sights. The awarding of an icon denotes unusual or exceptional qualities in the relevant category.

**RATINGS:** Fielding Award, Author Selection, Quality, Money Saver, Expensive, Inexpensive, Warning, Danger, Spacious, Cramped, Mild Disapproval

**WHERE TO STAY:** Simple, Luxurious, Cottage, Homey, Scenic, Business, Honeymoon, Chateau

**CULTURAL:** Museum/Art, Interesting Architecture, History, Book Reference, Artistically Important, Musically Interesting, Theatre, Crafts

**INTERESTS:** Singles, Romantic, Spectacular Cuisine, Wine Tasting, Shopping, Nightlife, Cafe Stops, Pro Sports

**SIGHTS:** Picturesque, Great Scenery, Market, Beaches/Resorts, Cultural, Fortress, Castles, Church

**TRAVEL TIPS:** Arrival/Departure, By Air, By Water, By Train, By Car, Bus/Local Transit, Calendar, Itinerary, Kids, Compass

**ACTIVITIES:** Relaxing, Workout, General Sports, Water Sports, Sailing, Swimming, Hiking, Walking, Cycling, Horseback Riding, Golf, Tennis, Scuba Diving, Snorkeling/Diving, Deep-sea Fishing, Freshwater Fishing

# TABLE OF CONTENTS

# LIST OF MAPS

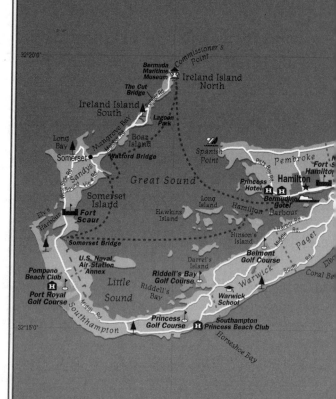

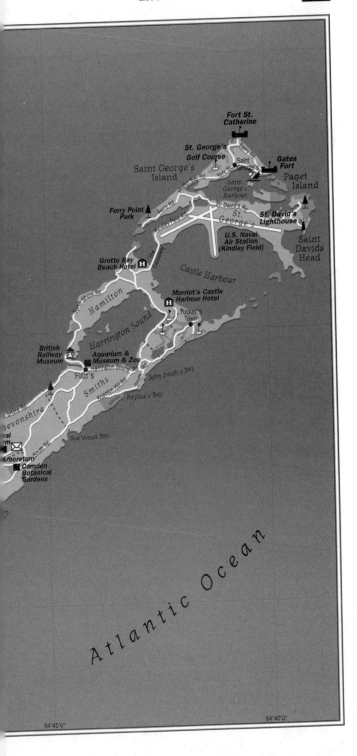

# INTRODUCTION

*Bermuda is famous for its stunning pink sand beaches.*

*"All the people who live on the said islands are very vicious but friendly when intoxicated, especially when Spanish wine, which they like, reaches the island."*

Perhaps Simon Zacharias, who made that observation of Bermuda in 1620, was right at the time, but his words could not be more off the mark today—except, possibly, that many Bermudians still like a good taste of Spanish wine. In fact, the astounding politeness of the people and their gracious hospitality are among the first things visitors to Bermuda notice. That is, once they stop gawking, hang-jawed, at the incredible beauty of the place. Sparkling water beckons from every vantage point, giant boulders jut up from the sea as if placed by the hand of an artistic giant, and stunning beaches await with their signature pink sand. It's hard to believe a more manicured locale can exist. Virtually every home oozes charm, front yards resemble botanical gardens, steeped white roofs and pastel colors are de rigueur, and cottages and mansions of the 17th and 18th centuries look as if they've just been fixed up for the cover of *Better Homes and Gardens.*

Unlike many destinations, this is not a manufactured charm, a mere facade to keep the tourists coming. Inside those impeccable homes is the same gracious living their outer appearance suggests. Bermudians enjoy one of the highest standards of living in the world, which they do not take for granted, but strive to maintain. The people are highly literate, hard-working and, above all, proud of their tidy little paradise.

They are also unfailingly polite—to each other, and to visitors. In fact, it is considered rude to begin an exchange—even one as innocuous as "Where's the ferry?" without first uttering the requisite "Good morning" or "Good afternoon." Though they must share their narrow and sinuous roadways with tourists who can barely negotiate their motor bikes, there's rarely heard the tooting of a horn or an impatient word. They'll simply wait till the coast is clear, then zoom around the hapless rider.

Bermuda's unique style is heavily influenced by its mother country of Great Britain, though many wags believe that Bermuda is actually more British than England itself. It's a real tribute to the colony that, despite the proximity to and heavy influx of visitors from the United States, it resists all efforts to become homogenized. There is just one fast-food outlet on the island and, despite the inevitable Benetton, virtually no chain stores. Though they get every U.S. network on their vast television cable system, Bermudian accents remain intact—and highly recognizable as British. And they have a dress code all their own—men in brightly colored Bermuda shorts, complete with matching tie and knee socks.

All of which make a visit to Bermuda an irresistible pleasure. The island is gorgeous, the beaches divine, the golf courses challenging, the restaurants sophisticated, the accommodations plush. There's just enough nightlife for those who seek such revelry, but, like all Bermuda, it's discreet, never overwhelming. The only drawback to a Bermuda holiday—and it can be a big one—is that such charms do not come cheap. Bermuda can be terribly expensive—but you do get what you pay for.

# WHAT'S NEW

*The power suit on the island includes Bermuda shorts.*

Those familiar with Bermuda know that it's a very stable destination; although the occasional restaurant changes hands and hotels are constantly in the process of being spiffed up, not much really changes on this lovely isle. A hotel moratorium assures that overdevelopment won't compromise Bermuda's many charms.

The Southampton Princess has added a three-acre habitat for six bottlenose dolphins on hotel grounds at East Whale Bay. The already-captive dolphins came from other such facilities, not the open ocean. Hotel guests can enter a lottery to experience a "Dolphin Encounter," in which they can swim and frolic with the creatures. But, if you'd rather not take a chance with the lottery, book a package that guarantees you a spot. (At press time, prices were not yet determined.) Meanwhile, the resort is spending $25 million through 1998 on renovations, including new green-colored decor in all guest rooms, as well as the addition of minibars and a second phone line with a speaker phone and data port.

In other hotel news, the Sonesta Beach Hotel & Spa, also in Southampton, has a brand-new marble-accented lobby that's quite pleasing and elegant. All guest rooms were redone in 1995 in shades of pinks and greens. The former Palm Court Bar has been turned into a sports bar, and changing rooms have been added to accommodate those with late flights. A children's pool has been added near the playground, and landscaping has been enhanced throughout the sprawling property.

The Hamilton Princess, a downtown landmark, has added 33 mini-suites for a total of 60. The new accommodations are designed with the business traveler in mind; the hotel primarily caters to individual and group business travelers.

# HOW TO USE THIS GUIDE

*Set on a cliff overlooking the beach in Southampton, The Whaler Inn offers delicious fish, spectacular views and Dixieland jazz.*

When planning a trip to Bermuda, one of your biggest considerations will be expense. Though it is a lovely spot to get away from it all in grand style, you'll pay the price for such pleasure. The prices listed in this guide were current as we went to press, but keep in mind they are constantly on the rise, with room rates usually going up at least $10 each year.

## Restaurants

The "Restaurant" chapter details all kinds of eateries, from elegant gourmet rooms to little holes-in-the-wall, and everything in between. The following guide is based on the per-person cost of a complete dinner, excluding alcoholic beverages.

| | |
|---|---|
| **Expensive:** | **More than $50** |
| **Moderate:** | **$25 to $50** |

# Hotels

The section on "Hotels" lists every property on Bermuda, from the posh resorts to the more-affordable guest houses and efficiency units. As detailed in that chapter, Bermuda offers a huge cross-section of accommodations, and is unique in its up-scale cottage colonies. Note that virtually every property tacks on a hefty daily service charge in addition to the published rates. The following gives you an idea of what it costs for a standard room for two on the European Plan (no meals), per day.

| | |
|---|---|
| Expensive: | More than $200 |
| Moderate: | $100–$200 |
| Inexpensive: | Less than $100 |

# Ratings

Fielding rates all hotels, restaurants and attractions (with the exception of sporting activities) with a star system of one to five. Obviously, ratings are highly subjective. Keep in mind that more stars does not necessarily mean more expensive.

| | |
|---|---|
| ★★★★★ | Doesn't get any better |
| ★★★★ | Excellent |
| ★★★ | Good |
| ★★ | Fair to middling |
| ★ | Nothing to write home about |

You'll note that not one entry in this book has just one star—an indication of just how special Bermuda is.

HOW TO USE THIS GUIDE

# THE BERMUDA TRIANGLE

*Secluded Jobson's Cove is a romantic hideaway.*

The Bermuda Triangle—an area between Florida, Puerto Rico and Bermuda—has intrigued people for years. According to legend, scores of ships and planes have disappeared from the area for no apparent reason. As far back as the discovery by Europeans of the New World, sea captains have logged unusual forces—usually electromagnetic—in the area. Even Christopher Columbus described an erratic compass, a great flame of fire and the appearance of a strange light in the Sargasso Sea, in the area now known as the Bermuda Triangle. Interest in the phenomenon peaked in the 1970s, when a slew of books, articles and television movies explored the sensational topic.

What makes the mystery especially puzzling is that many of the vanishing vessels left literally no trace—no wreckage, no survivors, not a scrap of clothing nor a slick of oil. Equally perplexing is how many disappearances occurred in good weather. In some instances, messages from aircraft gave no hint of trouble, but then simply vanished forever once entering the Triangle.

Even some vessels that traveled the Triangle unscathed have given eerie reports. For instance, according to the book *Without a Trace*, by Charles Belitz (the follow-up to his best-seller, *The Bermuda Triangle*), a Beechcraft Bonanza flew into a huge cumulus cloud off the Bahamian island of Andros and lost radio contact. Contact was regained four minutes later and the plane was then over Miami, with 25 more gallons of gas than it should have had—almost exactly the amount of gas it would have burned for the Andros–Miami trip. In another instance, a National Airlines 727 was lost on radar for 10 minutes, during which time the pilots reported flying through a light fog. Upon landing, all watches on board, and the plane's chronometer, had lost exactly 10 minutes—despite a time check half an hour before landing. In some cases, shipmasters sighting other ships at sea have entered their names in logs, only to later learn those ships had long been listed as sunk or disappeared.

Indisputably, the Bermuda Triangle is an area of magnetic aberration that frequently causes compass needles to spin, gyros to malfunction and radio communication to be sporadically interrupted. Many oceanographers and meteorologists attribute the mysterious wrecks to sudden weather changes and believe the lack of wreckage is due to the flow of the Gulf Stream. Other theories range from the mundane to the far out—freak seas, sea quakes, waterspouts, tidal waves, time warps, reverse gravity fields and even UFO abductions.                                    •

Lawrence David Kusche, author of *The Bermuda Triangle Mystery—Solved*, maintains that logical explanations have appeared for most of the mysterious incidents, and points out that ocean disappearances are hardly unique—just more publicized when they occur in the Triangle. He adds that many disasters occurred late in the afternoon or at night, so by the time rescuers arrived on the scene all wreckage had vanished. "The legend of the Bermuda Triangle," Kusche concludes, "is a manufactured mystery."

# TRAVELER'S GUIDE

*Bermudians and tourists find mopeds and scooters a great way of getting around the island.*

## When to Go

Bermuda's climate is semitropical, with annual rainfall of 57.6 inches. High season is May through October, when the temperature averages in the 80s Fahrenheit. This is when you'll pay the highest rates and share attractions with the most visitors. The off season is November through March, when you'll find lower rates, cooler temps and less humidity. Though it's usually too cold for the beach, the weather is ideal for golf and tennis.

Visitors during January, February and March enjoy a Temperature Guarantee Program that lops 10 percent off daily room rates on days when the temperature fails to reach 68°F. You'll also get free admission to many attractions and a one-day transportation pass for free travel on island buses and ferries. Twenty-six hotels participate in the program as well as most major attractions. Another advantage to off-season travel is the Dine-Around

Program, in which many restaurants offer discounted meals for a set price.

Expect springlike temperatures from November through March, with a few warmer days thrown in for good measure. To attract tourists during this low season, the country has a number of special events. February, for instance, is Golden Rendezvous Month, designed for the older traveler, with lectures on Bermuda's folklore, culture and flora and fauna, as well as bridge games, special tours and discount coupons to attractions. The Bermuda Festival, which takes place each January and February, is a series of cultural events with performances by noted groups such as the Royal Danish Ballet and Vienna Boys Choir. There are also lots of special sporting events, including the November to March Visitor Tournament with weekly prizes for golfers.

# Getting There

## By Air

Bermuda is serviced by American, Continental, Delta, USAir and British Airways from the United States, by Air Canada from Toronto, and by British Airways from London, South America and the Caribbean. It takes about two hours to fly to the islands from New York.

## By Sea

A number of cruise lines pull into Bermuda for several hours of exploring the islands' treasures. Most ships dock at the capital city of Hamilton, whereas others may pull into the Dockyard or St. George's.

If you've disdained the idea of cruising in the past, you may want to reconsider. It's a tremendously relaxing vacation, with all meals and onboard activities included in one price (drinks and tips, however, typically are extra). Cruise ships carry several dozen passengers all the way up to several thousand; the industry trend is toward much larger ships. The advantage is more activities and dining outlets; the disadvantage is that it can be hard to make friends on a floating city, as you may never run into the same people twice. Prices vary drastically by line, time of year and stateroom; if you can set sail on short notice (two to three weeks), you'll really save big. See "Cruising to Bermuda."

### Entry and Departure Procedures

Proof of citizenship is required to enter Bermuda. A passport is preferred, but U.S. citizens can get away with an original birth certificate or voter's registration card with a photo ID. You must show a return or onward ticket to prove you're not about to make Bermuda your new home. (Emigrating here is very difficult.) Canadians must show a passport, original birth certificate or certificate of citizenship. If you're coming from a country that is infected with smallpox, you'll need to show a vaccination certificate.

Visitors may bring in for their personal use and consumption 50 cigars, 200 cigarettes, one pound of tobacco, one quart of liquor and one quart of wine, all duty-free. Smokers should definitely bring their own cigarettes, which are at least double U.S. prices here (about $4.50 a pack at press time).

Departure tax is $20, collected in cash at the Bermuda Airport. To save time when leaving, you can purchase a voucher at any licensed hotel or guest house or from the airline counter at the airport. Children under two are exempt from the departure tax, and the $60 tax for cruise ship passengers is included in the overall fare. All hotels charge a 7.25 percent occupancy tax, while most also tack on a daily service charge.

### Pets

Small dogs, cats and other pets are permitted in the country only with a permit, secured in advance from the Department of Agriculture (*P.O. Box HM834, Hamilton HM CX, Bermuda*).

# What to Pack

Bermuda is not stuffy, but it is a lot more formal than the islands of the Bahamas and the Caribbean. Conservative dress is the norm—no bathing suits, cropped shirts or ultra-short shorts outside the pool or beach. Other no-nos: bare feet, hair in curlers, shirtless men, or women in swimsuit tops with shorts or skirts. Many restaurants and nightclubs require men to wear a jacket and tie in the evening, especially during the summer season. The basic rule of thumb is "smart casual," which means upscale sporty clothes.

If you're visiting from May to mid-November, pack summer-weight sports clothes, a raincoat or light windbreaker and casual but elegant clothes for evening. In the cooler months, December to late March, bring light woolens or fall-weight casuals, sweaters and a raincoat or warm jacket. Men don't necessarily need a suit, but shouldn't forget that mandatory jacket and tie(s).

Be sure to leave room in your bag for the stuff you'll be lugging home—there are good deals on imported merchandise, such as English bone china, Swiss watches, French perfumes, Danish silver and jewelry, Italian silks and cashmere sweaters. Locally made goodies include cedarware, pottery, blown glass and artwork. But be warned that prices are quite high throughout the island.

Naturally, you'll want to bring along any special medications, but rest assured you'll easily find over-the-counter items such as aspirin and feminine hygiene products with no problem.

| Temperature Chart | | | |
|---|---|---|---|
| **Month** | **Air Temp**<br>(°F, low/high) | **Sea Temp**<br>(°F) | **Rainfall**<br>(inches) |
| January | 60–69 | 64 | 6.0 |
| February | 59–69 | 64 | 4.7 |
| March | 60–69 | 65 | 4.6 |
| April | 62–71 | 69 | 4.5 |
| May | 66–77 | 75 | 2.3 |
| June | 71–80 | 79 | 4.1 |
| July | 75–84 | 83 | 4.0 |
| August | 76–86 | 84 | 4.1 |
| September | 74–84 | 80 | 4.8 |
| October | 71–80 | 76 | .6 |
| November | 67–75 | 70 | 3.7 |
| December | 61–71 | 67 | 4.5 |

*Gombey Dancers in colorful costumes celebrate many festivals.*

## Holidays/Festivals

Public holidays include New Year's Day, Good Friday, Bermuda Day (May 24), the Queen's Birthday (Mid-June), Labor Day (September), Cup Match & Somers Day (early August), Remembrance Day (November 11), Christmas and Boxing Day (December 26). Public holidays that fall on the weekend are normally observed the following Monday. On public holidays, as well as Sundays, all businesses and many shops and restaurants are closed, and buses and ferries operate on a limited schedule.

## Major Festivals

### January

**ADT Bermuda Race Weekend**
International and local athletes compete in foot races, including a marathon, half marathon and 10K.

**Bermuda Festival**
Classical music, jazz, dance, drama and pop concerts by international artists; continues through February.

### February

**Golf Tournaments**
Amateur duffers tee off in a tournament and golf festival.

### March

**Annual Street Festival**
Hamilton's Front Street becomes a colorful carnival with music, crafts and a fashion show.

### April

**Open Houses and Gardens**
Bermuda homes and gardens are open every Wednesday afternoon to visitors; continues in May.

**Agricultural Show**
A three-day exhibit of the island's best fruits, flowers and vegetables, as well as equestrian events.

**Peppercorn Ceremony**
The Masonic Lodge of Bermuda pays its annual rent for its headquarters, the Old State House, with lots of pomp and circumstance.

### May

**Beating Retreat Ceremonies**
A historical, musical military reenactment that runs through October (except August) and alternates between St. George's and the Royal Naval Dockyard.

**Invitational International Race Week**
Locals compete with yachtsmen from the United States, Canada and the United Kingdom.

**Bermuda Day**
A public holiday that celebrates all things Bermudian, with a parade, marathon and cycle and fitted-dinghy races.

### June

**Queen's Birthday**
A public holiday honoring the Queen of England and a good excuse for a military parade on Front Street in Hamilton.

**Boat Races**
In even years, yachtsmen from around the world compete in the famous Newport-Bermuda Yacht Race, while the Bermuda Ocean Race includes 45 blue-water racing and cruising yachts racing from Annapolis, Maryland.

## Major Festivals

### July

| | |
|---|---|
| **SOCA** | A Caribbean concert held annually in the Royal Naval Dockyard. |
| **Cup Match Cricket Festival** | A public holiday and two-day match between the east- and west-end cricket clubs. |

### August

| | |
|---|---|
| **Bermuda Reggae Sunsplash** | Local and Jamaican musicians keep the island swaying. |

### September

| | |
|---|---|
| **Bermuda Horse & Pony Association Fall Show** | Flat, jumping, western and driving classes and exhibitions. |

### October

| | |
|---|---|
| **Annual Bermuda Triathlon** | This annual sporting event is open to all as teams or individuals. |

### November

| | |
|---|---|
| **Convening of Parliament** | Traditional ceremony and a military guard of honor accompany this annual event, overseen by His Excellency the Governor. |
| **Bermuda Tattoo** | Lots of pomp and ceremony, as well as historical reenactments and a fireworks show. |
| **Remembrance Day** | A public holiday with parades to honor the men and women who died in service to their country. |

### December

| | |
|---|---|
| **Santa Claus Parades** | Three gala parades with bands, floats and good old St. Nick. |

# Getting Around

### By Moped

One of the things that sets Bermuda apart from other islands is that **visitors can't rent a car**. The best way to get around is by moped or scooter. Keep in mind, however, that they can be dangerous and scores of tourists are injured (though seldom seriously) each year. Bermuda's narrow, winding roads nearly always lack a shoulder (or even a sidewalk), and it can be tricky to get the hang of a moped. Nearly all rental dealers have a practice course, and it is highly recommended you take at least a few spins around until you feel comfortable enough to hit the road. Helmets are required by law and supplied by the rental agent. You don't have to have a driver's license to rent a moped, but you must be at least 16 and have a major credit card; a cash deposit is often required as well. It costs about $40–$50 a day to rent a moped; they come in one- or two-seaters.

Remember: DRIVING IS ON THE LEFT. A solid yellow line on the road means no passing and no parking, a solid white line means it's okay to pass and park, and a jagged line means pedestrians have the right of way. The speed limit is 35 kilometers (20 miles) per hour; although many locals ignore this, it's recommended for tourists.

Gas stations are open from 7 a.m.–7 p.m. daily; some stay open until 11 p.m. or later. Like everything else in Bermuda, gas is terribly expensive—at least $4 per gallon. You're generally required to return your moped or scooter with a full tank of gas.

One of Bermuda's biggest crime problems is cycle theft. Be sure to always lock your bike and helmet, or take your helmet with you when dining or shopping.

### By Taxi

Cabs can be hired by the hour, day (defined as six consecutive daylight hours) or mile. The rates are the same for one to six people. All taxis are metered; it costs $4 for the first mile and $1.40 for each additional mile. It adds up quickly—you'll pay at least $20 to get from the South Shore resorts into Hamilton, and more at night, on Sundays and public holidays, when a 25 percent surcharge is in effect from 10 p.m. to 6 a.m. Luggage in the trunk (or boot, as they call it here) costs 25 cents per article. Tip 10–15 percent. Cabdrivers are generally a courteous and friendly bunch.

For sightseeing by taxi, plan on paying $20 per hour for one to four people and $30 for five or six. Taxis licensed to offer sightseeing tours are identified by a blue flag on the hood of the car.

You'll have no problem finding a taxi in the city of Hamilton or outside the major hotels. To call ahead for one, contact **Bermuda Taxi Operators** (☎ *[441] 292-5600*) or **Radio Cabs Bermuda** (☎ *[441]-295-4141*).

### By Bus

Bermuda has a good and efficient bus system, and it's much cheaper than traveling by taxi. Passengers must use exact change for the fare. The system is broken into 14 zones, each about two  miles long. Regular fare (adults over 13) is $2.50 for up to three zones and $4 for more than three zones. Children ages 3 to 13 pay $1 for all zones, whereas kids under 3 are always free. Bus stops are marked with a striped pole or stone shelter. The main **Central Bus Terminal** is in the city of Hamilton *at Washington and Church streets;* ☎ *(441) 292-3854.*

If you plan to ride the bus a lot, consider purchasing a three-($20) or seven-day ($32.50) Transportation Pass, which allows unlimited use of buses and ferries. It also eliminates fretting over the sometimes confusing zone system. They are sold at the Central Terminal, the Visitors Service Bureau in Hamilton and at authorized outlets. Bus and ferry schedules can be found in the lobby of most hotels.

## By Ferry

Ferries run to and from Hamilton, Paget, Warwick, Somerset and the Dockyard. They are a wonderful way to get around and are especially picturesque at night. Ferries run from about 7:15 a.m. to 11:30 p.m. weekdays; there is an abbreviated schedule on Sundays and public holidays. One-way fares: Hamilton to Paget and Warwick $2; Hamilton to Somerset and Dockyard $3.50. Children ages 3 to 12 pay $1; kids under 3 are free. Mopeds can be taken only onboard the Somerset/Dockyard ferry; there's a $3.50 charge. Bicycles can be brought aboard any ferry for free.

The main ferry terminal is on the Hamilton waterfront; call ☎ *(441) 295-4506.* When riding the ferry from Hamilton, pay by dropping a token in a turnstile—and make sure you get on the right ferry! When arriving in Hamilton, pay with a token when exiting the terminal. (If you're using a transportation pass, go to the window, where they'll give you a token to exit.) Ferry schedules are posted at each stop and in most of the complimentary tourist magazines. In the city of Hamilton, it's about a 10-minute walk from the ferry to the bus terminal.

## By Carriage

Horse-drawn carriages are available for hire by the half-hour. They are a romantic—albeit corny—way to see the city. Rates are $20 per half-hour for up to four passengers. Five or more passengers pay $5 each for a half-hour. Catch one on Hamilton's Front Street.

# Directory

### Electricity

Electricity is 100 volts, 60 cycles AC, the same as in the United States and Canada.

### Money

Legal tender is the Bermuda dollar, which is pegged to the U.S. dollar one to one. U.S. currency is accepted everywhere at face value, so there's no need to convert your dollars. American Express, Visa and MasterCard are the most frequently accepted credit cards (note, however, that many restaurants and even some hotels don't accept plastic). Diner's Club cards are also in use, but leave your Discover card at home. It's not accepted in many Bermuda establishments.

Some Automatic Teller Machines (ATMs) are part of the Cirrus and Plus networks; you can also use them to get cash off your credit card. Most major hotels will cash personal checks for guests, but limit the amount to $100 per day.

If you're a frequent visitor to the island, you may want to consider obtaining a Bermuda Club Visa card, for which participating restaurants, merchants and attractions offer 10 percent discounts and other goodies, such as free film developing. For information, call ☎ *(800) 847-7378.*

## Telephone

The area code is 441, which came into effect in late 1995 (before that it was 809). Direct dialing is possible to and from Bermuda worldwide. When using a pay phone, dial first and then drop in your coins once the party has answered.

Calling anywhere overseas is extremely expensive. Full rates are in effect from 10 a.m.–7 p.m., and the so-called "discount periods" won't save you much. It costs from 80 cents to $1.15 per minute to call the continental United States and $1 to $1.15 to phone Canada. Many 800 numbers can't be reached from Bermuda; instead, you can reach them via the "Call 400" service by replacing the 800 with a 400—but then these calls are not free and the usual rates apply. For more information on overseas calling, consult the Bermuda Telephone Directory, which details charges to nearly every country. Many hotels charge about $1 per local call.

## Tipping

Many hotels and guest houses add a (high) service charge to your bill, so extra tipping is not necessary; ask if you're not sure. Otherwise, the standard tip is 15 percent.

## Water

Water is safe to drink throughout Bermuda. Tourists are asked to conserve water.

## Mail

First-class mail to the United States and Canada is 60 cents for postcards and letters. Airmail leaves and arrives daily, but note it can take weeks for a simple postcard to reach the United States. If you don't want to take that chance, use Federal Express (☎ *[441] 295-3854).*

## Business Hours

Stores and businesses are open Monday through Saturday from 9 a.m.–5 p.m.; some later. Most stores close on Sunday and legal holidays. Most restaurants open at 11 a.m. weekdays and noon on Saturday. Many are closed on Sunday.

## Time

Bermuda is an hour later than Eastern Standard Time, and observes daylight-savings time from the first Sunday in April until the last Sunday in October, the same as in the United States.

## Getting Married in Bermuda

Couples who wish to take the plunge in Bermuda must plan ahead. First, file a Notice of Intended Marriage form with the Registrar General *(Government Administration Building, 30 Parliament Street, Hamilton HM 12, Bermuda;* ☎ *[441] 295-5151 or fax [441] 292-4568)*, accompanied by a fee of $150 in the form of a money order, cashier's check or bank draft (made payable to the Accountant General, Hamilton, Bermuda). Keep in mind that mail from the United States and Canada can take six to 10 days—at least. You can pick up one of the forms at Bermuda Department of Tourism offices throughout the United States; call ☎ *(800) 223-6106* in the United States and ☎ *(416) 923-9600* in Canada for the office nearest you.

After the Notice has been received by the Registrar General, it is published in two local newspapers. Assuming there is no formal objection, the Registry will issue a marriage license 14 days after receiving the Notice. The license remains valid for three months from the date of issue.

Civil ceremonies are performed at the elegant Marriage Room at the Registry by appointment only Monday through Friday, 10 a.m.–4 p.m., and Saturdays between 10 a.m. and noon. The fee is $153, which includes the ceremony and marriage certificate.

Non-Bermudians who wish to marry in a Roman Catholic church are considered on a case-by-case basis. Contact the Bishop of Hamilton, *P.O. Box HM 1191, Hamilton, HM EX, Bermuda.*

You can also have the ceremony at a number of hotels; the Sonesta has a particularly scenic spot that's perfect for taking your vows. Several firms supply wedding consultants to assist with details, including **The Wedding Salon** *(☎ [441] 292-6577)*, **The Bridal Suite** ☎ *[441] 238-0818)* and **Bermuda Wedding Association** *(☎ [441] 293-4033)*.

## Visitor Information

The **Department of Tourism** is in Hamilton at the Global House, *43 Church Street (P.O. Box HM 465, Hamilton, HM BX Bermuda)*. Radio Station VSB 1160 airs local music and information on special events. In the United States, call the Department of Tourism at ☎ *(800) 223-6106;* in Canada ☎ *(416) 923-9600* and in the United Kingdom ☎ *(071) 734-8813.*

# HISTORY AND CULTURE

*St. George's Unfinished Church is the island's most picturesque ruin.*

## A Brief History

The first known person to visit the uninhabited cluster of re-mote islands now called Bermuda was Spaniard Juan de Bermu-dez—and this was by accident, as his ship was wrecked there in 1503. Spain did not claim the land, however, and it was basically the province of pirates (an activity that continued well into the 18th century), whose nefarious activity gave Bermuda the nick-name "Isles of Devils." Seamen were terrified of Bermuda, not only because of the pirates (and supposed ghosts), but because its jagged coast and reefs could—and often did—rip a ship to shreds.

In 1609, Admiral Sir George Somers wrecked off the coast of what is today St. George. His ship, the *Sea Venture*, was carrying 150 British colonists to Jamestown, Virginia, which was in dire straits with rampant disease and starvation. William Shakespeare is thought to have based his play, *The Tempest*, on the harrowing shipwreck. Somers claimed the islands for England, but only stayed long enough to build two ships from his wrecked vessel to continue the journey to Jamestown.

Three years later, more settlers arrived from England, and in 1620 British colonial government was installed. In 1684, Bermuda became self-governing. Today it is the oldest self-governing British colony in the world. St. George's was the capital city from 1612 to 1815, but then the government was moved to the more central city of Hamilton (located in Pembroke Parish, not Hamilton). Islanders exploited slaves from the West Indies and Africa, but finally abolished slavery in 1834.

Farming was a major industry in the late 19th century, with large exports of the Bermuda onion. (To this day, Bermudians are known as "onions.") But that market died when American farmers learned how to successfully grow the vegetable themselves. Today, tourism is Bermuda's chief money-maker.

## Government and Economy

As the oldest British Colony, Bermuda follows the English mode of government, with a Parliamentary Democracy. In fact, theirs is the third-oldest in the world, after that of its mother country of England and then Iceland's. And while it is officially a dependency of England, Bermuda is self-governing and gets little economic assistance from Great Britain. The governor, appointed by the Queen of England, holds a primarily ceremonial position; the democratically elected premier wields the real power. The elected legislature, known as the Legislative Council, consists of a 40-person House of Assembly and an 11-member Senate. The conservative United Bermuda Party (UPB), formed in 1964, is currently in power; its chief rival is the liberal Progressive Labor Party (PLP), founded in 1963. Each of the island's nine parishes is managed separately by an advisory council. Justices and barristers wear the traditional wigs and robes associated with British government. Tourists are welcome to sit in at a session of the Assembly and Supreme Court at Sessions House (Parliament Street, Hamilton); call ☎ *(441) 292-7408* for a schedule.

There are more than 8000 offshore companies based on the island (only 275 are actually located in Bermuda), though tourism remains by far the biggest industry, bringing in some $450 million per year. The international companies are the island's second-largest source of employment. Other major economic drivers are the insurance, oil, computer software, shipping, communications and investment holding and finance industries. Major exports include pharmaceuticals, concentrates, essences and beverages. Some 80 percent of foodstuffs are imported, as are virtually all alcoholic beverages, clothing, furniture, fuel, motor vehicles and electrical appliances. Bermuda's major trading partners are the United States, Canada, Great Britain, the Netherlands and islands of the Caribbean. The island produces bananas, vegetables, citrus fruits, flowers and dairy products.

# The People

Some 58,460 people live in Bermuda on 20 of the colony's 150 islands. The population density is high—3054 people per square mile—though it doesn't seem that way to a visitor, thanks to the law that stipulates that only one member per household can own a car. The capital city of Hamilton has 2000 residents.

Bermudians have one of the world's highest standards of living, with a per-capita income of $20,420. Minimum wage is $8.75—substantially higher than that of the United States. However, many residents hold several jobs to meet the island's very steep prices; it's not just tourists who feel the pinch of Bermuda's high lifestyle.

About 61 percent of the population is black, and 39 percent is white. The largest minority group is the Portuguese. Some 64 percent of Bermudians have a heritage of several generations on the island, and everyone speaks English.

Though the races mingle peacefully, blacks do face a glass ceiling. One prominent hotel executive (who is white) summed it up well when he said, "We live together very well because everyone is so friendly and we're all very proud of the island. However, it's the whites who are making the money, though many blacks also do extremely well and there's a general spreading of the wealth. Blacks do face a glass ceiling—but the racism is firmly under the table."

Bermuda has one of the highest literacy rates (98 percent) in the world. School is mandatory for children from age 5 to 16, and many students go on to college in Canada or the United States. The island has just one center of higher education, Bermuda College, whose Hospitality and Culinary Institute of Bermuda runs—with smashing results—the Stonington Beach Hotel.

Bermuda has virtually no pollution and barely a piece of litter mars the well-tended lawns and gardens that make the island so picturesque. Outdoor advertising and neon signs are banned, and most hotels and guest houses are marked with little more than a discreet sign. Only one person per household may own a car (which weren't even allowed until 1947), so it's common to see the men of traditional families motor-scootering to work—rain or shine—while mom lugs the kids around in the car. If that's a trial, you'll never hear complaints—Bermudians are savvy enough to realize their small chain of islands are a gem, and they are determined to keep them that way.

Bermuda has more than 90 houses of worship, representing everything from Roman Catholic to Baha'i. Thirty-seven percent of the islanders are Anglican, followed by Roman Catholic (14 percent) and African Methodist Episcopal (Zion, 10 percent).

The islanders have retained much of the stiff-upper-lip properness of the English. Afternoon tea is a time-honored tradition—at least for the tourists. Dress is always proper, and people are exceedingly polite.

# Bird's-Eye View

*An aerial view of Tucker's Town beach*

Though it is generally referred to as one island, Bermuda actually consists of 150 islands and isles that form a fishhook shape. Located in the Atlantic Ocean 650 miles east of Cape Hatteras, North Carolina, Bermuda is not in the Caribbean, contrary to popular misconception. (The Caribbean is actually 1000 miles to the south.) Bermuda's land mass stretches over 21 miles in a northwest to southwest formation. Just 20 islands are inhabited, most connected by causeways and bridges and so close together you barely realize you're changing islands. An efficient ferry system also links many islands.

Bermuda has 79 national parks and nature reserves that stretch from east to west, creating a ribbon of green—though virtually the entire colony is so lush and verdant that the parks just seem like a natural extension. The terrain is hilly, though the highest point (Town Hill) only stands 260 feet above sea level. The best of the island's 34 beaches are along the South Shore, which slopes to the sea, so you'll often have to negotiate a steep hill or stairway to reach the ocean.

Bermuda has no rivers or freshwater lakes, so all drinking water comes from rainfall, captured in underground tanks by the ingeniously designed, white-steeped limestone roofs that grace each house. Nearly all residents supply their own water. Annual rainfall is 57.6 inches. While October is the wettest month, rainfall is generally scattered throughout the year. The average daily temperature is 70°F.

The island is amazingly clean and tidy; it's rare to spot litter, graffiti or other eyesores. In fact, neon signs and outdoor advertising are forbidden by law. Smog is nonexistent thanks to a law that allows only one car per household. Hotel development is restricted under a moratorium that forbids new properties and limits the expansion of current ones to 10,000 beds.

Bermuda is broken into nine parishes: Sandys, Southampton, Warwick, Paget, Devonshire, Pembroke, Smith's, St. George's and Hamilton. It can be confusing for a visitor to remember that the capital city of Hamilton is actually located in Pembroke Parish—not Hamilton Parish. (It helps that locals will always assume visitors inquiring about Hamilton are referring to the city—which, for all practical purposes, will usually be the case.)

# THE PARISHES

*St. George's St. Peter's Church is one of the most photographed sights.*

Bermuda is broken into seven districts, known as parishes. The major sites for tourists are the city of Hamilton (in Pembroke), the beach resorts of Southampton, the historic attractions of St. George's and the Royal Naval Dockyard in Sandys. Here's a rundown of what to expect in each parish, from east to west.

# St. George's

Located on the far eastern end of Bermuda, St. George's is where Bermuda's history began. It is here that the shipwrecked passengers of the *Sea Venture* came aground in 1609. Though they stayed only long enough to build two new ships to get them to their planned destination of St. James, Virginia, Admiral Sir George Somers claimed the land for England. In 1612, settlers from England came to Bermuda to stay, and founded St. George's, naming it in honor of Somers, as well as England's patron saint. St. George's was Bermuda's capital city until 1815, when the government was moved to the city of Hamilton, in Pembroke, a more central location. St. George's is Bermuda's most spread-out parish, consisting of several large islands. Much of the land by the airport, on St. David's Island, was until recently a U.S. Naval Air Station, but that base has been closed for good. What will become of the land is as yet uncertain; the parliament is bandying about proposals that range from turning it into parkland to constructing government buildings.

A visit to historic St. George's is a must for any tourist, and there's enough to see to while away an entire day. (Hint: Unless you have money to burn, you're better off taking one of the many buses that make the run from Hamilton to St. George's, rather than a taxi.) The city is a real charmer, with its narrow, windy roads, old churches and vintage structures from the 1700s, most in impeccable shape. Don't miss St. Peter's Church and the old cemetery that surrounds it, the massive Unfinished Church (currently under restoration by the Bermuda Trust) and the Tucker House, where you can get a good impression of how Bermudians lived in the 18th and 19th centuries. Also of interest to history buffs are the *Deliverance*, a replica of the ship Somers and crew built to carry them to Jamestown; and the Confederate Museum, which explores Bermuda's anti-Yankee role in the U.S. Civil War. On the outskirts of town are two old forts, the most important being Fort St. Catherine, which has interesting historical exhibits and a replica set of the Crown Jewels of Great Britain.

St. George's main center, King's Square, is a lovely spot to begin a walking tour. Known in past days as King's Parade or Market Square, it is a picturesque spot, made more atmospheric by the Town Crier, who each Wednesday at 11:45 a.m. bellows out the news of the day and convenes a tribunal that metes out (mock) punishments in the nearby stocks, pillory, whipping post or dunking stool—the latter used to chastise gossips and nags and test the flotation of witches. Those props are up all the time for the many tourists who delight in taking pictures of each other undergoing old-style humiliation.

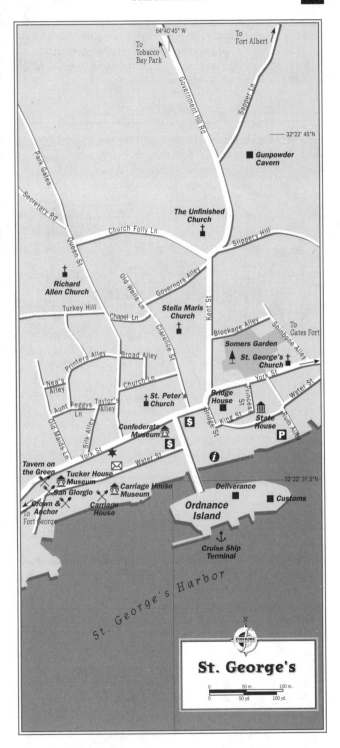

THE PARISHES

64°40'45" W

To
Tobacco
Bay Park

To
Fort Albert

Government Hill Rd

Sapper Ln

32°22' 45"N

■ **Gunpowder
Cavern**

Park Gates

Secretary Rd

Queen St

Church Folly Ln

*The Unfinished
Church* ✝

Slippery Hill

To
Gates Fort

Old Wells Ln

Governors Alley

✝ **Richard
Allen Church**

Turkey Hill

Chapel Ln

**Stella Maris
Church** ✝

Clarence St

Kent St

Blockade Alley

Shinbone Alley

Printers Alley

Broad Alley

Church Ln

Nea's
Alley

Aunt Peggys
Ln

Taylor's
Alley

✝ **St. Peter's
Church**

*Somers Garden*
🌲
**St. George's** ✝
**Church**

York St

Water St

Princess St

**Bridge
House** ■

King St

**State
House** 🏛

Shinbone Alley

Old Maids Ln

Silk Alley

**Confederate**
**Museum** 🏛

York St

$

$

Bridge St

🅿

Water St

ℹ

**Tavern on
the Green**

✉

**Tucker House
Museum** 🏛

*Deliverance*

32°22' 37.5"N

**San Giorgio**

🍴 **Carriage House
Museum** 🏛

**Crown &**
✝ **Anchor**
To
Fort George

**Carriage
House**

***Ordnance
Island***

■ **Customs**

⚓
***Cruise Ship
Terminal***

*S t.  G e o r g e ' s   H a r b o r*

N

FIELDING

## St. George's

0          50 m.          100 m.
0          50 yd.          100 yd.

Except for the St. George's Club, a time-share facility that also accommodates tourists, the parish has little in the way of lodging. There's a slew of good restaurants, however, as well as numerous art galleries and upscale shopping in boutiques and branches of Hamilton's department stores.

# Hamilton

*Bermuda's Aquarium and Zoo features more than 100 species of marine life plus a number of native and imported animals.*

The parish that borders St. George's to the west is Hamilton, but just to keep things interesting, it does not house the city of Hamilton, which is in Pembroke. Many a tourist—and not a few locals—have been confused by this state of affairs. The parish borders most of Harrington Sound inland (a large saltwater lake) and the Atlantic Ocean to the north and south. The only major facilities for lodging are the Grotto Bay Beach Hotel and Marriott's Castle Harbour Resort, but there are few attractions that can't be seen in a half-day.

Not to be missed are Hamilton's limestone caves, which vexed explorer Captain John Smith in 1623 (he grumbled about the island's "vary strange, dark, and cumbersome caves"). Two are open to tourists for guided tours. Crystal Caves is the largest and most impressive, with its giant stalactites and stalagmites, though the nearby Leamington Caves are also an awesome sight.

Another major attraction is the Bermuda Aquarium, Natural History Museum and Zoo, located in Hamilton's Flatts Village. You can take a self-guided audio walking tour among the aquariums that house more than 100 species of fish. You'll also enjoy meandering through the museum's excellent exhibits on the whaling industry, shipwrecks and the environment, and peering at primates, birds and reptiles in the zoo.

Also of note is Bermuda Perfumery, where they've been producing sweet scents in a 250-year-old cottage since 1935. The grounds include some pleasing gardens to explore, and admission is free. Nearby is the Swizzle Inn, where they claim to have invented the potent rum punch of the same name.

# Smith's

Smith's is one of Bermuda's quieter parishes, at least as far as visitors are concerned. It has just one housekeeping facility (Angel's Grotto), one cottage colony (Pink Beach Club) and a handful of attractions. Like Hamilton Parish, it borders Harrington Sound and the sea to the north and south.

The parish is predominantly residential, though it does have a few attractions to lure tourists. Verdmont, a 17th-century home off Collector's Hill, is the grandest of the Bermuda National Trust's holdings and should not be missed if you're interested in antiques. The Georgian-style mansion is filled with an excellent collection of Bermuda cedar furniture and other period pieces, and the views from here are splendid. Another Bermuda National Trust site, Spittal Pond, located to the south, is the island's largest nature reserve. Its 60 acres are home to a number of birds, including the colony's only pair of flamingos.

You'll find the Underwater Wonderland in Flatts Village, one of Bermuda's earliest settlements. This is one of two spots on the island where you can try helmet diving, in which you walk around the ocean floor wearing a large helmet that supplies air and keeps your hair dry—a neat idea for nonswimmers and children.

# Devonshire

Like Smith's, Devonshire is predominantly residential, though it has some sites worth visiting. The Old Devonshire Church, a replica of one built in 1716, is noted for its fine cedar woodwork and old silver pieces. (The original church burned down after an explosion on Easter Sunday, 1970.) For natural beauty, head for the Edmund Gibbons Nature Reserve, a marshland where the birding is good. The gardens at Palm Grove, a private estate dotted with the lifelike statues of Desmond Fountain, are highlighted by a pond that houses a "living" map of Bermuda, done in relief with different lengths of grass. Devonshire also has the public Ocean View Country Club, the island's only nine-hole golf course.

This very quiet parish is home to just one cottage colony (Ariel Sands) and a few restaurants. Notable is the Clay House Inn, a nightclub on North Shore Road, with a lively revue that features the best of African-Caribbean entertainment.

# Pembroke (City of Hamilton)

*Reid Street in the city of Hamilton is a busy avenue of shops.*

Located on a peninsula that juts into the Atlantic, and bordering Hamilton Harbour to the south, Pembroke is best known as the home of Hamilton, Bermuda's capital since 1815. Though it is technically a city, locals refer to it as "Town," a tribute to its laid-back livability and pleasant atmosphere. Whatever the moniker, Hamilton is a beautiful and delightful place to spend time, and it is easily explored on foot.

Front Street, the main thoroughfare that winds along the waterfront, oozes with charm with its gaily painted 19th-century buildings that house upscale shops on the ground floor and, more often than not, restaurants up above. A traffic cop keeps things moving from a "bird cage" on the corner of Front and Queen streets, where the ferry drops off passengers.

Front Street is a shopper's dream, with its three grand department stores—A.S. Cooper & Son, Trimingham's and Smith's—as well as countless smaller boutiques and galleries. The street's many pubs and cafés—virtually all located up a steep set of steps—are wonderful spots for an outdoor meal on the terrace, though in the summer months cruise ships often block the sweeping views of the sound.

One block up and running parallel to Front is Reid Street, another busy avenue of shops and restaurants. The smaller streets linking the two are well worth exploring; don't miss Fagen's Alley and Walker Arcade for off-the-beaten-track shops. Up another block is Church Street, named for the Gothic-style Bermuda Cathedral (formally known as the Cathedral of the Most Holy Trinity), Bermuda's most spectacular church. Nearby is City Hall, which houses both the Bermuda National Gallery and the Bermuda Society of Arts Gallery, where you can buy paintings and other works by local artisans.

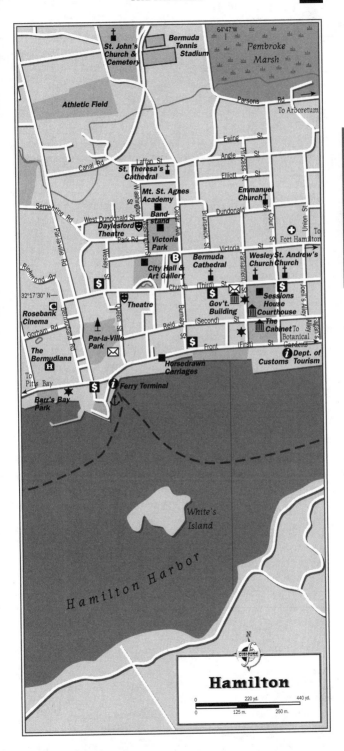

Hamilton

When you're ready for a rest, make tracks for Par-la-Ville Park, off Queen Street, a lovely oasis of flowering trees and gardens, where many Bermudians spend a peaceful lunch hour. If you're a friend of felines, you may want to tote along a can of cat food, to feed the many strays who live in the park.

If you think Front Street is pretty by day, wait until you see it at night, when tiny lights and attractively lit store windows, combined with the twinkling lights from houses across the harbor in Paget, make a scene right out of a picture book. It is generally quite safe to walk along the city streets once the sun goes down, but avoid the "back of town" (far from the waterfront, around Angle Street), where drug dealers ply their wares—and use the same common sense as you would in any metropolitan area.

To the west, Front Street turns into Pitts Bay Road, where several fine hotels are found, including Waterloo House, Rosedon and the landmark Hamilton Princess. There's also a generous sprinkling of guest houses for those on a budget.

# Paget

Located across the harbor from the City of Hamilton to the south, Paget is among Bermuda's most upscale neighborhoods. The area is mainly residential and heavily populated, but still manages to look gorgeous with its beautifully maintained 17th- and 18th-century mansions, wide lawns and flowering gardens. Paget's central location makes it an ideal base for those who will spend lots of their vacation sightseeing around the island.

To the west, along the border of Devonshire, are the delightful Botanical Gardens, a 36-acre preserve with all kinds of ecosystems, including a small forest and the sweetly scented Garden for the Blind. On the grounds is Camden, the official residence of Bermuda's premier, which can be toured on Tuesdays and Friday afternoons, assuming no government functions are in progress.

Nature lovers should also check out Paget Marsh, an 18-acre woodland and mangrove swamp that looks just as it did when the first settlers arrived on the island. While admission is free, arrangements to visit must be made by calling the Bermuda National Trust (☎ [441] 236-6483) in advance. Speaking of the Trust, you can visit its headquarters and browse through its fine gift shop, both housed in an 18th-century cottage known as Waterville, on the corner of The Lane and Pomander Road.

Among Paget's excellent lodging choices is Newstead, a gorgeous old mansion turned into gracious and luxurious accommodations. The views from here of Hamilton are breathtaking, especially at night. Paget is also home to the atmospheric Fourways Inn, famed for its gourmet cuisine and deluxe cottages, as well as the scrumptious Horizons and Cottages, and a number of homey guest houses and housekeeping units clustered in charming Salt Kettle. To the south are good stretches of sand, particularly at Elbow Beach, where the resort of the same name offers outstanding full-service lodging.

# Warwick

*Warwick Bay has the longest stretch of continuous beach.*

The site of two good golf courses (Belmont and the private Riddles Bay) and some scenic beaches, Warwick is a small parish sandwiched between Paget and Southampton, with the Little Sound to the north and the Atlantic to the south. A fair number of accommodation choices are found here, from resorts (Belmont), to small hotels (Mermaid Beach Club) to efficiency units, most within walking distance of the beach.

At half a mile long, Warwick Long Bay is the island's largest and sports an interesting coral outcrop that's the subject of many a photo. The surrounding South Shore Park is a great place to stroll among the dunes in relative isolation.

Found in the center of the parish is Warwick Pond, a good place for bird watchers. Also of interest is Christ Church on Middle Road, opposite the Belmont Golf Course, a Scottish Presbyterian church built in 1719.

## Southampton

A sun worshipper's delight, Southhampton is known for its excellent South Shore beaches, choice resorts (Princess and Sonesta) and smaller hotels, including the Pompano Beach Club and The Reefs. There's also a sprinkling of guest houses that are much more economical than the full-service establishments. This is an expensive neighborhood, and it shows in the generally immaculate look of the parish.

Southampton has two public golf courses (Princess and Port Royal) as well as one of Bermuda's biggest tourist attractions, Gibbs Lighthouse. The views from atop the world's oldest cast-iron lighthouse are spectacular (but not for the acrophobic). Even if you'd rather not huff and puff your way to the top, you can still enjoy sweeping panoramics from the base, or indulge in a traditional spot of tea at the Lighthouse Tea Room. From here, it's a short walk down the hill to Henry VIII, a popular restaurant where the servers don medieval costumes. Over on the sound, dining is more sophisticated at Waterlot, which pampers those who can afford it.

Most beaches are reached via a steep hill or set of stairs. One of the most spectacular is Horseshoe Bay, where the sand is pink, and lifeguards keep watch in the summer months. Also lovely is the Princess Beach Club, though it's open only to guests of the Hamilton and Southampton Princesses. The Sonesta has several fine beaches, including a romantic cove, seemingly made just for two.

Though Southampton is an ideal vacation spot, you may wish to consider staying closer to the city of Hamilton in the winter months, when it's generally too cold to use the beach, as taxi fares to and from the city are quite high.

## Sandys

Reached via Somerset Bridge—billed as the world's smallest drawbridge—the parish of Sandys consists of several islands so close together you could practically hop from one to the next. The parish is known primarily for the Royal Naval Dockyard, Bermuda's largest tourist attraction, though it has much more to offer than man-made charms. The U.S. Navy has abandoned its Air Station Annex on the peninsula between the Great Sound and the Little Sound, near the border of Southampton, and the acreage may be turned into parkland, a new resort or some sort of attraction; nothing had been decided at press time.

Several nature reserves, including Gilbert and Heydon Trust, are always open for leisurely hikes and good bird watching. Fort Scaur, off Somerset Road, offers grand views of the Great Sound and Ely's Harbour. Also be on the lookout for St. James Church, one of the island's prettiest. Check out the old tombstones at the small cemetery that surrounds it.

Tiny Somerset Village, a former shipbuilding center, is Sandys' largest commercial center, though it remains a sleepy hamlet with limited shopping, except for a few branches of Bermuda's larger department stores.

You can (and should) easily spend a day exploring the attractions of Dockyard. Shopping is fun at the picturesque Clocktower Mall, but if handcrafted goods are more your thing, head for the Craft Market and Island Pottery, where you can watch local artisans at work. You can also pick up original artworks at the Bermuda Arts Centre, where the exhibits change monthly.

The highlight of Dockyard is the Maritime Museum, a truly fascinating spot with excellent exhibits on the island's past, including the many shipwrecks that brought fear to the heart of any sailor venturing near Bermuda's treacherous reefs.

Sandys boasts some lovely cottage colonies, including the impeccable Cambridge Beaches and the very lovely Lantana Country Club. Willowbank is primarily known as a Christian retreat, but it is open to all.

Though many buses ply the route from Hamilton to Dockyard, the best way to get there is via ferry, a 45-minute ride that is as scenic as it is practical.

THE PARISHES

# ATTRACTIONS

*Ft. St. Catherine offers spectacular views of the reefs and displays dioramas of important events in Bermuda's history.*

Whether your idea of a good time is poking into an old fort, strolling through a verdant garden, sportfishing on the high seas or touring historic homes, Bermuda delivers. The island is blessedly free of tacky tourist attractions, and even the sites that have been developed chiefly for visitors, such as the Royal Naval Dockyard, have been done with the refined understatement that makes Bermuda so veddy proper.

In you're coming in the off-season (November to March), keep in mind the Temperature Guarantee Program, in which many attractions give visitors free admission the day after the temperature fails to reach 68°F as well as a one-day transportation pass on the ferry or bus to get you there. Participating properties include the Aquarium, Museum and Zoo; the National Gallery; the holdings of the Bermuda Trust; the Maritime Museum; and Leamington Caves.

**WEST END**

# BEST OF BERMUDA

**WEST END**
This spread

**EAST END**
Next spread

**LEGEND**

🚢 Ferry stop

🏰 Historic site

🚩 Golf course

## ROYAL NAVAL DOCKYARD

Plan on spending an entire day exploring Bermuda's biggest tourist attraction, a former naval dockyard that now houses the spiffy Clocktower Center, several art galleries and the fascinating Maritime Museum.

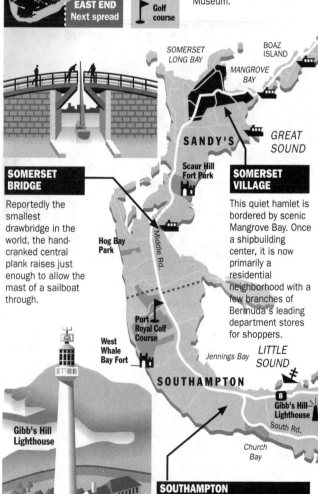

BOAZ ISLAND

SOMERSET LONG BAY

MANGROVE BAY

**SANDY'S**

GREAT SOUND

Scaur Hill Fort Park

## SOMERSET BRIDGE

Reportedly the smallest drawbridge in the world, the hand-cranked central plank raises just enough to allow the mast of a sailboat through.

Hog Bay Park

Middle Rd.

## SOMERSET VILLAGE

This quiet hamlet is bordered by scenic Mangrove Bay. Once a shipbuilding center, it is now primarily a residential neighborhood with a few branches of Bermuda's leading department stores for shoppers.

Port Royal Golf Course

West Whale Bay Fort

Jennings Bay

LITTLE SOUND

**SOUTHAMPTON**

8 Gibb's Hill Lighthouse

South Rd.

Church Bay

Gibb's Hill Lighthouse

## SOUTHAMPTON

Bermuda's most beautiful pink beaches are found in this parish as well as several golf courses and two posh resorts. Gibb's Hill Lighthouse, rising 362 ft. high and dating from 1846, is one of the most famous attractions.

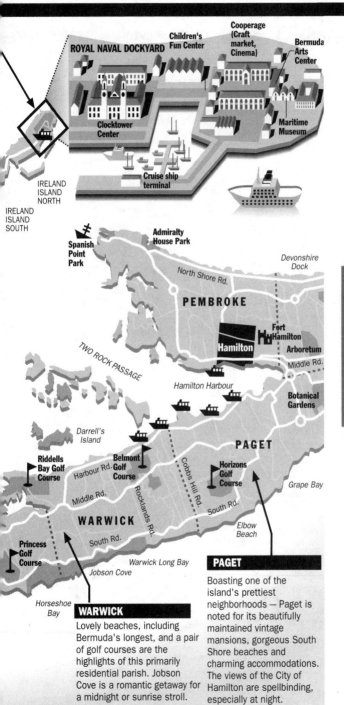

ROYAL NAVAL DOCKYARD

Children's Fun Center

Cooperage (Craft market, Cinema)

Bermuda Arts Center

Clocktower Center

Maritime Museum

Cruise ship terminal

IRELAND ISLAND NORTH

IRELAND ISLAND SOUTH

Spanish Point Park

Admiralty House Park

Devonshire Dock

North Shore Rd.

**PEMBROKE**

Fort Hamilton

Hamilton

Arboretum

TWO ROCK PASSAGE

Middle Rd.

Hamilton Harbour

Botanical Gardens

Darrell's Island

**PAGET**

Riddells Bay Golf Course

Belmont Golf Course

Harbour Rd.

Cobbs Hill Rd.

Horizons Golf Course

Grape Bay

Middle Rd.

Rocklands Rd.

South Rd.

Elbow Beach

**WARWICK**

Princess Golf Course

South Rd.

Warwick Long Bay

Jobson Cove

Horseshoe Bay

**WARWICK**

Lovely beaches, including Bermuda's longest, and a pair of golf courses are the highlights of this primarily residential parish. Jobson Cove is a romantic getaway for a midnight or sunrise stroll.

**PAGET**

Boasting one of the island's prettiest neighborhoods — Paget is noted for its beautifully maintained vintage mansions, gorgeous South Shore beaches and charming accommodations. The views of the City of Hamilton are spellbinding, especially at night.

**ATTRACTIONS**

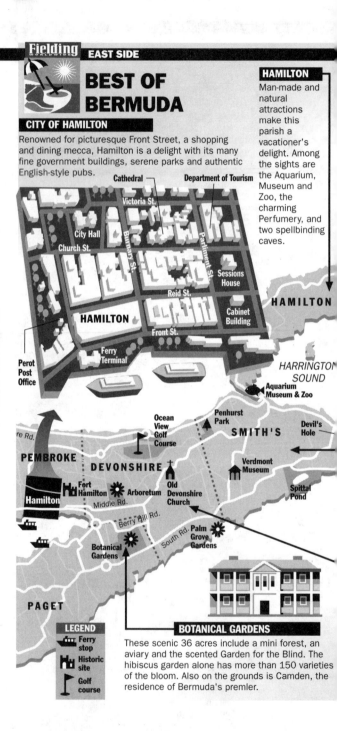

**Fielding** EAST SIDE

# BEST OF BERMUDA

## CITY OF HAMILTON

Renowned for picturesque Front Street, a shopping and dining mecca, Hamilton is a delight with its many fine government buildings, serene parks and authentic English-style pubs.

### HAMILTON

Man-made and natural attractions make this parish a vacationer's delight. Among the sights are the Aquarium, Museum and Zoo, the charming Perfumery, and two spellbinding caves.

Cathedral — Department of Tourism

Victoria St.

City Hall

Church St.

Burnaby St.

Parliament St.

Sessions House

Reid St.

HAMILTON

Cabinet Building

Front St.

Ferry Terminal

Perot Post Office

HAMILTON

HARRINGTON SOUND

Aquarium Museum & Zoo

Ocean View Golf Course

Penhurst Park

SMITH'S

Devil's Hole

PEMBROKE

DEVONSHIRE

Verdmont Museum

Fort Hamilton    Arboretum    Old Devonshire Church

Spittal Pond

Hamilton

Middle Rd.

Berry Hill Rd.

South Rd.    Palm Grove Gardens

Botanical Gardens

PAGET

### LEGEND

- Ferry stop
- Historic site
- Golf course

### BOTANICAL GARDENS

These scenic 36 acres include a mini forest, an aviary and the scented Garden for the Blind. The hibiscus garden alone has more than 150 varieties of the bloom. Also on the grounds is Camden, the residence of Bermuda's premier.

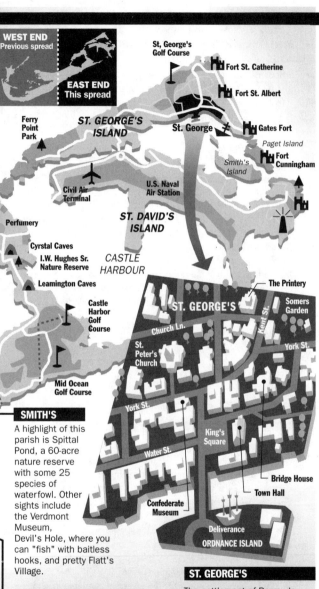

**WEST END**
Previous spread

**EAST END**
This spread

St. George's Golf Course

Fort St. Catherine

Fort St. Albert

**ST. GEORGE'S ISLAND**

St. George

Gates Fort

*Paget Island*

Ferry Point Park

*Smith's Island*

Fort Cunningham

Civil Air Terminal

U.S. Naval Air Station

**ST. DAVID'S ISLAND**

Perfumery

Cyrstal Caves

I.W. Hughes Sr. Nature Reserve

*CASTLE HARBOUR*

Leamington Caves

Castle Harbor Golf Course

The Printery

**ST. GEORGE'S**

Somers Garden

Kent St.

Church Ln.

York St.

St. Peter's Church

York St.

King's Square

Mid Ocean Golf Course

Water St.

Bridge House

Town Hall

Confederate Museum

Deliverance

**ORDNANCE ISLAND**

**ATTRACTIONS**

## SMITH'S

A highlight of this parish is Spittal Pond, a 60-acre nature reserve with some 25 species of waterfowl. Other sights include the Verdmont Museum, Devil's Hole, where you can "fish" with baitless hooks, and pretty Flatt's Village.

## DEVONSHIRE

This peaceful parish is mainly residential but does lure tourists with the historic Old Devonshire Church and the scenic gardens at Palm Grove.

## ST. GEORGE'S

The settlement of Bermuda first began here in 1612. Easily explored on foot, the City of St. George's is a treasure trove of historic buildings and fine museums .

# Historical Sites

Just a walk down a residential street is akin to a historical stroll in Bermuda, as the island teems with vintage cottages and stately mansions dating back as early as the 1600s. Among the island's 70 houses of worship are a generous handful of historic churches—not to be missed, in particular, are the **Bermuda Cathedral** in Hamilton, **St. Peter's** in St. George's and **St. James** in Sandys. The latter two have old and well-preserved **cemeteries**, well worth a gander. If military history is more to your liking, march to the island's handful of old forts; **St. Catherine** in St. George's is in especially good shape.

### Bermuda Cathedral　　　　　　　　　　　★★★★

*Church Street, Hamilton, Bermuda, ☎ (441) 292-4033.*
*Hours: 8 a.m.–4:45 p.m.*

This towering early English-style Gothic structure adds much character to Hamilton's skyline. Formally known as the Cathedral of the Most Holy Trinity, it is the seat of Bermuda's Anglican Church. Begun in 1885 and consecrated in 1911 to replace the 1872 Trinity Church, which was torched by an arsonist, the cathedral is made of Bermuda limestone and imported materials—some coming from as far as France and Scotland. (Incidentally, the arsonist, who also destroyed several other buildings in Hamilton, including the Roman Catholic church, was never caught.)

The High Altar is made of marble; its mosaics, crafted by an Italian artist, depict the Annunciation, Nativity and Crucifixion. The large statues of Mary and several saints are simply gorgeous. The Canterbury Cross on the wall near the Lectern is a copy of one made in Kent in the 8th century, and is set in stone taken from the walls of the Canterbury Cathedral. Also impressive is the organ, a four-manual instrument that has seen extensive repairs and additions through the years. Also note the lovely stained-glass windows, especially the one high up on the east wall of the north transept, whose angel playing a harp represents "Heavenly Music." In the south transept is the Warriors Chapel, dedicated to those who served in the Armed Forces of the Crown, particularly in the first two world wars. The Great Warrior Window, which depicts well-known Warrior Saints, is a memorial to the 85 Bermudians who died in World War I. The flags beneath it represent Bermuda's military units. Sunday services are held at 8, 9:30 and 11 a.m. There is also a Holy Communion service the first Sunday of the month at 12:15 p.m. (otherwise, the sacrament takes place at the 8 a.m. service) and an evening service at 7 p.m. (6 p.m. October to May). Ongoing work keeps the cathedral in all its splendid glory; donations are gratefully accepted. For splendid views of Hamilton and the harbor, climb to the top of the tower ($3 admission charge), which rises up some 143 feet.

### Bridge House　　　　　　　　　　　★★★

*1 Bridge Street, Bermuda, ☎ (441) 297-8211.*

This 17th-century mansion, located just off King's Square, was home to several governors and Bridger Goodrich, a Virginian Loyalist. Its name refers to the fact that it used to straddle a creek (now gone). Today it is a Bermuda National Trust property and houses an interesting art gallery and gift shop. Goods for sale include antique prints, old maps, vintage bottles and books, handcrafted Bermudian items and original works by local artists.

### Cabinet Building ★★★

*Front and Parliament streets, Hamilton, Bermuda, ☎ (441) 292-5501.*
*Hours: 8:30 a.m.–5 p.m.*

Home to the Senate, the upper house of Parliament (but less powerful than the House of Assembly), the landmark Cabinet Building dates to 1836. Visitors are welcome to watch the proceedings in the Council Chamber, where the Senate meets each Wednesday at 10 a.m., except during the summer. The official opening of Parliament takes place here each fall with great pomp and circumstance—the governor arrives in full regalia via horse-drawn carriage and accompanied by a full military escort. If you're in town in late October or early November, call to find out exactly when the ceremony takes place—it's a true "Kodak" moment.

### Fort Hamilton ★★★

*Happy Valley Road, Hamilton, Bermuda.*
*Hours: 9:30 a.m.–5 p.m.*

Located on the outskirts of the city of Hamilton (and a bit of a walk from downtown), the fort was completed in 1889 but, like Bermuda's other fortresses, never saw action. In fact, it was considered obsolete before it was even finished. It was open to the public in 1963 after extensive renovations, and the best reason to visit is for the sweeping views of Hamilton and the harbor. The old moat is now a lovely garden of native plants and shrubs. Each Monday at noon from November to March, the Bermuda Isles Pipe Band (properly outfitted in traditional kilts) performs a skirling ceremony.

### Fort St. Catherine ★★★

*Barry Road, Bermuda, ☎ (441) 297-1920.*
*Hours: 10 a.m.–4 p.m.*
*Special hours: kids under 12 free.*

Built on the spot where survivors of the 1609 Sea Venture shipwreck first came ashore, this impressive fort was built in 1614 and constantly fortified over the next 250 years with redoubts, forts, towers and gun batteries. In 1865, a massive reconstruction added 25-foot-thick concrete embrasures and casemates, and the fort was rearmed with five-rifled, 18-ton muzzle loaders—which could send a 400-pound projectile half a mile. Despite all that readiness, the fort never saw action, and was opened as a museum in the early 1950s. Exhibits include dioramas depicting Bermuda's history, an audiovisual show on the island's military past, a re-created cook house, replicas of Britain's crown jewels and an antique weapons collection. Closed Christmas. General admission: $2.50.

### Gates Fort ★

*Cut Road, Bermuda.*
*Hours: 10 a.m.–4 p.m.*

This reconstruction of a small fort from the 1620s was originally a sea battery of three guns. It overlooks Gates Bay, and is not worth a spe-

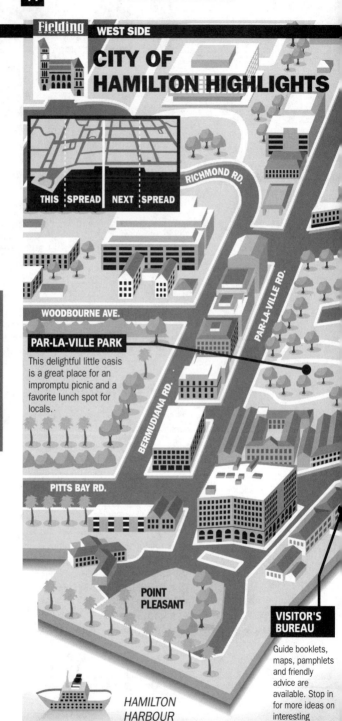

**ATTRACTIONS**

**Fielding** WORLDWIDE   **WEST SIDE**

# CITY OF HAMILTON HIGHLIGHTS

THIS SPREAD   NEXT SPREAD

RICHMOND RD.

PAR-LA-VILLE RD.

WOODBOURNE AVE.

**PAR-LA-VILLE PARK**

This delightful little oasis is a great place for an impromptu picnic and a favorite lunch spot for locals.

BERMUDIANA RD.

PITTS BAY RD.

POINT PLEASANT

HAMILTON HARBOUR

**VISITOR'S BUREAU**

Guide booklets, maps, pamphlets and friendly advice are available. Stop in for more ideas on interesting places to visit.

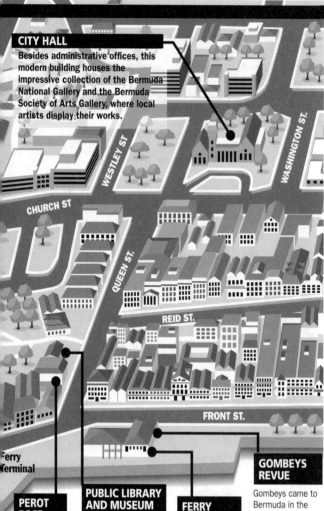

## CITY HALL

Besides administrative offices, this modern building houses the impressive collection of the Bermuda National Gallery and the Bermuda Society of Arts Gallery, where local artists display their works.

WESTLEY ST.

WASHINGTON ST.

CHURCH ST

QUEEN ST.

REID ST.

FRONT ST.

Ferry Terminal

## PEROT POST OFFICE

The two-story building dates to 1840 and is still a functioning post office. It's named after William Bennett Perot, who created Bermuda's first book of stamps, which now sells for a large fortune.

## PUBLIC LIBRARY AND MUSEUM

Mark Twain was said to have been disappointed that the giant rubber tree out front wasn't laden with hot water bottles and other rubber wares. The first floor of this vintage building is occupied by the Museum of the Historical Society, with excellent exhibits on the island's past. The library upstairs has a good collection of historical documents.

## FERRY TERMINAL

The Number One terminal is where you'll catch the ferry to all points, and also where you'll disembark in Hamilton. Note the "bird cage" across the street from which a traffic cop keeps things moving. From here it's an easy walk around town

## GOMBEYS REVUE

Gombeys came to Bermuda in the 17th century, and their colorful costumes and music delight locals and tourists to this day. Once a New Year's tradition, today Gombeys perform in parades and special events all year round. The Gombey Review takes place on Tuesdays at 3 p.m.at Passenger Terminal #I in Hamilton.

## CITY OF HAMILTON HIGHLIGHTS    EAST SIDE

VICTORIA ST.

CEDAR AVE.

CHURCH ST.

BURNABY HILL

REID ST.

FRONT ST.

*HAMILTON HARBOUR*

### VICTORIA PARK

Built in 1887 to honor Queen Victoria's Golden Jubilee, this pretty park consists of four acres of sunken gardens and a bandstand where concerts are held.

### FRONT STREET

This fascinating street along the harbour is lined with a plethora of shops selling wares ranging from cameras, watches and jewelry to designer fashions, Scottish kilts, Persian carpets and Royal Doulton china.The area also boasts several art galleries and antique shops.

### BERMUDA CATHEDRAL

An imposing sight on the city's skyline, the Cathedral dates to 1911. The Gothic-style church is spendid in its details and stained-glass windows. Inspiring views reward those who climb to the top of the tower.

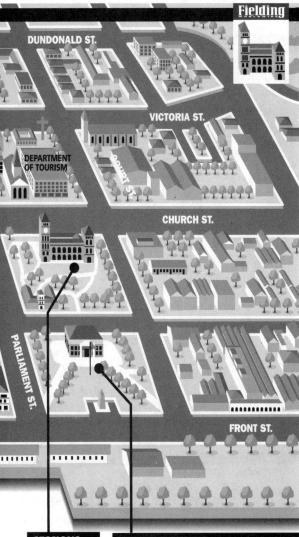

Fielding

## DUNDONALD ST.

## VICTORIA ST.

COURT ST.

DEPARTMENT
OF TOURISM

## CHURCH ST.

PARLIAMENT ST.

## FRONT ST.

## SESSIONS HOUSE

This Italianate structure houses the House of Assembly and the Supreme Court. Built in 1817, the impressive clock tower was added in 1983 to celebrate Queen Victoria's Golden Jubilee.

## CABINET BUILDING

Home of the Senate, this elegant building dates to 1836. Each November the convening of Parliament takes place here with great pomp and circumstance. The Cenotaph Memorial in front honors Bermuda's soldiers.

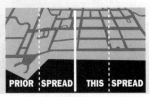

PRIOR | SPREAD    THIS | SPREAD

cial trip unless you're really into military history. The small fort was built by Sir Thomas Gates, one of the passengers on the Sea Venture.

*Before Gibbs Hill Lighthouse was erected in 1846, many ships were wrecked on coral reefs off Bermuda's western end.*

### Gibbs Hill Lighthouse ★★★★

*Lighthouse Road, Bermuda, ☎ (441) 238-8069.*
*Hours: 9 a.m.–4:30 p.m.*
*Special hours: kids under five free.*

This lighthouse, perched on a 245-foot-high hill and itself towering 117 feet, is one of the few in the world made of cast iron, due to a lack of steel during its construction in 1844. The need for a lighthouse was painfully obvious—in the decade before its completion, 39 vessels were wrecked off Bermuda's western end, where the reefs extend some 16 miles out to sea. Ships 40 miles away can see the 1000-watt light, as can planes flying 10,000 feet 120 miles away. One hundred and eighty-five spiral steps wind their way to the top, where the panoramic views are fantastic—but not recommended for those with a fear of heights. (Claustrophobics won't enjoy the tight climb, either.) Each of the eight landings has exhibits that tell of the lighthouse's past—not only are they interesting, they're a great excuse to catch your breath. Consider the plight of the original keepers, who worked in alternate shifts 365 days a year, hand-winding the giant clockwork mechanism each half-hour to keep the light revolving. Things got quite a bit easier in 1964, when the lighthouse was fully automated. In 1987, two women were hired (and are still on duty) as keepers—a first. Before climbing the tower, buy a ticket in the gift shop, which has some interesting displays on old shipwrecks, some as far back as 1838. Among the relics are pieces of cargo salvaged from the *Constellation*, the 1943 wreck used as the setting for the film "The Deep". After descending the tower, stop by the Lighthouse Tea Room for a light snack (see "Restaurants"). General admission: $2.

### Old Devonshire Church ★★★

*Middle Road, Bermuda, ☎ (441) 236-3671.*
*Hours: 9 a.m.–5:30 p.m.*
An explosion on Easter Sunday, 1970, caused a fire that virtually destroyed the church that stood on this site since 1716 (an even earlier version dates to 1612). The present church, which looks more like a simple Bermudian cottage than a house of worship, is a complete re-creation and houses some important relics that survived the blast, including silver from 1590—believed to be the island's oldest—and a candelabra.

### Perot Post Office ★★

*Queen Street, Hamilton, Bermuda, ☎ (441) 295-5151.*
*Hours: 9 a.m.–5 p.m.*
This small, whitewashed building dates to around 1840 and still functions as a post office. It is named for the island's first postmaster, William Bennet Perot, who printed Bermuda's first postage stamp in 1848—apparently to give himself more time to putter in the adjacent Par-la-Ville gardens. (Before he came up with the ingenious idea, he made each stamp by hand and resented the time and trouble.) Only 11 of those stamps are known to exist today; they are extremely valuable to collectors—one of whom paid $350,000 to own one!

### Royal Naval Dockyard ★★★★★

*Bermuda, ☎ (441) 234-3824.*
Though it is undeniably one giant tourist attraction, don't be too quick to dismiss the Royal Naval Dockyard as something too gimmicky. The site, set on Bermuda's far western end on Ireland Island (connected by bridge to the rest of Bermuda), is well worth visiting for its interesting architecture, good shopping and excellent Maritime Museum (see separate listing). Lord Wellington purchased the land in 1795 to build a huge fortified compound that quickly became known as "the Gibraltar of the West." The six-acre complex was created by slave laborers and thousands of British convicts—many of whom died of the yellow fever then rampant in the area. During the War of 1812, a British fleet sailed from Dockyard to sack and burn Washington, D.C. It was used as a shipyard for some 150 years; then, in 1951, Dockyard was open to the public, and today has become Bermuda's number-one tourist attraction.

*Royal Naval Dockyard's Clocktower rises above a shopping mall.*

The flagship of the site is the 1856 Clocktower Centre, an upscale shopping mall situated in two adjoining naval storehouses. With its cobblestone floors, high ceilings and three-foot-thick stone walls, the mall is a lovely place to drop some bucks (see "Shopping" for details). The two handsome clocktowers served two purposes: The one on the south tower, made in England in 1857 by John Moore & Sons, told the time, while the one on the north has just a single hand set daily to indicate high tide, when it was easiest to navigate Bermuda's treacherous reefs. Clocktower is open daily from 10 a.m.–5 p.m.—making it one of the few places in Bermuda that you can shop on a Sunday.

After you've hit the shops at Clocktower, stroll over to the Crafts Market (same hours), which is housed in the old Cooperage building. The 1831 building manufactured and maintained barrels that held salted perishables—the way it was done before refrigeration. Chances are good you'll spot a local artist or two creating jewelry, cedar pieces and other Bermudian souvenirs—all, of course, for sale. The Cooperage also houses the Art Centre (open 10 a.m.–4:30 p.m. Monday-Saturday and noon–5 p.m. Sundays from June to September and 10 a.m.–4 p.m. Tuesday-Saturday and noon–5 p.m. Sunday the rest of the year), christened by England's Princess Margaret in 1984. The nonprofit organization features changing exhibits of the works of Bermudian sculptors, painters, photographers and craftspeople.

Over at Island Pottery (9 a.m.–5 p.m.), set in a high-ceilinged old shipbuilding facility, artisans are at work on ceramics, pottery, tableware, vases and ornamental house signs. The grounds also include pretty lawns and gardens and a number of restaurants. Guided walking tours of Dockyard, some free, are frequently offered. Times vary, so check with the complex's Visitor's Center for details. Dockyard, about 40 minutes from the city of Hamilton, can be reached by bus or, better yet, ferry, which makes the scenic chug daily.

### Scaur Hill Fort                    ★★

*Scaur Hill, off Somerset Road, Bermuda,* ☎ *(441) 234-0908.*
*Hours: 9 a.m.–4:30 p.m.*
The best reasons to visit this 22-acre site are for its pretty gardens, picnic areas and sweeping views of virtually all of Bermuda; the free telescope on hand is a welcome amenity. The fort dates to the 1870s and never saw action—though it was home to British soldiers during World War I and American troops during World War II. (The fort was originally planned by the British to defend the Royal Naval Dockyard from a feared U.S. invasion.) On the eastern slope, a milestone is inscribed, "London 3076 miles" on one side and "27 Regiment, RE 1906" on the other.

### Sessions House                    ★★★

*Parliament Street, Hamilton, Bermuda,* ☎ *(441) 292-7408.*
*Hours: 9 a.m.–4:30 p.m.*
The Italianate structure houses Bermuda's House of Assembly and Supreme Court. It dates to 1817, though the striking Victoria Jubilee Clock Tower (made to commemorate Queen Victoria's Golden Jubilee) was added in 1893. Bermuda's parliament is the third-oldest in the world, following England's and Iceland's. Visitors are welcome to watch the proceedings in the Assembly and the Supreme Court (call for a schedule), but are asked to dress appropriately (no jeans or shorts). Traditional white wigs and gowns (red for judges, black for barristers) are always worn in the Supreme Court, but are donned only on special occasions in the House of Assembly.

### Somerset Bridge                   ★★★

*Somerset Road, Bermuda.*
This tiny drawbridge, which dates to the 17th century, is said to be the world's smallest—and seeing is believing. The hand-operated bridge opens just 22 inches—just enough to let the mast of a sailboat pass through. It joins Somerset Island with the rest of Bermuda—though in a pinch, you could probably just leap from one land mass to another.

*Somerset Bridge is the smallest drawbridge in the world.*

### St. David's Lighthouse ★★

*St. David's Road, Bermuda, ☎ (441) 236-4201.*
Splendid views abound from this 208-foot-high lighthouse, built of Bermuda stone in 1879. It is generally open from May 20 to Sept. 4, but hours can vary, so call first.

### St. James Church ★★★★

*Main Road, Somerset, Bermuda, ☎ (441) 234-0834.*
*Hours: 8 a.m.–7 p.m.*
Among the island's prettiest, this Anglican church is just lovely inside, with its highly polished wooden pews, stained-glass window gracing the altar, and brass lanterns hanging from large white pillars. It was built in 1789 to replace the original building, which was destroyed by a hurricane in 1780; the imposing wrought-iron entrance gates were added in 1872. The first organ was built by a prisoner in 1902, but was replaced by the present instrument in 1902. In 1937, the church was struck by lightning, which caused all the windows and doors to blow out and the spire to fall into the center aisle. Undeterred, church members quickly fixed the place back up to its present glory. After admiring the church's interior, take a stroll through the surrounding graveyard, where many tombstones date to the 1800s. Sunday services are held at 8 a.m.

### St. Peter's Church ★★★★

*York Street, Bermuda, ☎ (441) 297-2459.*
*Hours: 9:30 a.m.–5 p.m.*
The oldest Anglican church in the Western Hemisphere, St. Peter's sits regally atop steep, steep stairs in downtown St. George's (there's an easier entrance around back for the physically challenged). Parts of the structure were built in 1620, 1713 and 1833; the old three-decker pulpit dates to 1660. The church is famed for several articles, including St. George's Chalice, presented in 1625 and still in common use for the sacrament of Holy Communion. Made of rare silver, the bowl and cover feature intricate engravings of the coat-of-arms of the old Bermuda Company. Another item of historical significance is the King's Set, which includes a large chalice and cover, a round paten on a foot, two half-gallon-size flagons and an arms basin. Made of

"Higher Standard" silver (which is softer and purer than sterling), the set dates to 1679. Also look out for the Christening Bowl, a fine piece of Adam-period silver given to the church by William Browne of Salem, Massachusetts, who was Bermuda's governor from 1782-1788; and a model of the ship *Sea Venture*, which, when wrecked on the reefs in 1609, began Bermuda's modern history. A baptismal register from 1834 and many commemorative plaques from the 1800s adorn the walls.

St. Peter's is surrounded by a small graveyard that is well worth a walking tour. A fair amount of Americans are buried here and there's also a section for "slaves and free blacks." Though some of the crumbling tombstones are now illegible, many poignant inscriptions can be easily made out. One honors the memory of a 19-year-old man who "died of the prevailing fever" in 1819. Another marks the grace of a man who died at age 27 in 1853 "on board Her Majesty's ship Weymouth of the epidemic then raging in these islands....leaving a wife and two children to deplore their loss." Visitors are welcome to the services held each Sunday; dress conservatively.

### Unfinished Church                    ★ ★ ★

*Blockade Alley, Bermuda.*

True to its name, this giant church was never completed, and was considered the folly of St. George's. It was designed in the 1870s to replace St. Peter's (which is still very much in existence), but a schism in the Anglican church, financial difficulties and a devastating storm put the kabosh on the entire project, which was abandoned by the turn of the century. It's now run under the auspices of the Bermuda National Trust, which is currently stabilizing the gothic structure.

*James Thurber and E.B. White were two famous guests at the Waterville Mansion at the foot of Hamilton Harbour.*

### Waterville                    ★ ★

*5 The Lane, Bermuda, ☎ (441) 236-6483.*
*Hours: 9 a.m.–5 p.m.*

This charming 18th-century house is the headquarters of the Bermuda National Trust, the nonprofit organization that oversees Verdmont, the Confederate Museum, Tucker House, the Unfinished Church and Spittal Pond Nature Reserve, among others. It's a good

ATTRACTIONS

place to stop by and pick up information on the island as well as peruse the gift shop (open Tuesday-Saturday 10 a.m.–4 p.m.), which has high-quality handcrafts and the Trust's palmetto palm logo items for sale.

# Museums and Exhibits

*The Maritime Museum at the Royal Naval Dockyard offers fascinating glimpses into Bermuda's history.*

Among the highlights of Bermuda's many museums are the **Maritime Museum** at Royal Naval Dockyard, whose displays on shipwrecks are especially fascinating, and the two museums run under the auspices of the Historical Society, both of which give visitors a glimpse of long-ago island life. The Bermuda National Trust, a nonprofit group dedicated to preserving Bermuda's past and open spaces, runs many other worthwhile museums and exhibits, including its showpiece, the historical home Verdmont.

### Bermuda Aquarium, Museum and Zoo     ★★★★
*Flatts Village, Bermuda,* ☎ *(441) 293-2727.*
*Hours: 9 a.m.–4:30 p.m.*
One of the island's most visited attractions, this complex is easily reached by bus from Hamilton. The aquarium, which opened in 1928, displays in 26 tanks and a giant reef tank more than 100 species of marine life indigenous to the area, including large eels, parrotfish, wrasses, barracuda and sharks. A self-guided audio tour gives details on their behavior. The stars of the show are two harbor seals named Charlotte and Archie; Charlotte has given birth to pups twice. At the museum, fascinating displays tell the story of Bermuda's natural development (did you know the island formed from a volcano?) and the exploits of Dr. William Beebe, who dove half a mile down off the shores of Bermuda in 1934. (A replica of his "Bathysphere" is on display out front.) Over at the zoo, which dates to the 1950s, native and imported animals such as alligators, Galapagos tortoises, exotic birds and small primates are on display. The zoo scores points for its breeding programs. Children get a kick out of the Invertebrate House, where a beehive, wet lab and touch tank await, and the Discovery

Room, which has kids-friendly educational games. The aquarium is ramped for wheelchair-access. General admission: $6.00.

*The park surrounding the Aquarium and Museum features quaint bridges and botanical gardens.*

### Bermuda Glassblowing ★★

*Bailey's Bay, Bermuda,* ☎ *(441) 293-2234.*
*Hours: 9 a.m.–5 p.m.*
Drop by anytime and watch the ancient art of flame-working and glassblowing at this privately owned shop and studio, which employs six artisans. The glassware features Bermudian themes and colors and ranges from the functional to the fanciful. Bermuda Glassblowing pieces are also available at Triminghams department stores, the Craft Market at the Royal Naval Dockyard and Queen Street Glass in the city of Hamilton.

### Bermuda Journey ★★★

*Town Hall, King's Square, Bermuda.*
This audiovisual show spotlights the best of Bermuda and its people. A good all-around orientation to the island and its past. Open Monday-Thursday 11:15 a.m. to 2:15 p.m. and Saturday 12:15 to 2:15 p.m. Hours are limited from December to April. Admission for seniors over 65 and kids under 13: $2. General admission: $3.

### Bermuda Maritime Museum ★★★★★

*Royal Naval Dockyard, Bermuda,* ☎ *(441) 234-1333.*
*Hours: 9:30 a.m.–5 p.m.*
*Special hours: 10 a.m.–4:30 p.m. December-April.*
Housed in the Keep (fortress) that was built to protect the Royal Naval Dockyard and store munitions, the Maritime Museum is a must for anyone interested in Bermudian history. The complex consists of six buildings made of hard Bermuda limestone built between 1837 and 1852. Pick up a brochure upon entering and leisurely make your way through the grounds—you can easily spend several hours poring over the well-tended exhibits.

Building one, the Queen's Exhibition Hall, has displays on navigation, whaling and pilots as well as models of historic ships. Building two, the three-gabled Shifting House, is one of the most interesting, with details on the 1609 wreck of the *Sea Venture*—which led to per-

**ATTRACTIONS**

manent settlement of the island—and a large chart that pinpoints shipwrecks around the colony. One particularly fascinating exhibit details how the *Sea Venture* was excavated, and there's also a good collection of artifacts, including pieces of eight, a large gold bar and breathtaking gold jewelry, recovered from 16th- and 17th-century wrecks.

In the third building, the Bermuda Monetary Authority displays the island's history in coins and notes. Building four, the 1849 Shell House, tells of Bermuda's past reputation as the "Isle of Devils" (due to its treacherous reefs, the undoing of many a sailor) and celebrates the 500th anniversary of Christopher Columbus' "discovery" of the New World. Over in the Forster Cooper Building (building five), there are exhibits on the Royal Navy and the Bromby Bottle Collection, which consists of some 2000 antique bottles found around the island.

Finally, the Boatloft (the large building at the end of the Parade Ground) houses the original Store House Clock, a fully rigged Bermuda fitted dinghy and a 42-foot pilot gig, as well as displays on weather forecasting, watercraft and turtling. The Boatloft also contains exhibits that detail the 50 years the U.S. military maintained a station in Bermuda.

Standing above on a bluff is the Commissioner's House, built in 1823. Its design incorporates cast-iron girders and trusses to support the floors and roofs, and it is believed to be the world's first prefabricated building. It is currently under restoration and not yet open to the public. The views from the bluff are worth the short climb—that distant point of land is St. George's, all the way on Bermuda's far eastern point. All buildings are accessible by wheelchair, with the exception of the upper floor of the Boatloft. Note: The museum's extensive grounds include a resident flock of sheep that are quite skittish and best left alone. Admission is $6 for seniors over 60 and $3 for kids 5-18 (under 5 free). Inquire about special family rates that run from $9 to $15. General admission: $7.50.

## Bermuda National Gallery                    ★★★★

*In City Hall, 17 Church Street West, Hamilton, Bermuda, ☎ (441) 292-1234.*
*Hours: 10 a.m.–4 p.m.*
*Special hours: open Sunday 12:30-4 p.m.*

Located on the second floor of City Hall, a pretty building completed in 1960, the National Gallery has among its permanent collection Renaissance and old master works by Gainsborough, Reynold and Palma Vecchio. Also on display are depictions of Bermuda by such famed artists as Georgia O'Keefe, Winslow Homer and Charles Demuth. As you climb the sweeping stairway to the gallery, note the large oil painting of Queen Elizabeth II, painted by Curtis Hooper in 1987. Tours are conducted Monday-Friday at 1 p.m. The gallery has an excellent gift shop. Admission is free to the adjacent Bermuda Society of Arts Gallery, open Monday through Saturday from 10 a.m.–4 p.m., which features and sells the works of local artists. General admission: $3.

### Bermuda Perfumery                    ★★★

*North Shore Road, Bermuda,* ☎ *(441) 293-0627.*

The sweet little tour of the Bermuda Perfumery, set in a cedar-beamed cottage amid six acres of manicured gardens, is blessedly free of high-pressure sales tactics—though you are, of course, welcome to buy some of the men's and women's fragrances concocted here. The perfumery has been in constant operation since its inception in 1929; the short tour details the process from A to Z. Afterwards, you're free to explore the gardens (pick up a complimentary map) that supply many of the flowers used in the perfumes. Stop by the Orchid House, home of Bermuda's most extensive collection; the formal Ornamental Garden with its many exotic plants, and the Tea Garden, a trestled garden with Bermuda roses. Also on the grounds is the Cobweb Shop, a nice gift shop with locally made and imported goods. Open April through October 9 a.m.–5 p.m. Monday-Saturday and 10 a.m.–4 p.m. Sundays and holidays. November through March: 9 a.m.–4:30 p.m. Monday-Saturday; closed Sunday and holidays.

### Bermuda Railway Museum                    ★★

*Flatts Village, Bermuda,* ☎ *(441) 293-1774.*
*Hours: 10 a.m.–4 p.m.*

The Bermuda Railway was one of the most expensive per-mile railways ever built—but when cars were introduced to the island in 1946, it quickly fell by the wayside. This small museum pays homage to the "Old Rattle and Shake" with memorabilia and vintage photos from the era. Donations accepted. The adjacent Curiosity Shop is well worth a browse.

### Biological Station for Research                    ★★★

*Ferry Reach, Bermuda,* ☎ *(441) 297-1880.*

Those interested in the environment should not miss this scientific research station, in operation since 1903. Ongoing projects at the U.S. nonprofit organization include studies of the Gulf Stream, global warming and acid rain. The grounds include 13 laboratories, a 20,000-volume library, a simulated coral reef and research ships. Visitors are welcome for a free, hour-long guided tour each Wednesday at 10 a.m.; coffee and donuts are served, and donations are appreciated.

### Confederate Museum                    ★★★

*King's Square, Bermuda,* ☎ *(441) 297-1423.*
*Hours: 9:30 a.m.–4:30 p.m.*
*Special hours: Open 10 a.m.–4 p.m. Nov. 1-March 31. Closed: Sun.*

Many Americans don't realize that Bermuda was headquarters for a principal Confederate agent during the U.S. Civil War. Housed in the former Globe Hotel (which saw its heyday in the mid-1800s), this historic structure was built as a governor's mansion in 1698-1700 and is noted for its four great chimneys and decorative roof line. The small museum houses artifacts, Confederate currency, and a parlor and bedroom furnished with period pieces and other memorabilia from the era. It also tells the story of a blockade running during the war and chronicles the life of Joseph Hayne Rainey, the first black man to become a member of the U.S. House of Representatives, originally as a congressman and later as a senator. (Rainey, a free man who fled from South Carolina to Bermuda aboard a blockade-runner, returned to the United States in 1866.) The museum is a Bermuda National Trust property. General admission: $4.

### Deliverance II                                      ★★★

*Ordnance Island, Bermuda,* ☎ *(441) 297-1459.*
*Hours: 9 a.m.–7 p.m.*
*Special hours: 9 a.m.–3 p.m in winter.*

This is a full-scale replica of the ship *Deliverance*, one of two built by Sir George Somers and crew after they wrecked the *Sea Venture* in Bermuda in 1609 on their way to the colonial settlement of Jamestown, Virginia. The short, self-guided tour is interesting; note the small sleeping bunks that attest to both a hard life at sea and how man has evolved (the average height back then was 5 feet, 4 inches). Those looking for something different can get married aboard—it's never been done, but they're willing! Nearby in King's Square is a grand statue of Somers and some vintage canons. General admission: $3.

*Two seals named Charlotte and Archie steal the show at the Aquarium Seal Pool.*

### Devil's Hole Aquarium                               ★★★

*Harrington Sound Road, Bermuda,* ☎ *(441) 293-2072.*
*Hours: 10 a.m.–4:30 p.m.*

You can fish with a line and bait to your heart's content, but don't count on catching anything, as hooks are prohibited at this preserve. Devil's Hole claims to be Bermuda's first tourist attraction, open to tourists since 1830. Early visitors gave the 400-foot-deep pool "formed by a collapsed cave" its name because the wind traveling through the hole sounded like Satan. Actually, this place is quite benign, with some 400 marine creatures "living in absolute harmony," including colorful reef fish and the more dramatic sharks, giant groupers, moray eels and huge sea turtles. General admission: $5.

### Dolphin Quest                                       ★★★

*Southampton Princess, Bermuda,* ☎ *(441) 238-8000.*

Just opened in the fall of 1996, Dolphin Quest is the newest feature of the sprawling Southampton Princess Resort. Six bottlenose dolphins (which already were in captivity before being moved to Bermuda) live in a $1.2 million, three-acre ocean habitat, including a protected nursery cove for hopeful future births. Hotel guests have the opportunity to swim (Princess calls it "interact") with the creatures if their number comes up in a lottery, but if your heart is set on this experience, book the special Princess promotional package that guarantees a spot. Hours of operation and prices were not set at press time. Part of the proceeds from Dolphin Quest go to organizations that support marine education, research and conservation.

*St. George's Featherbed Alley contains an 18th century press and the St. George's Historical Society Museum.*

### Featherbed Alley Printery                              ★★

*Featherbed Alley, Bermuda,* ☎ *(441) 297-0009.*
*Hours: 10 a.m.–4 p.m.*
*Special hours: Closed 11-2 Wednesdays. Closed: Sun.*
The Printery has a working replica of a vintage Gutenbergess, invented by German Johannes Gutenberg in 1440. Worth a quick peek.

### Historical Society Museum                           ★★★★

*Featherbed Alley and Duke of Kent Street, Bermuda,* ☎ *(441) 297-0423.*
*Hours: 10 a.m.–4 p.m.*
This little gem in a former private mansion from the 1700s has a slew of interesting exhibits that chronicle Bermuda's early days. Besides the re-created bedrooms and other living spaces, there is a great variety of artifacts from the era. Among them: the second issue of the island's first newspaper, the *Bermuda Gazette* (Jan. 24, 1784), decoratively painted snuffboxes and tins, vintage clothing and a knife for cutting whale blubber. Note the backboard made of English oak, which was inserted in the back of a girl's dress to make her stand up straight. Well worth a visit. General admission: $2.

### Museum of the Bermuda Historical Society             ★★★★

*13 Queen Street, Hamilton, Bermuda,* ☎ *(441) 295-2487.*
*Hours: 9:30 a.m.–3:30 p.m.*
Set in the Bermuda Public Library on the grounds of Par-La-Ville Park, this museum is chock-full of artifacts from Bermuda's past. The Georgia-style two-story building dates to 1814 and was the lifelong

home of William Bennet Perot, Bermuda's first postmaster. The museum's fine collection of Bermuda cedar furniture dates almost entirely from the 18th century. The re-created living room has the original pitch pine flooring imported from the Carolinas, high-back prayer chairs from the 1700s and a bracket clock made on the island by Thomas Blatchley between 1784 and 1791. In the dining room, you'll find a mahogany and walnut table, an important collection of silver flatware, English and Oriental porcelain, a pair of Queen Anne cedar side chairs from about 1740 and a two-handled Worcester caudle cup from 1765. Note the portraits of Sir George Somers and his wife, Winifred, in the entranceway and a model of their ship, the *Sea Venture*, whose wreck in 1609 began permanent settlement of the island. Other interesting items include a Bermuda map by Blaeuw, dated 1622, that shows how Bermuda was divided into 25-acre strips by the original Bermuda Company; a fish-shaped lace maker by a Boer prisoner-of-war, made on the island in 1902; the "hog" coin, issued by the Bermuda Company in 1615, and Victorian stereoscopic viewers that present three-dimensional images of photographs.

Upstairs is the library, which was founded in 1839 and moved to this house in 1916. Among the stacks are rare books, as well as local newspapers on microfilm dating to 1784. The balcony is a pleasant spot to watch the hustle and bustle of Hamilton below.

### Palmetto House

*North Shore Road, Bermuda, ☎ (441) 295-9941.*
This early 18th-century house was built in the shape of a cross, a common style at the time. Three rooms furnished with fine Bermudian pieces are open to the public, but only on occasion, so call the Bermuda National Trust first to make arrangements.

### Springfield & Gilbert Nature Reserve

*Somerset Road, Somerset, Bermuda, ☎ (441) 234-1980.*
Another property run under the auspices of the Bermuda National Trust, Springfield is a 17th-century plantation house, complete with slave quarters, a buttery and a kitchen built around an open courtyard. Today, it houses the Somerset Public Library. The house is surrounded by five acres of mostly wooded land—a nice place to take a stroll. The reserve never closes, while the house is open to visitors on Mondays, Wednesdays and Saturdays from 9 a.m. to 5 p.m.

### Tucker House ★★★★

*Water Street, Bermuda, ☎ (441) 297-0545.*
*Hours: 9:30 a.m.–4:30 p.m.*
*Special hours: 10 a.m.–4 p.m. from Nov. 1-March 31.*
It may not look like much on the outside, but inside this early 18th-century merchant's house is a treasure trove of family heirlooms that date to the late 18th century, when the site was home to Henry Tucker, president of the Governor's Council from 1775 to 1807. Family silver, fine portraits, handcrafted quilts, crystal chandeliers and antique English and Bermudian furnishings pay silent tribute to the family's fortunes. Later, the home was occupied by Joseph Hayne Rainey, a free black man who escaped to Bermuda during the U.S. Civil War. Though he toiled as a barber on the island from this very house, he returned triumphant to the United States to become the

first black elected to the House of Representatives. Also check out the basement, where an exhibit of vintage artifacts uncovered on the site are displayed. General admission: $4.

### Verdmont ★ ★ ★ ★

*Collector's Hill, Bermuda,* ☎ *(441) 236-7369.*
*Hours: 9:30 a.m.–4:30 p.m.*
*Special hours: 10 a.m.–4 p.m. from Nov. 1-March 31. Closed: Sun.*
This Bermuda National Trust property is a Georgian-style mansion that dates to around 1710. It is considered the most important of the Trust's houses, and each of Verdmont's eight rooms has its own fireplace. The re-created rooms contain fine examples of antique Bermuda cedar furniture, as well as imported period pieces, English and Chinese porcelain, portraits and Victorian children's toys. The upstairs nursery is especially charming. A visit to Verdmont and its lovely gardens is a must for those interested in antiques and anything Bermudian. General admission: $4.

# Parks and Gardens

*Railway trail offers some of Bermuda's most scenic views.*

All the islands of Bermuda are practically one giant park, so well-manicured and landscaped are both its commercial and residential areas. No visit would be complete without a dazzling walk though one of the two limestone caves open to the public, and a jaunt or bike ride along the **Railway Trail** is practically de rigueur.

### Botanical Gardens ★ ★ ★ ★ ★

*Point Finger and South roads, Berry Hill, Bermuda,* ☎ *(441) 236-5291.*
*Hours: from dawn–dusk.*
Thirty-six acres of riotous color and sweet scents make the Botanical Gardens a must for visitors seeking natural beauty. The garden has 15 permanent exhibits and more than 1000 varieties of plant life, most of which were transported to the island in the 18th and 19th centuries. Stroll through a small forest, a hibiscus garden with 150 varieties of the colorful flower, subtropical fruit groves and a formal garden. The grounds also include an aviary and the Garden for the Blind, where

the scent of spice trees, lavender, lemon mint, oregano and geranium fills the air. Free 75-minute tours are offered on Tuesdays, Wednesdays and Fridays at 10:30 a.m. (Tuesdays and Fridays only from November to March); meet at the visitors center. The gardens also include a gift shop and tearoom (open 10 a.m.–4 p.m.), where you can try English cream teas each Tuesday from 3-4 p.m. Camden, located on the grounds, is the official residence of the island's premier. The two-story house, built around 1775, was lavishly embellished during the Victorian era. You can take a free tour of the house on Tuesdays and Fridays (noon–2:30 p.m.) if no official functions are in progress.

*Mark Twain described Bermuda's Crystal Caves as "the most beautiful in the world." One glowing group of stalagmites resembles Manhattan's skyline at night.*

### Crystal Caves      ★★★★★

*Wilkinson Avenue, Bailey's Bay, Bermuda, ☎ (441) 293-0640. Hours: 9:30 a.m.–4:30 p.m.*

This astoundingly beautiful cave was discovered in 1907, when two boys playing cricket saw their ball disappear down a hole. The resourceful lads climbed down the hole via rope and lantern, and soon forgot the ball upon discovering the cavern. (Incidentally, the ball has never been found.) A tour guide takes groups into the large main cavern some 80 feet underground. The cave is lit by white lights—not those obnoxious colored lamps you see at some commercial caves—and save for a few comments, the tour is not too corny. A wooden pontoon bridge traverses the subterranean Cahow Lake, which is so clear you can easily peer all the way down to its 55-foot bottom. The cave features giant stalagmites and stalactites; the constant sound of dripping water attests to the cave still busy very much alive—and growing at the glacial pace of one cubic inch per century. The cave is eerily beautiful—especially if you come early to avoid the crowds that inevitably show up when cruise ships are in port. Otherwise, it's a tight fit and all those people detract from the experience. General admission: $5.

### Heydon Trust      ★★★

*Somerset Road, Somerset, Bermuda, ☎ (441) 234-1831.*

*Hours: from dawn–dusk.*

Located across from Willowbank, the Christian retreat, this virginal slice of land encompasses 43 acres of orchards and gardens. A great place for birders, and lovely for anyone looking for a peaceful respite, with picturesque views of the Great Sound. Located on the grounds is Heydon Chapel, a sweet little house of worship that dates to around 1620.

### Leamington Caves ★★★

*Harrington Sound Road, Bailey's Bay, Bermuda,* ☎ *(441) 293-1188.*
*Hours: 10 a.m.–4 p.m.*

Though not as impressive as Crystal Caves, the Amber Caves at Leamington are worth a visit for their underground lakes and grand stalagmites and stalactites. The caves are located on the site of the Plantation Restaurant (see "Restaurants"), one of the island's best eateries. Spend $15 per person on lunch, and they'll give you free admission to the caves—not a bad deal. General admission: $4.

### Paget Marsh ★★★★

*Middle Road, Bermuda,* ☎ *(441) 236-6483.*

If you'd like to see Bermuda the way it looked when the first settlers came ashore, make arrangements with the Bermuda National Trust to tour this 18-acre site. The pristine woodland includes a mangrove swamp, regal cedar and palmetto trees and some endangered plants.

### Palm Grove Gardens ★★★

*South Shore Road, Bermuda.*
*Hours: 9 a.m.–5 p.m.*

Located on an 18-acre private estate, the gardens at Palm Grove are lovely, with spectacular ocean views a fitting backdrop to the well-tended citrus groves, lush blooms, wishing well, Chinese moon gate and a relief grass map of Bermuda set in a pond. Open Monday-Thursday.

### Par-la Ville ★★★★★

*Queen Street and Par-la-Ville Road, Hamilton, Bermuda.*
*Hours: from dawn–dusk.*

Probably one reason why Bermudians are able to stay so remarkably polite is this little gem of a park, located in downtown Hamilton behind the Perot Post Office and Public Library. The park is a tranquil oasis right in the heart of the city and beautifully done up with meandering pathways and well-tended gardens—a splendid place to enjoy a picnic lunch or catnap under the shade of a flowering tree. (Speaking of cats, a slew of the critters call this place home.) The park is crowded at noontime with businessfolk on their lunch hour, but that does little to detract from its peaceful ambience. Charming!

### Railway Trail ★★★★

Before the days of motorcars on Bermuda (which weren't allowed on the island until 1946), locals got from one end of the island to the other via the old "Rattle and Shake," a picturesque railway that threaded its way from St. Georges down to Sandys. When it finally opened in 1931 (after being conceived in 1899), it had a few dubious distinctions. Not only was it the costliest railway per mile ever built, but it was the slowest in terms of construction, with just 2.5 miles

ATTRACTIONS

added per year—due in part to the fact that one-tenth of the 21 miles of track is carried on 33 trestle bridges, 16 of which are over water.

The railway was quite popular with locals, but during World War II, equipment was hard to come by to keep it up and running. Meanwhile, Bermudians began a perhaps inevitable love affair with the automobile, and the railway met its final demise in 1946. The government bought it out but then quickly sold the entire system to Guyana (then called British Guiana). The original investors lost everything, and Bermuda, in a classic moment of shortsightedness, lost a fine method of mass transit.

After being virtually ignored for decades, the government cleared the overgrown track and opened the Railway Trail in 1984. It follows the old railway line from Sandys to St. George's, with frequent interruptions, including a three-mile section around the city of Hamilton. Broken into seven sections that form 18 miles of trails, the Railway Trail is a marvelous way to explore Bermuda on foot and enjoy some spectacular scenery. Part of the trail can be explored by horseback or motor scooter, and frequent signage helps keep visitors (literally) on track. To best enjoy the trail, pick up the free brochure (available at visitors centers and major hotels), which is chock-full of history, maps and reference guides to help you along. It is not recommended to use the deserted trail at night, and women should always use caution when traveling it alone—even in well-heeled Bermuda, there are still a few louts.

**ATTRACTIONS**

### Somers Garden

★★★★

*Duke of York Street, Bermuda.*

*Hours: 7 a.m.–4:30 p.m.*

Named for the man who started Bermudian history—Sir George Somers—this picturesque little park is a pleasant spot in which to take a break when exploring St. George's attractions. Local lore has it that Somers' heart was buried in the garden upon his death in 1610 by his nephew, who then took the body to England.

### Spittal Pond

★★★★

*South Shore Road, Bermuda.*

*Hours: dawn–dusk*

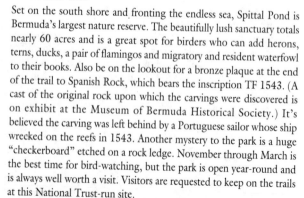

Set on the south shore and fronting the endless sea, Spittal Pond is Bermuda's largest nature reserve. The beautifully lush sanctuary totals nearly 60 acres and is a great spot for birders who can add herons, terns, ducks, a pair of flamingos and migratory and resident waterfowl to their books. Also be on the lookout for a bronze plaque at the end of the trail to Spanish Rock, which bears the inscription TF 1543. (A cast of the original rock upon which the carvings were discovered is on exhibit at the Museum of Bermuda Historical Society.) It's believed the carving was left behind by a Portuguese sailor whose ship wrecked on the reefs in 1543. Another mystery to the park is a huge "checkerboard" etched on a rock ledge. November through March is the best time for bird-watching, but the park is open year-round and is always well worth a visit. Visitors are requested to keep on the trails at this National Trust-run site.

# Sports

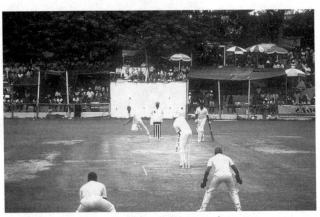

*Cricket remains one of the island's most popular sports.*

If you're into spectator sports, don't miss a game of cricket, played with great enthusiasm throughout the months of April to September. For information on where to find games, call the **St. George's Cricket Club** (☎ *[441] 297-0374*) or the **Somerset Cricket Club** (☎ *[441] 234-0327*). And don't miss the annual **Cup Match Cricket Festival**, held the Thursday and Friday before the first Monday in August. The tournament, between the East and West End cricket clubs, draws thousands who come to party (it's a national holiday) and cheer their teams to victory. You'll find more than bats and balls at cricket games; there's also the popular **Crown and Anchor**, a dice game with a minimum bet of $1 and unlimited maximum bets. This side action is fast and furious—and can be costly.

Rugby is also popular, with the season running from September to April. Local teams play on weekends at the National Sports Club (*Middle Road, Devonshire,* ☎ *[441] 236-6994*), while two major events, the **Easter Rugby Classic** (spring) and the **World Rugby Classic** (November), draw international players.

There are also plenty of opportunities for those who would rather participate than watch. The island has some 80 tennis courts—virtually every hotel has at least one—and is the perfect place to play all year, especially in the so-called "off" season of November to May. There are also horseback riding, snorkeling and scuba diving, fishing and other watersports.

### Helmet Diving

If you're not ready to try scuba diving and want a closer look at marine life than you can get from snorkeling, try this unique adventure, available April through November. After a boat cruise, you climb down a ladder with a helmet on your head that supplies air. The helmet allows you to walk around the ocean bottom at a depth of about 10 to 12 feet without getting your hair wet or having to remove your glasses—"as simple as walking through a garden," as the ad says. Swimming ability is not necessary. Helmet diving costs $44 for adults, $33 for kids under 12. Two outfits offer helmet diving: **Underwater Wonderland** *(Flatts Village, ☎ [441] 292-4434)* and **Undersea Adventures** *(Somerset, ☎ [441] 234-2861)*. Reservations recommended.

### Horseback Riding

Bermuda has just a handful of horses for hire, and they cannot be taken out without guides. The island's largest stable is **Spicelands Riding Centre** *(Warwick, ☎ [441] 238-8212)*, which offers lessons and excursions such as a one-hour trail ride (about $40) and a two-hour, early morning breakfast trip along the south shore (about $50). **Lee Bow Riding Centre** *(Devonshire, ☎ [441] 236-4181)* also offers trail rides (about $30 per hour) and lessons.

### Jet-skiing

Zipping along the surf in a motorized jet ski is becoming a popular watersport of the '90s, and the views of the shoreline here can be breathtaking. You can rent a Wave Runner at **Club Wet'n' Wild** at the Royal Naval Dockyard Marina, ☎ *(441) 234-2426*. Rates are about $70 per hour.

### Parasailing

Want to hang suspended by a parachute while a boat tugs you along? The views are great, and you can impress the folks back home. Call **Parasail Watersports** *(St. George's, ☎ [441] 297-1542)* and **South Side Scuba** *(Southampton, ☎ [441] 293-2915)*. The experience will set you back about $50.

### Scuba Diving

Surrounded by colorful coral reefs, crystal-clear water, teeming schools of tropical fish and literally hundreds of shipwrecks, Bermuda is perfect for diving. However, the sport has not been exploited much until recent years, though it is now coming on strong as an island activity. A comprehensive mooring system is being implemented to mark and protect dive sites, and commercial fishers are forbidden to use traps to catch fish and lobsters.

Bermuda's diving season starts in mid-March and runs through November, though some operators stay open past Christmas if the weather is good (Nautilus and Blue Water stay open year-round). Summer visibility is about 100 feet on the island's northern and western reefs, and about 80 feet on the southern and eastern reefs, which are closer to shore. Though Bermuda has a vibrant and healthy reef, the real lure for divers is the island's many shipwrecks—called "turtles in the net" by early sailors. Most of the wrecks are on shallow reefs; in fact, none past 80 feet is frequented by the dive operators, though deeper wrecks can be explored with a guide.

From July through September, water temperatures are in the mid-80s, and an eight-inch shorty wet suit is sufficient. During April, May, most of June and October and November, a full quarter-inch wet suit is advised.

Dive shops: **Nautilus Diving** *(Hamilton Princess, ☎ [441] 238-2322 and Southampton Princess, ☎ [441] 295-9485)*, **Blue Water Divers**

*(Somerset, ☎ [441] 234-1034),* **Fantasea** (Warwick, *[441] 236-6339)* and **Dive Bermuda** *(Sandy's, ☎ [441] 234-0225).* Expect to pay about $50 for a one-tank dive, $70 for two tanks and $35 if you need to rent equipment.

## Bermuda's Top Shipwrecks

Aristo *(maximum depth, 50 feet): This Norwegian steamer sank under tow during a rescue effort. Its cargo included a vintage fire truck, the remains of which are still on the forward deck.*

Constellation *and* Montana *(maximum depth, 30 feet): The 200-foot-long* Constellation, *an American four-masted schooner, was the inspiration for the novel and film "The Deep." It wrecked on the western reefs in 1943. Less than 50 yards away is the 236-foot-long* Montana, *an English paddle-wheel steamer built to penetrate the Union blockade during the Civil War. It wrecked in 1863.*

Cristobal Colon *(maximum depth, 55 feet): Bermuda's largest shipwreck, the 480-foot Spanish luxury liner ran aground in 1936. It's believed the ship was smuggling Loyalists out of Spain during the Spanish Civil War.*

Hermes *(maximum depth, 75 feet): This U.S.-built freighter, 160 feet long, is the island's most intact wreck. After being abandoned in Bermuda, the island's Dive Association scuttled her off the south shore in 1985, where she sits upright on the ocean floor.*

Mary Marie Celeste *(maximum depth, 60 feet): The paddle wheeler, a Confederate gunrunner, sank in 1864. Its rifles are still onboard.*

Minnie Brelauer *(maximum depth, 70 feet): The English freighter, en route from New York to Portugal, wrecked on its native voyage on New Year's Day, 1873.*

North Carolina *(maximum depth, 40 feet): Another New Year's Day wreck, this time in 1880, the* North Carolina *was a 150-foot-long English sailing barge with a cargo of cotton (which was salvaged). Considered one of Bermuda's most photogenic wrecks.*

Pelinaion *(maximum depth, 70 feet): This ill-fated Greek cargo steamer sank less than a mile from shore and is noted for its massive swim-through arches on either side.*

Pollockshields *(maximum depth, 30 feet): This German-built steamer ran aground during a hurricane in 1915 on the south shore. Many of its shell casings and projectiles are now cemented into the reef on the site. (They are considered unstable and should not be touched.)*

Rita Zovetta *(maximum depth, 65 feet): The 50-foot-long Italian freighter, which sank off the east end during a storm in 1924, is semipenetratable with many swim-throughs.*

Taunton *(maximum depth, 40 feet): A Norwegian freighter that wrecked to the northeast in 1920, despite having made many similar runs over 18 years. Her shallow depth and photogenic bow section make this a good dive for novices.*

ATTRACTIONS

*Church Bay beach is a choice spot for swimmers and sunbathers.*

### Snorkeling

*Bermuda.*

Bermuda's shallow reefs make snorkeling right off the beach both easy and accessible. Among the better spots to try: Tobacco Bay in St. George's, where rock columns some 25 feet high separate the bay from the sea; Shelly Bay on North Shore, where the water is shallow all the way up to the reef that starts about 50 yards offshore; John Smith's Bay on South Shore, where a solid reef starts 50 yards out; Elbow Beach, where the reef begins just 10 yards from the beach and continues out for more than a mile; and Achilles Bay, near Fort St. Catherine on the eastern end, where the water is shallow and the patch reef colorful.

If your hotel can't supply you with snorkel equipment, check out one of these outfits, which also arrange glass-bottom cruises and half- or full-day excursions: **Bermuda Cruises** *(Devonshire,* ☎ *[441] 234-7038),* **Bermuda Water Tours** *(Pembroke,* ☎ *[441] 295-3727),* **Bermuda Watersports** *(Grotto Bay,* ☎ *[441] 293-8333),* **Blue Water Divers** *(Somerset,* ☎ *[441] 234-1034),* **Fantasea Diving** *(Warwick,* ☎ *[441] 236-6339),* **Hayward's** *(Paget,* ☎ *[441] 292-8652),* **Jesse James Cruises** *(Warwick,* ☎ *[441] 236-4804),* **Nautilus Diving** *(Southampton,* ☎ *[441] 238-2332),* **Pitman's** *(Somerset,* ☎ *[441] 234-0700)* and **South Side Scuba** *(Paget,* ☎ *[441] 293-2915).*

### Water-skiing

*Bermuda.*

If you've got a hankering to ski on the crystal-clear sea, try one of these outfits (local law says only a licensed skipper can provide water-skiing): **Bermuda Water Ski Centre** *(Somerset,* ☎ *[441] 234-3354),* **Fantasea Diving** *(Warwick,* ☎ *[441] 236-6339),* **Island Water Skiing** *(Grotto Bay,* ☎ *[441] 293-3328)* and **Wake Up Ski School** *(Smith's,* ☎ *[441] 234-8924).* Plan on spending anywhere from $50 to $100, including lessons. **Kiteski Bermuda** *(*☎ *[441] 293-1968, or [441] 234-8768 in the evenings)* offers a new twist on the sport: kite-skiing, wherein a kite pulls the skier along the water to clock speeds as high as 50 m.p.h. They also claim the world's only "flying water-ski," a sit-down ski that rides above the water on a hydrofoil.

### Windsurfing

*Bermuda.*

The constant wind may be the bane of golfers, but it makes for great windsurfing, especially at Elbow Beach, the Great Sound and Shelly Bay. To rent equipment or take lessons, call **Mangrove Marina** *(Somerset,* ☎ *[441] 234-0914)* and **Windsurfing Bermuda Sail On** *(city of Hamilton,* ☎ *[441] 295-0808).*

# Boat Cruises

One of the best ways to see Bermuda is from the water, where you can really appreciate the great beauty of the island and its vintage, lovingly tended structures. If money is tight, the ferry can be just as enjoyable—at a fraction of the price. It's especially romantic at night.

### Boat Cruises

*Bermuda.*

One of the best ways to see Bermuda is from the water, where you can really appreciate the great beauty of the island and its vintage structures. Bermuda's many cruise companies offer everything from two-hour-long narrated tours (about $20 per person), to all-day excursions (about $60), to evening parties that include a buffet dinner, live music, entertainment and drinks (about $65). Another option is to board one of the many glass-bottom boats that showcase reefs and wrecks (about $30 for two hours). You can charter a 60-foot luxury yacht (call **Andrea Christine Charters,** ☎ *[441] 295-1240*) or join one of the more economical, regularly scheduled cruises for tourists. Most operate from April to October. Among those offering everything from sunset sails to booze cruises: **Bermuda Longtail** *(*☎ *[441] 292-0282),* **Bermuda Watersports** *(*☎ *[441] 293-2640),* **Bermuda Water Tours** *(*☎ *[441] 295-3727),* Champagne Cruises *(*☎ *[441] 236-7435),* **Coral Sea Cruises** *(*☎ *[441] 236-7637)* **Jesse James Cruises** *(*☎ *[441] 236-4804),* **Reef Roamers** *(*☎ *[441] 292-8652),* **Sea & See Cruises** *(*☎ *[441] 295-2580)* and **Somerset Bridge Cruises** *(*☎ *[441] 234-2738).*

For a completely different experience, hop aboard the Submarine Enterprise *(*☎ *[441] 234-3547),* which carries 44 passengers far beneath the water's surface to examine coral reefs and the wreck of the Lartington, which sank in 1878. Trips depart from Dockyard and Hamilton during high season.

**ATTRACTIONS**

# Fishing

Bermuda is a great spot for fishers, especially from May through November—though the fishing season runs year-round. For general information, contact the **Bermuda Game Fishing Association** *(P.O. Box HM 1306, Hamilton HM FX, Bermuda)*. Reef fishing is popular around the three major reef bands that lie off the shore. The closest runs a half-mile from the coast and goes out about five miles, the Challenger Bank is about 14 miles out, and Argus Bank goes out about 30 miles. Generally, the farther out you go, the bigger the fish (and the more expensive the outing). Shore fishing is good along the South Shore, West Whale Bay, Spring Benny's Bay, Great Sound and St. George's Harbour. Deep-sea fishing is also available through numerous charter firms.

### Fishing

*Bermuda.*

Visitors don't need a license to fish, though they may not take lobsters or use spear guns. Shore and shallow-water fishers can expect to snag snapper, bonefish and pompano, while those combing the reefs may bag grouper, Bermuda chub, rainbow runners, amberjack and snapper. Look for blue and white marlin, yellowfin tuna, barracuda and wahoo in deeper waters. Night fishing for shark (about $100) is also popular. To charter a deep-sea fishing boat, expect to pay about $675 for up to four people for four hours, and $875 for up to six people for eight hours. Reef fishing on a scheduled excursion goes for about $70 per person for a half-day.

Among the numerous companies that provide you with equipment and take you out on the deep blue sea or along the reefs: **Albatroll IV** (☎ *[441] 297-0715*), **Baxter Reef Fishing** (☎ *[441] 234-2963*), **Bermuda Big Game Fishing** (☎ *[441] 234-0198*), **Sea Scorpion II** (☎ *[441] 295-0140*), **Mako Charters** (☎ *[441] 234-8626*), **Early-bird Charters** (☎ *[441] 293-0813*), **Edness Fishing Charters** (☎ *[441] 236-3702*), **Captain Sinclair Lambe** (☎ *[441] 234-3081*), **Messaround Big Game Fishing** (☎ *[441] 297-8093*), **Princess Charters** (☎ *[441] 295-5813*), **Robinson's Boat Works** (☎ *[441] 234-1409*), **Sea Wolfe** (☎ *[441] 234-1832*) and **Striker I** (☎ *[441] 234-9294*).

# RESTAURANTS

*Ascots offers diners gourmet food in an antique-filled house, under the stars or poolside.*

Though Bermuda is almost more British than its motherland, you can forget all those jokes about bad English cooking—at least on the colony. While English pubs do abound, the food is traditional, true—and tasty. You can get everything from bangers and mash (beef sausages served with mashed potatoes and onion gravy), cottage pie (seasoned ground beef in a rich gravy with onions and vegetables and topped with mashed potato), steak-and-kidney pie or the ploughman's platter (cheeses, pickled onions, sweet pickle and crusty bread)—and, of course, fish and chips.

Besides their pub fare, Bermudians also love a good meal from Italy. The island has a slew of Italian restaurants that offer up everything from pizzas to pastas to lasagna. The British love of curried food is also apparent in the many Indian dishes offered at continental restaurants.

Some things you must try: Bermuda fish chowder (a tasty seafood concoction served with black rum and sherry peppers on the side), conch fritters, cod cakes, shark hash, onion-and-mussel pie, and cassava pie, a spicy meat pie traditionally served on Christmas Day. You'll often see "local Bermuda fish" on the menu, which simply means whatever fish they caught that day. "Bermuda lobster" differs from the Maine variety in that it is more spiny and lacks claws. It can only be caught from Sept. 1 to March 31; the rest of the year the lobster is from Maine.

For some reason, the presentation of butter has become a high art form in Bermuda. Take the time to notice and you'll see that virtually every restaurant has its own uniquely designed pats.

One thing Bermuda lacks is what makes it so special: chain and fast-food restaurants. While there is a KFC in the city of Hamilton, you won't find any Burger Kings or McDonald's. However, as a result, dining out in Bermuda can be, and often is, a very expensive proposition. Except for local seafood and some fruits and vegetables, virtually all food is imported.

Most people dress for dinner, especially in the summer (high) season and year-round at the fancier resorts, hotels and restaurants. Gentlemen are often required to wear not just a jacket but a tie as well, while women can get away with a dress or fancy pants suit. Otherwise, it's a jacket for men and something suitably dressy for women. In most cases, jeans, T-shirts, beach clothes, cropped shirts, short-shorts and too-revealing clothing are not acceptable.

Many restaurants add a 15 percent service charge onto the bill, which takes care of the tip. If you're not sure, ask. Reservations are often required during the summertime, when many places fill up.

The island has few nonsmoking restaurants, though many have designated smoking sections.

## The Dine-Around Program

To help lure tourists during the off (winter) season, many restaurants participate in the Dine-Around Program that runs from Nov. 1 to March 31. These special-dinner menus include three or four courses for a fixed price that is often quite reasonable. You usually get two or three choices of appetizers, entrées and desserts. However, drinks and tip are not included in the price. If you're visiting the island during that time, you'll have no problem finding a brochure that details the Dine-Around Program; participating restaurants display a symbol in the window.

## Hamilton

**Halfway House**                    **$**                    ★★

*8 North Shore Road, Flatts Village, Hamilton,* ☎ *(441) 295-5212.*
No, it's not run by people poised to re-enter society—the name comes from the location, which is halfway between the cities of St. George's and Hamilton. Despite the sometimes-lacking service, this place is liked by locals for its casual atmosphere and decent burgers,

chicken dishes and the like. The fountain drinks are especially good. Credit cards: MC, V.

### Mikado     $$$     ★★★★

*Marriott's Castle Harbour Resort, Hamilton,* ☎ *(441) 293-2040.*
*Japanese cuisine.*
*Dinner: 6:30-9:30 p.m., entrées $25–$40.*
After passing through a stylized Japanese garden, you'll find all the razzle-dazzle of a traditional Japanese steak house—where chefs prepare teppanyaki meals right at the table amid lots of showmanship. Mikado is the island's only major Japanese restaurant; you can order either a la carte or a complete dinner. It also has one of the island's few sushi bars. After dinner, continue the Japanese theme by singing karaoke at the resort's Blossoms Oriental Lounge. Reservations required. Credit cards: A, DC, MC, V.

### Swizzle Inn     $$$     ★★★

*Blue Hole Hill, Bailey's Bay, Hamilton,* ☎ *(441) 293-9300.*
*English cuisine.*
*Lunch: Noon–6 p.m., entrées $6–$9.*
*Dinner: 6-10:30 p.m., entrées $12–$22.*
"Swizzle in—swagger out" is the motto of this old favorite, which has been around for decades. Housed in a 350-year-old building, the Swizzle is famous for the creation of the rum swizzle, Bermuda's national drink. The bar is happening and lots of fun—tack your business card to the wall, as countless others before you have done, or borrow a felt-tip pen and inscribe a witticism. Come for happy hour (4:30-6:30 p.m. in the summer, 5-7 p.m. in the winter), and spin the large carnival wheel, which determines how much you'll pay per drink (not much of a gamble, as the price only varies by 35 cents). Also, ask to see the old guest books, which date to 1941. Lunch fare consists of typical English pub food as well as homemade soups, salads and sandwiches, while dinner is a bit more elaborate, with specialties such as Asian lemon chicken, vegetarian curry and the artery-clogging mixed grill (lamb, liver, sausage, bacon, mushrooms and grilled tomato). With its high-quality rattan furnishings, the upstairs dining room is a good escape for those who don't want to be part of the rowdy bar scene, which rocks till 1 a.m. There's also a gift shop offering logo apparel. Credit cards: A, MC, V.

### The Plantation     $$$     ★★★★

*Harrington Sound Road, Bailey's Bay, Hamilton,* ☎ *(441) 293-1188.*
*cuisine.*
*Dinner: 7-9:30 p.m., entrées $24–$34.*
If you're interested in trying "real" Bermudian food, look no further than The Plantation, long a local favorite. The dining room, filled with greenery and high-quality rattan furnishings, is lovely. The menu offers up all kinds of eclectic dishes, including a good selection of steaks and chicken, though the emphasis is on fresh local seafood. Service is professional and hospitable. If you spend at least $10 on lunch (which is not hard to do), they'll give you a free ticket to Leamington Caves. The Plantation closes each January and part of February. Jacket requested. Reservations recommended. Credit cards: A, MC, V.

### Tom Moore's Tavern     $$$     ★★★★

*Harrington Sound Road, Bailey's Bay, Hamilton,* ☎ *(441) 293-8020.*

*cuisine.*
*Dinner: 7-9:30 p.m., entrées $24–$32.*
Named for the Irish poet who frequented this spot in the early 1800s, the Tavern is set in a former private mansion that dates to 1652. The French/continental gourmet fare is quite grand, but don't fill up too much on the divine appetizers and main courses (the seafood is especially good), because the dessert soufflés are not to be missed. Plan on spending about $40 per person at this posh spot. Open for dinner only. Jacket and tie requested. Reservations required. Credit cards: A, MC, V.

## Paget

**'Brellas**                                 **$$$**                              ★★★★
*Newstead Hotel, Harbour Road, Paget,* ☎ *(441) 236-6069.*
*Dinner: 7-10 p.m., entrées $18–$29.*
This outdoor cafe at Newstead Hotel is open only from May to October and is a fabulous place to watch the lights of Hamilton across the harbor. Start with an appetizer like warm asparagus salad or homemade shrimp-and-spinach ravioli, then move onto a main dish such as grilled New Zealand lamb fillet, fillet of suckling pig or grilled seafood on the skewer. Or try the traditional cassava meat pie—a local favorite. Features: outside dining. Reservations required. Credit cards: A, MC, V.

**Fourways**                                 **$$$**                         ★★★★★
*1 Middle Road, Paget,* ☎ *(441) 236-6517.*
*Dinner: 6:30-9:30 p.m., entrées $27–$56.*
Long considered one of Bermuda's finest restaurants, Fourways consistently delivers for those who can afford its charms. The restaurant is set in a 1727 mansion and is breathtaking with its traditional beamed ceiling, thriving hanging plants, stone walls and arches and cedar furnishings and trim. Though you can sit outdoors on the patio, the ambience inside is just too good to pass up. The large menu offers up many hors d'oeuvres—such as beluga caviar at $86 per ounce and more (relatively) affordable appetizers in the $16–$29 range. Among the highlights on the menu are baked fillet of rockfish with lobster and herb crust, Bermuda lobster, loin of venison, chateaubriand for two ($80) and a good selection of vegetarian dishes, such as filo parcels with a variety of fillings and fondue of leek. Save room for both the fresh-baked breads and dessert—Fourways is justifiably famous for its wonderful pastries made on the premises. (They also have a shop in Hamilton on Reid Street for those who can't get enough.) The excellent wine list has won awards from the *Wine Spectator*, and the lobby proudly displays the signature of George Bush, who dropped by for lunch in 1991. Jacket and tie requested. Reservations recommended. Credit cards: A, MC, V.

**Newstead**                                 **$$$**                              ★★★★
*Harbour Road, Paget,* ☎ *(441) 236-6060.*
*Dinner: 7:30-9:30 p.m., prix fixe $42.*
The formal dining room at the Newstead hotel offers views of Hamilton, right across the harbour, and will put anyone in the mood for romance. On a more practical note, you can eat as much as you want with the prix-fixe dinners, which makes this spot especially popular

with big eaters. The food is marvelous and there's frequently entertainment to go with it. Vegetarians should not be shy about speaking up—if there is nothing suitable on the menu (which changes daily) the chef will happily whip something up. While there, be sure to check out the wonderful ambience of Newstead's gracious and elegant public rooms. Jacket and tie requested. Reservations required. Credit cards: A, MC, V.

### Norwood Room      $$$      ★ ★ ★ ★

*Stonington Beach Hotel, Paget,* ☎ *(441) 236-5416.*
*Lunch: Noon–2 p.m., entrées $8–$19.*
*Dinner: 7-8:15 p.m., prix fixe $45.*
The formal dining room at the Stonington Beach hotel features wood-beamed ceiling, black chandeliers and arched windows that overlook the sea. Like the hotel, the chefs and staff are mostly students of the Hospitality and Culinary Institute of Bermuda, so you're ensured friendly, enthusiastic service. The food is wonderful and highly gourmet—try the crabmeat-stuffed mushrooms for starters—and fresh local seafood is especially recommended. Arrive before 8:15 p.m. for dinner, as that is when the last order is taken. Jacket and tie requested. Reservations required. Credit cards: A, DC, MC, V.

### Peg Leg Bar      $$      ★ ★ ★ ★

*1 Middle Street, Paget,* ☎ *(441) 236-6517.*
*American cuisine.*
*Lunch: Noon–3 p.m., entrées $7–$15.*
Located in the same mansion that's home to the famed Fourways Restaurant, this cozy spot is housed in the original kitchen. It's quite charming with an enormous stepped and whitewashed Bermuda-style fireplace, slanted walls rising to a pitched ceiling, tiny paned windows and white walls accented with brass lanterns and antique golf prints. The Caesar salad is excellent, or try luscious entrées such as grilled shitake mushrooms and goat cheese, roasted free-range chicken and Bermuda codfish cake. A good choice for a tasty lunch. Credit cards: A, MC, V.

## Pembroke

### Ascots      $$$      ★ ★ ★ ★

*Rosemont Avenue, Hamilton, Pembroke,* ☎ *(441) 295-9644.*
*Lunch: Noon–2:30 p.m., entrées $10–$13.*
*Dinner: 6:30-10:30 p.m., entrées $23–$29.*
You'll have as hard a time deciding where to sit as what to order at this fine gourmet spot just outside of downtown Hamilton. You can dine in a cozy antique-filled room (the house was built circa 1870), out under the stars surrounded by garden greenery or on the pool terrace. The menu highlights provincial European dishes, with lots of local fish enchanced by freshly picked fruit. There's also a good selection of daily specials, vegetarian entrées and, for later, the award-winning Crepe Garibaldi. Lunch is served Mondays–Friday. Jacket requested. Reservations recommended. Credit cards: A, MC, V.

### Bombay Bicycle Club      $$$      ★ ★ ★

*75 Reid Street, Hamilton, Pembroke,* ☎ *(441) 292-0048.*
*Indian cuisine.*
*Lunch: Noon–2:30 p.m., prix fixe $12.*
*Dinner: 6:30-11 p.m. Mon.-Sat., entrées $14–$22. Closed: Sun.*

RESTAURANTS

Get your dinner to go, or better yet, dine in the atmospheric room with ceiling fans, sitar music and large peacock wicker chairs. Located in the Rago Furniture Building, this restaurant offers 15 curries as well as Bengali and tandoori specialties such as chicken parkora, bastimi rice biryanis and spiced shrimp in coconut sauce. The "Taste of India" lunch buffet is good value at $11.95. For dinner, expect to pay about $30–$40 per person. The Bombay Bicycle Club is located on the third floor of the building, and can be reached by stairs or an elevator. Lunch is not served on Saturdays. Jacket requested. Reservations required. Credit cards: A, MC, V.

### Botanic Garden Tea Room          $                    ★ ★ ★

*37 Front Street, Hamilton, Pembroke,* ☎ *(441) 295-1183.*
*English cuisine.*
*Lunch: 11:30 a.m.–3 p.m., entrées $3–$8. Closed: Sun.*

Despite the name, this cozy tea room is actually located in Trimingham's Department Store—not the Botanic Gardens. But lots of greenery justifies the name. A pleasant spot for afternoon tea or a light snack; the menu features sandwiches, pastries and other home-baked concoctions.

### Buckaroo                          $                    ★ ★

*Church Street West, Hamilton, Pembroke,* ☎ *(441) 295-1231.*
*Lunch: 6 a.m.–3 p.m., entrées $3–$12. Closed: Sun.*
Few tourists patronize this no-nonsense spot that promises home-cooked meals. With its formica counter and unadorned booths, this no-frills place provides good eats at cheap prices. Besides the typical salads and sandwiches, you can get grilled specials such as deep-fried scallops or fried calf's liver. Best of all are the old-fashioned sundaes and milk shakes. Breakfast is served until 11:30 a.m.

### Chancery Wine Bar                 $$$                  ★ ★ ★ ★

*Chancery Lane, off Front Street, Hamilton, Pembroke,* ☎ *(441) 295-5058.*
*Lunch: Noon–2:30 p.m., entrées $8–$20.*
*Dinner: 6:30-10:30 p.m., entrées $17–$27.*
One reason locals like this place so much is that the menu changes each season, so there is always something new and different. You can sit in the small trellised courtyard for an al fresco meal, or inside the restaurant, housed in a former wine cellar that dates to the early 1900s. True to the name, the restaurant has a huge wine list (more than 160 types), and many vintages can be ordered by the glass. Another plus: dress and ambience here is strictly casual. Reservations recommended. Credit cards: A, MC, V.

### Chopsticks                        $$$                  ★ ★ ★

*88 Reid Street, Hamilton, Pembroke,* ☎ *(441) 292-0791.*
*Chinese cuisine.*
*Lunch: Noon–2:30 p.m., entrées $11–$28.*
*Dinner: 6-11 p.m., entrées $11–$28.*
Feeling daring? Order the "hot and numbing chicken," but beware, as the dish lives up to its name. This pretty-in-peach restaurant offers specialties from China and Thailand, including such delicacies as five-spiced hanging duck, tom yum kung dim sum, green curry chicken and varied vegetarian dishes. If you're hankering for Peking duck, order 24 hours in advance. Dinner for two will run about $60. Lunch

is served Monday–Friday. Reservations recommended. Credit cards: A, MC, V.

## Cock & Feather          $$          ★★★

*Front Street, Hamilton, Pembroke,* ☎ *(441) 292-2263.*
*English cuisine.*
*Lunch: 11 a.m.–5:30 p.m., entrées $4–$17.*
*Dinner: 6-10 p.m., entrées $8–$20.*
The cruise-ship dock is right across the street, so expect lots of tourists at this casual spot, located up a steep set of stairs, where you can dine indoor or out. Locals hang out here, too, and buy "bingo" tickets—a sort of instant lottery. At times, the Cock & Feather has the atmosphere of a casino as everyone from the bartender to the doorman gets into the act of testing Lady Luck. (Warning: These $1 tickets are a rip-off!) The menu features sandwiches in the $6 range, as well as more filling fare such as Bermuda red bean soup, fish chowder, steaks, rack of lamb, seafood and cottage pie (seasoned ground beef in a rich gravy with onions and vegetables and topped with mashed potatoes). Bands play nightly in the summer and Thursday–Sunday during winter. Those with late-night munchies appreciate the pizza served from 10:30 p.m.–1 a.m. Lunch is served Monday–Friday. Credit cards: MC, V.

## Fisherman's Reef          $$$          ★★★

*Burnaby Hill, Hamilton, Pembroke,* ☎ *(441) 292-1609.*
*Seafood cuisine.*
*Lunch: Noon–2:30 p.m., entrées $8–$24.*
*Dinner: 6:30-10:30 p.m., entrées $22–$33.*
As the name suggests, it's all quite nautical at this intimate restaurant located above the popular Hog Penny Pub. The walls, painted blue and scalloped to resemble waves, are punctuated by "portholes" that look onto reefs and colorful fish. Oak furnishings and brass lanterns complete the effect. Lunch fare consists of soups, Cajun or garlic shrimp, and conch and corn fritters, as well as the usual salads and sandwiches. The dinner menu is much more extensive and includes the house specialty, Angels on Horseback (lobster wrapped in bacon). Stop at the Hog Penny for a before- or after-dinner drink. Lunch is served Mondays–Fridays. Jacket requested. Reservations recommended. Credit cards: A, MC, V.

## Flanagan's Irish Pub          $$          ★★

*69 Front Street, Hamilton, Pembroke,* ☎ *(441) 295-8299.*
*Dinner: to 9:30 p.m., entrées $8–$20.*
If you're weary of Bermuda's many English-style pubs, here's an Irish pub with cuisine to match—try Dublin Skins, Wexford spicy chicken, and all the traditional pub foods. There's also a decent selection of local dishes such as the award-winning Bermuda fish chowder. A great selection of imported beers and ales and frequent live entertainment keep the joint jumpin'. Credit cards: A, MC, V.

## Harbourfront          $$$          ★★★★

*21 Front Street, Hamilton, Pembroke,* ☎ *(441) 295-4207.*
*Seafood cuisine.*
*Lunch: 11:30 a.m.–6 p.m., entrées $7–$19.*
*Dinner: 6:30-10 p.m., entrées $16–$28.*
Enjoy views of the harbour from this upstairs eatery located on busy Front Street. Sit on the porch or inside the dining room made pretty

with its cloth linens, hurricane lamps and flickering candles. Up on entering, you'll encounter the sushi bar, with a good selection of tempura, sashimi, nigiri, temaki and norimaki, along with sake and Sapporo beer to wash it all down. The sushi bar costs $4–$6 for two to six pieces, but if you come during happy hour (4:30-6:30 p.m. every day), everything is just $3.75 with complimentary miso soup.

Lunch is informal (served Monday–Saturday), with the usual soups, salads, pastas and burgers. Dinner is more formal and elaborate; the extensive menu includes appetizers with saffron snails in a puff pastry and mussels baked in Cajun spicy sauce, mushrooms and herbs. For an entree, try ravioli topped with lobster meat and rockfish; angel hair pasta with sun-dried tomatoes, eggplant, mushrooms and white wine; or ricotta and spinach gnocchi. Seafood entrées include the "Bermuda Triangle"—the three best catches of the day topped with saffron, basil and honey-mustard sauces. Credit cards: A, MC, V.

### Hog Penny                  $$$                  ★★★★

*5 Burnaby Hill, Hamilton, Pembroke,* ☎ *(441) 292-2534.*
*English cuisine.*
*Lunch: Noon–3 p.m., entrées $7–$17.*
*Dinner: 5:30-10 p.m., entrées $9–$24.*

This wonderfully atmospheric English pub is a favorite gathering spot of locals who come to sample the latest from the Bermuda Triangle Brewing Company and unwind after a day in the office. The small bar features specialty drinks, including the national favorite, "Dark & Stormy" (black rum with ginger beer) and, of course, the "Bermuda Triangle" (black rum, Bermuda gold, orange and pineapple juices). The lunch menu consists of burgers and pub fare such as shepherd's pie, steak and kidney pie, and as well as bangers and mash. A selection of Indian curries, sandwiches and salads also are available. Dinner is much the same, with the addition of Angus beef, surf and turf combinations, along with coffees from around the world. This is a great spot to rub elbows with young local professionals. Lunch is served noon–4 p.m. on Fridays and Saturdays and dinner is served Saturdays–Thursdays. On Sundays the pub is open only for dinner. Credit cards: A, MC, V.

### Little Venice              $$$                  ★★★★

*32 Bermudiana Road, Hamilton, Pembroke,* ☎ *(441) 295-3503.*
*Italian cuisine.*
*Lunch: 11:45 a.m.–2:15 p.m., entrées $9–$15.*
*Dinner: 6-10 p.m. daily, entrées $16–$28.*

Twin lions guard the door of this Italian restaurant, a favorite hangout of locals who head upstairs to The Club for a few dances after dinner (admission is free to diners). The dining room is sedate, with a black-and-white checkered floor, pressed tin ceiling and paintings of Italy. Lunch consists of pizzas, a variety of salads and pasta dishes and heavier fare such as Bermuda fish, calf's liver and roasted cornish hen. Dinner features the same, plus hot and cold appetizers and meat entrées. Try to snag one of the plush booths as they're much more comfortable than the tables. Lunch is served Mondays–Fridays. Credit cards: A, MC, V.

## Lobster Pot       $$$        ★ ★ ★ ★

*6 Bermudiana Road, Hamilton, Pembroke, ☎ (441) 292-6898.*
*Seafood cuisine.*
*Lunch: 11:30 a.m.–4:30 p.m., prix fixe $0.*
*Dinner: 6-10:30 p.m. Mon.-Sat., entrées $22–$28. Closed: Sun.*

True to the name, there are lots of lobsters awaiting their demise in this cute restaurant that's been around since 1973. Outside the building looks like a wharf, with a wooden boardwalk and large barrels; inside the nautical theme continues with wooden lobster crates, fish nets and bamboo accents. The business lunch, served weekdays from 11:30 a.m.–2 p.m., is a good deal, costing $14.75 for three courses. The menu, which is essentially the same for lunch and dinner, offers seafood pasta dishes, sandwiches, salads and some interesting concoctions such as curried fish in a pancake glazed with mango chutney and hollandaise sauce. Depending on the time of year, you can order Bermuda spiny lobster (Sept. 1-March 31) or ones from Maine. Your lobster can be cooked, steamed, broiled, stuffed or cold. Prices vary so much that they are written on the menu in pencil, but expect to pay at least $28. The menu also advises guests to ask for rare kinds of fish, just in case they are on hand. This accommodating attitude makes the Lobster Pot a favorite of both locals and visitors. Incidentally, its fishing vessel, the *Lobster Reef*, can be chartered for deep-sea or reef fishing; call for details. Lunch is served Monday–Friday and dinner is served Monday–Saturday. Credit cards: A, MC, V.

## M.R. Onions       $$$        ★ ★ ★

*Par-la-Ville Road, Hamilton, Pembroke, ☎ (441) 292-5012.*
*Lunch: Noon–2:30 p.m., entrées $11–$24.*
*Dinner: 5 p.m.–1 a.m., entrées $11–$24.*

It's inevitable Bermuda would have at least one restaurant named for its national vegetable—here it is in the form of this fun place with a friendly bar. Expect to see lots of families lured by the casual atmosphere and "Kidds Korner" menu that's offered from 5-7 p.m. Everyone can enjoy the budget-priced, early-bird menu that is served until 6:30 p.m. Prices are reasonable and the food good and simple—burgers, salads, fish, ribs, steaks and the like. Lunch is not served on Saturdays or Sundays. Reservations recommended. Credit cards: A, D, MC, V.

## Monte Carlo       $$$        ★ ★ ★ ★ ★

*9 Victoria Street, Hamilton, Pembroke, ☎ (441) 295-5453.*
*Mediterranean cuisine.*
*Lunch: Noon–3 p.m., entrées $9–$14.*
*Dinner: 6:30-11:30 p.m., entrées $19–$25. Closed: Sun.*

Located just behind City Hall, Monte Carlo scores time and again with its wonderful Mediterranean menu featuring goodies from Italy and Southern France. The cozy restaurant has French provincial furnishings, impressionist artwork painted directly onto the walls, and white linen service. Lunchtime is highlighted by the wonderful pizzas and yummy appetizers—two appetizers make a perfect meal. After enjoying the complimentary rosemary focaccia with olive paste tapenade at dinner, feast on such specialties as bouillabaisse Marseillaise or angel hair pasta with roasted peppers, sun-dried tomatoes and kalamata olives. Save room for the tempting desserts presented via table-

RESTAURANTS

side trolley. Lunch is served Monday–Friday and dinner is served Monday–Saturday. Reservations recommended. Credit cards: A, MC, V.

### New Captain's Lounge                $$                ★

*Reid Street, Hamilton, Pembroke,* ☎ *(441) 293-9546.*
*American cuisine.*
*Lunch: 11:30 a.m.–3:45 p.m., entrées $5–$14.*

This local bar is open from 11 a.m.–1 a.m. and offers up a basic lunch and some imaginative burgers such as one decked out with pineapple. You can also get roast beef or a hot turkey sandwich served with fries, coleslaw or peas and rice. Lunch is served Monday–Saturday. No sneakers after 9 p.m.

### New Queen                $                ★★★

*Par-la-Ville Road, Hamilton, Pembroke,* ☎ *(441) 295-4004.*
*Chinese cuisine.*

The New Queen has been feeding hungry diners for more than 70 years, so you know the food will be good at this casual restaurant noted for its reasonable prices. Specialties are Chinese Cantonese and hot-spicy Szechuan dishes, and there's also English and American fare, including lots of sandwiches. Open Sunday from 5:30 p.m.–midnight. Reservations recommended. Credit cards: A, DC, MC, V.

### Once Upon a Table                $$$                ★★★★

*49 Serpentine Road, Hamilton, Pembroke,* ☎ *(441) 295-8585.*
*French cuisine.*
*Dinner: 6-9 p.m., entrées $20–$47.*

Elegance is the byword at this ultra-deluxe restaurant housed in an 18th-century mansion dolled up in lace, velvet, antiques and candlelight. Dinner is usually a fabulous event, with freshly baked herb-scented rolls and interesting appetizers such as hot camembert with strawberry conserve. If that doesn't sound sinful enough, consider chicken and truffles in a puff pastry, chateaubriand bearnaise or grilled tournedos maison. Fresh seafood, vegetarian and low-fat items are available as well. It's all quite lovely and romantic here, but be prepared to drop a bundle—at least $40 to $50 per person. And though this spot has a reputation as one of Bermuda's finest restaurants, it's only fair to report that not everyone agrees: One person reports that dinner here "was one of the worst dining experiences I have ever had" due to indifferent service, poorly prepared food and small portions. Complaints have also been received about the restaurant's participation in the off-season dine-around program—it seems the promised last course of a "four-course" dinner is merely coffee. Jacket and tie requested. Reservations required. Credit cards: A, DC, MC, V.

### Pasta Basta                $                ★★

*One Elliott Street, Hamilton, Pembroke,* ☎ *(441) 295-9785.*
*Italian cuisine.*
*Lunch: 11:45 a.m., entrées $5–$9.*

Sister restaurant to St. George's Pasta Pasta, this informal place is perfect for tasty Italian dishes available in half or full portions. The decor is welcoming and so are the prices—a steal by Bermuda standards. No liquor is served.

### Pink's Front Street Deli                $                ★★

*55 Front Street, Hamilton, Pembroke,* ☎ *(441) 295-3524.*
*American cuisine.*

*Lunch: from 7:30 a.m., entrées $4–$8.*
*Dinner: to 10 p.m., entrées $4–$8. Closed: Sun.*

This basic, but spotlessly clean, delicatessen is a good place to pick up sandwiches on white, wheat, French, multigrain bread or an onion roll; salads (great Caesar) or continental breakfast. It also offers picnic box lunches if you call ahead. You can get food to go, or sit on the porch overlooking Front Street. Closes at 5 p.m. during the spring and winter.

### Port O' Call      $$$       ★★★★

*87 Front Street, Hamilton, Pembroke, ☎ (441) 295-5373.*
*Seafood cuisine.*
*Dinner: from 5 p.m., entrées $20–$36. Closed: Sun.*

At this atmospheric seafood spot the walls are painted wedgewood blue, blending nicely with the naval uniforms worn by the wait staff. Prepare to be spoiled with the likes of grouper cordon bleu, whole English dover sole and seafood crepes and ravioli. A few meat dishes are offered for carnivores. Money-saving early bird specials are served from 5–6:30 p.m. nightly. Reservations recommended. Credit cards: A, MC, V.

### Portofino      $$$       ★★★★

*Bermudiana Road, Hamilton, Pembroke, ☎ (441) 292-2375.*
*Italian cuisine.*
*Lunch: 11:30 a.m.–4 p.m., entrées $8–$18.*
*Dinner: 6 p.m.–1 a.m. Mon.-Sat, entrées $10–$23.*

It's cozy inside this locals' favorite, but the tables are a bit too close together for intimate conversation. No matter, because the food is so good you'll be too busy eating to talk. The lunch and dinner menus, which are virtually the same, feature pasta dishes, seafood, homemade pizzas (daring souls try the "Portofino Special"—pizza with tuna fish and onions) and specials such as *fegato alla veneziana* (liver with onions). Open Sunday from 6 p.m.–midnight; other days, get here before 11:45 p.m. to place a dinner order. Lunch is served Monday–Friday. Credit cards: A, MC, V.

### Red Carpet      $$$       ★★★★

*37 Reid Street, Hamilton, Pembroke, ☎ (441) 292-6774.*
*Italian cuisine.*
*Lunch: 11:30 a.m.–3 p.m., entrées $7–$19.*
*Dinner: 6:30-10:30 p.m., entrées $13–$28.*

The carpeting is indeed red at this tiny Italian bistro (decorated more like an English pub) that draws lots of locals, especially for lunch. Signature dishes include penne with vodka, smoked salmon and cream; veal cooked with cream, ham and mushrooms; and fresh fish sautéed in white wine, clams and baby shrimp. Keeping with the Italian theme, there's even a ravioli dish named in honor of Frank Sinatra. Lunch is served Monday–Saturday. Reservations recommended. Credit cards: A, MC, V.

### Ristorante Primavera      $$$       ★★★★

*69 Pitts Bay Road, Hamilton, Pembroke, ☎ (441) 295-2167.*
*Italian cuisine.*
*Lunch: 11:45 a.m.–2:30 p.m., entrées $16–$23.*
*Dinner: 6:30-10:30 p.m., entrées $15–$23.*

A comfortable place to fill up on luscious pasta dishes and other Tuscany specialties, Primavera consistently delivers with good, friendly service. Choose from a wide selection of fresh seafood, including soft shell crab, mussels, clams and lobster. Cap it all off with a tasty espresso or cappuccino. Come between 6:30–7:30 p.m. and enjoy price-saving early bird specials. Closed for lunch on the weekends. Reservations required. Credit cards: A, DC, MC, V.

**Robin Hood**                         **$$**                         ★★★

*Richmond Road, Hamilton, Pembroke,* ☎ *(441) 295-3314.*
*English cuisine.*
*Lunch: Noon–2 p.m., entrées $7–$12.*
*Dinner: 6-11 p.m., entrées $8–$19.*

Off the beaten track from downtown Hamilton, Robin Hood is a favorite of young locals, especially expatriates from England. The Tudor-style building is wonderfully atmospheric from the outside; once through the doors, though, the decor is more generic. Lunch consists of soups, salads, quiches, and hot and cold sandwiches; ask about the day's "Merrymen" specials. The more extensive dinner menu offers up platters of grilled steaks, cottage pie, liver and bacon—even lasagne. Robin Hood is best known for its pizzas—served all day—which you can order off the menu or create yourself. The small room upstairs is the place to go to play pool. Credit cards: A, MC, V.

**Romancing the Scone**                **$**                         ★★★

*Front Street, Hamilton, Pembroke,* ☎ *(441) 295-3961.*
*English cuisine.*
*Lunch: 11:30 a.m.–4 p.m., entrées $3–$13. Closed: Sun.*

Set on a porch above Cooper & Sons Department Store, this is the perfect spot to relax and enjoy a light nibble. Enjoy views of Front Street and the harbour beyond—providing no cruise ships are in port. The decor is charming, with white glass-topped tables and striped umbrellas. Breakfast, served from 10-11:30 a.m., includes eggs benedict and homemade waffles. Lunch, offered from 11:30 a.m. on, features gourmet sandwiches and hot dishes such as quiches, vegetarian lasagne and baked avocado stuffed with chicken, shrimp, tuna or crab and topped with provolone cheese. Afternoon tea is served from 2:30-4 p.m., the perfect complement to a fresh-baked scone.

**Romanoff**                          **$$$**                        ★★★★

*34 Church Street, Hamilton, Pembroke,* ☎ *(441) 295-0333.*
*Lunch: Noon–2:30 p.m., prix fixe $17.75.*
*Dinner: 7-10 p.m., entrées $33–$42. Closed: Sun.*

Be prepared to spend a bundle for dinner at this stately restaurant, where the service is impeccable and the cuisine ranges from continental specialties to Russian and French dishes, all created by chef/owner Anton Duzevic. Some favorites include traditional Russian borscht, local fish and poultry dishes, you'll also can try vodka and black caviar. The ever-present trolley makes dessert impossible to resist, but you'll be glad you indulged. A bit overpriced, though, even by Bermuda standards. Lunch is served Monday–Friday. Jacket and tie requested. Reservations required. Credit cards: A, DC, MC, V.

**Rosa's Cantina**                     **$**                         ★★★

*121 Front Street, Hamilton, Pembroke,* ☎ *(441) 295-1912.*
*Mexican cuisine.*
*Lunch: from noon, entrées $7–$10.*

Bermuda's only Tex-Mex restaurant pulls out all the stops with its fiesta-inspired decor of ceiling fans, Mexican sombreros and brightly colored tablecloths. The reasonable prices and relaxed dress code draw locals by the score. The food is not too overwhelmingly spicy, and includes everything you'd expect, from iguana eggs to burritos to fajitas. Not surprisingly, Rosa's makes a mean margarita, too. Reservations not accepted. Credit cards: A, MC, V.

**The Porch**                    **$$$**                    ★★★

*93 Front Street, Hamilton, Pembroke,* ☎ *(441) 292-4737.*
*English cuisine.*
*Lunch: 11:30 a.m.–5 p.m., entrées $5–$19.*
*Dinner: 5:30–10 p.m., entrées $14–$23.*
With its fanciful white wrought-iron gingerbread trim, The Porch is a distinctive landmark on Front Street. The restaurant is housed on the second floor, as are many other Front Street eateries. Guests are seated indoors in the atmospheric English-style pub, decorated with horse brasses and a wall lined with books, or outside, where patrons can enjoy splendid views of Hamilton Harbour. For lunch, try hot sandwiches such as breaded fish or steak, or specialties such as grilled or Cajun chicken breast or a Bermuda-style codfish cake. Salads, burgers and fish and chips are offered, too. Dinner is a bit more formal, with entrées such as sautéed venison kabobs flamed with Drambuie liquor, seafood, English steak and mushroom pie and the "roast of the evening." Vegetarians have a few choices as well. Open on Sundays for dinner only. Credit cards: A, MC, V.

**The Wok**                    **$**                    ★★★

*10 Bermudiana Road, Hamilton, Pembroke,* ☎ *(441) 295-7789.*
*Chinese cuisine.*
*Lunch: entrées $9.*
*Dinner: entrées from $15.*
Though you can eat at the small counter, most folks get their food to go from this small Chinese fast-food restaurant, then dine under the sun at adjacent Par-la-Ville park. Everything tastes—and smells—divine, and your biggest problem will be deciding what to order. Besides sandwiches and salads, there's chop suey, sweet and sour pork, chow mein, stir fry and even burgers. Be sure to grab a free fortune cookie. Hours are Monday–Friday 7 a.m. to midnight, Saturdays 8 a.m.–1 a.m. and Sundays 11:30 a.m.–midnight. American and Chinese breakfasts are served until 11 a.m.

**Tuscany**                    **$$$**                    ★★★★

*95 Front Street, Hamilton, Pembroke,* ☎ *(441) 292-4507.*
*Italian cuisine.*
*Dinner: 6–10:30 p.m., entrées $10–$23.*
Though it just opened in 1994, this Italian eatery looks much older, with the traditional beamed ceiling, brick walls and colorful murals reminiscent of Tuscan. The food is as good as the atmosphere, with a wide selection of fish, meat and pasta dishes. Great pizza, too. Dine indoors or al fresco on the terrace. Reservations recommended. Credit cards: A, MC, V.

**Waterloo House**                    **$$$**                    ★★★★

*Pitts Bay Road, Hamilton, Pembroke,* ☎ *(441) 295-4480.*
*Lunch: Noon–2:30 p.m., entrées $10–$21.*

*Dinner: 7:30–9:30 p.m., entrées $25–$28.*

This pretty dining room at the lovely Waterloo House is painted rose and has coordinated floral drapes, brass chandeliers, linen tablecloths and large windows overlooking the harbour. Meals are also served outdoors when the weather permits. Lunch consists of vegetarian sandwiches, burgers, codfish cakes and salads. Dinner is a much more formal affair with offerings such as baked red snapper, tiger prawns, roasted rack of lamb, quail, and chicken and duck dishes. Be sure to try one of the imaginative soups such as wild berry or chilled cherry tomato with curried crabmeat. Jacket and tie requested. Reservations recommended. Credit cards: A, MC, V.

## Sandys

**Frog & Onion Pub**          **$$**          ★★★★

*Royal Naval Dockyard, Sandys, ☎ (441) 234-2900.*
*English cuisine.*
*Lunch: Noon–3 p.m., entrées $7–$18.*
*Dinner: 6–9:30 p.m., entrées $8–$22.*

This large pub boasts a huge fireplace, thick stone walls and a happening bar. The extensive lunch menu features English pub fare as well as sandwiches, salads and vegetarian specials. Try a traditional pub pie filled with pork and lentils or vegetables and cheese. Dinner is much the same, with the addition of appetizers such as black pudding served with apple chutney. Daily specials are named for famous old English pubs; Wednesday, for instance, is "Cat & Fiddle"—linguini with mussels, shrimp, clams and crab with a creamy white sauce. Friday evenings include a barbecue with meats grilled in the fireplace. There's also a reasonably priced kids' menu. On Sundays, lunch is served from noon–4 p.m. and dinner from 5:30-9 p.m. The bar stays open until midnight daily, and there's nightly entertainment in the summer. If you like pool or darts, check out the back room. Lunch is served Monday–Saturday. Credit cards: A, MC, V.

*Diners at Lantana Colony Club are surrounded by paintings, sculptures, flowers and trees as they dine on classic French cuisine.*

**Lantana Colony Club** $$$ ★★★★
*Somerset Bridge, Sandys,* ☎ *(441) 234-0141.*
*French cuisine.*
*Dinner: 7:30-9:30 p.m., prix fixe $45.*
The menu changes daily at this lovely dining room, which enhanced by trees and colorful fresh flowers, as well as sculptures and paintings. The classical French food is as scrumptious as the surroundings, and those put off by heavy cream sauces will be delighted by the selection of lighter, health-conscious entrées. While it's OK to dress casually for outdoor dining, indoors gentlemen are required to wear a jacket and tie. Jacket and tie requested. Reservations required. Credit cards: A, DC, MC, V.

**Loyalty Inn** $$$ ★★★
*Mangrove Bay, Somerset Village, Sandys,* ☎ *(441) 292-6978.*
*Lunch: 11:30 a.m.–4 p.m., entrées $7–$16.*
*Dinner: 6:30–10 p.m., entrées $26–$49.*
Located a short stroll from the Watford Bridge ferry, this charmer is housed in a 250-year-old Bermuda mansion. You can eat indoors or out, where the singing of tiny tree frogs is a pleasant musical backdrop (there's man-made entertainment as well on the weekends). Try one of the homemade soups, then dig into a well-prepared entrée of seafood or meat. Locals frequent this spot. Lunch is served Monday–Saturday. Reservations recommended. Credit cards: A, DC, MC, V.

**Pirate's Landing** $$$ ★★★
*Royal Naval Dockyard, Sandys,* ☎ *(441) 234-5151.*
*Lunch: 11:30 a.m.–4 p.m., entrées $4–$17.*
*Dinner: 6–10 p.m., entrées $13–$23.*
This informal spot in Royal Naval Dockyard is decorated with terra cotta floors, lanterns and ceiling fans. Lunch consists of salads, burgers, pastas and a small selection of gyros—try the Hu-Ha-Si-Sa, a combination of chicken, beef and chorico (Portugese sausages) in very hot Indian sauce. The more extensive dinner offerings include grilled specialties such as chicken and tenderloin, as well as several dishes flavored with Indian spices and herbs. Credit cards: A, MC, V.

**Somerset Country Squire** $$$ ★★
*Mangrove Bay Road, Somerset, Sandys,* ☎ *(441) 234-0105.*
*English cuisine.*
*Lunch: 11:30 a.m.–4 p.m., entrées $11–$26.*
*Dinner: 6:30–10 p.m., entrées $11–$26.*
You'll find the ambience of a traditional English pub at this casual spot near the Watford Bridge Ferry. Pretty views of Mangrove Bay abound, and if the weather permits, you can dine outdoors under the stars. Among the English and Bermudian specialties are a wonderful curried mussel pie and traditional Bermuda fish chowder. During the summer, barbecues are offered Sunday, Monday and Tuesday nights. Frequent live entertainment also is offered. Reservations recommended. Credit cards: A, MC, V.

## Smith's

**Inlet Restaurant** $$$ ★★
*Palmetto Bay Hotel, Flatts Village, Smith's,* ☎ *(441) 293-2323.*
*Lunch: Noon–2:30 p.m., prix fixe $12.*
*Dinner: 7–9:30 p.m., entrées $18–$30.*

**RESTAURANTS**

A good place to drop by for a light lunch or dinner, this small eatery serves guests in a pleasant dining room or outdoors on the patio. The food is decent but nothing to rave about with reasonable prices and friendly service. Enjoy the great views of Harrington Sound. The traditional English dinner served each Sunday from noon–2 p.m. is popular. The bar in the Ha'penny Pub stays open until 1 a.m. Credit cards: A, MC, V.

**Specialty Inn**                    $                         ★★
*Collector's Hill, Smith's,* ☎ *(441) 236-3133.*
*Italian cuisine.*
Extremely reasonable prices and good, home-style Italian pizza and specialties make this laid-back restaurant a frequent choice of locals—who don't mind the decided lack of atmosphere. Stuff yourself with yummy pasta or fried seafood, and you won't either.

## Somerset

**Il Palio**                         $                         ★★★
*Middle Road, Somerset,* ☎ *(441) 234-2323.*
*Italian cuisine. Closed: Mon.*
Craving great pizza? Head for this West End spot, about a 10-minute walk from the village. If pizza won't do, try some of the mouthwatering pasta or seafood dishes—or perhaps roast duckling. Save room for dessert! Reservations recommended. Credit cards: A, MC, V.

## Southampton

**Cafe Lido**                        $$$                       ★★★★
*Elbow Beach Resort, Southampton,* ☎ *(441) 236-9884.*
*Italian cuisine.*
*Dinner: entrées $18–$29.*
Set right on lovely Elbow Beach at the resort of the same name, this Italian eatery often has a lively bar scene. The food is fantastic—try the vermicelli with shrimp—and the service good. Besides wonderful pastas, the menu features fish and meat dishes. Check out the great antique clock at the bar. Reservations recommended. Credit cards: A, MC, V.

**Coconuts**                         $$$                       ★★★
*The Reefs Hotel, South Shore Road, Southampton,* ☎ *(441) 238-0222.*
*Dinner: prix fixe $39.*
There's nightly entertainment and dazzling views of the sea at this outdoor restaurant at The Reefs. The prix-fixe dinner is a good deal and includes an appetizer, soup, salad, main course and coffee and dessert. Don't worry about eating so much—you're sure to burn off more than a few calories on the walk back up the hill. Open only from May to October. Reservations required.

**Henry VIII**                       $$$                       ★★★
*South Shore Road, Southampton,* ☎ *(441) 238-1977.*
*English cuisine.*
*Lunch: Noon–2:30 p.m., entrées $9–$18.*
*Dinner: 6:30–10 p.m., entrées $20–$26.*
With its beamed ceilings, large-paned windows, dark woods and brass railings, Henry VIII's is a tudor charmer. Despite the fact that the staff dresses in Olde England garb and the "King" and "Queen" occasionally hold court, the food is really good, and you'll find locals

mixed in with the inevitable tourists. Lunch fare consists of salads, sandwiches (try the liverwurst and Bermuda onion) and English favorites such as fish and chips, steak and kidney pie and the plough-man's platter (cheeses, pickled onions, sweet pickle and crusty bread). The huge dinner menu, presented on a scroll, has fish, "fowls" and meat dishes. Specialities include chateaubriand, rack of lamb and duck l'orange. The bar is a nice and cozy place to meet new folks, and rocks until 1 a.m. with a live band. Credit cards: A, DC, MC, V.

### Lighthouse Tea Room $ ★★

*Gibbons Lighthouse, Southampton,* ☎ *(441) 238-8679.*
*English cuisine.*
*Lunch: 9 a.m.–5 p.m., entrées $4–$9.*
This cute little spot is located in the base of Gibbons Lighthouse—treat yourself to a snack after tackling the many stairs to the top. Enjoy the views from the windows, and take note that all the artwork and knick-knacks pay homage to the glory of tea, with some amusing old advertisements and quaint teapots. Unfortunately, a plethora of signs reduce it all to tackiness. There are signs urging you to buy souvenirs, signs saying tea room caters to groups, signs suggesting you buy a gift certificate—even a sign saying "please don't take our menus," which are not the slightest bit special anyway! Ah well, the food is good and reasonably priced. The menu consists of the quiche of the day, smoked salmon, English smoked trout (especially good), even baked beans served on toasted herb bread. Besides the soothing traditional English and specialty teas, there are espressos, cappuccinos and mochas for the coffee crowd.

### Lillian's $$$ ★★★★

*Sonesta Beach Hotel, Southampton,* ☎ *(441) 238-8122.*
*Dinner: 6–10 p.m., entrées $14–$28.*
The prices are quite reasonable for a hotel gourmet dining room, and the atmosphere is elegant. The dining room is enchanced by fine woodwork, subdued lighting and colorful table runners over white linen. A pianist provides delightful background music. Among the more interesting appetizers are smoked mozzarella ravioli with a spicy tomato sauce and excellent minestrone made with a tomato broth. Save room for the main course—anything from sautéed breast of pheasant or grilled salmon to sirloin steak or fettuccine. Light eaters can order a "petit entree" of chicken, pasta, layered eggplant and smoked gouda cheese or seasonal specials. Credit cards: A, MC, V.

### Newport Room $$$ ★★★★★

*Southampton Princess, Southampton,* ☎ *(441) 238-8000.*
*French cuisine.*
*Dinner: 6:30–9:30 p.m., entrées $25–$32.*
You'll feel as if you're in the stateroom of a luxurious—and huge—yacht at this very nautical spot in the Southampton Princess. This place is so popular that it still looks exactly as it did when it first opened in 1972. The menu changes frequently, and the cuisine, dubbed "nouveau French," has modern American and United Kingdom touches. Meals are served on Wedgwood china and German crystal. Jacket and tie requested. Reservations required. Credit cards: A, MC, V.

RESTAURANTS

### Rib Room    $$$    ★★★★

*Southampton Princess, Southampton,* ☎ *(441) 238-8000.*
*American cuisine.*
*Dinner: 6:30–9:30 p.m., prix fixe $35.*

One of the few places at the Princess Southampton where you can dress casually at night, this dinner-only spot specializes, as the name suggests, in ribs—and lots of them. There's also lamb, beef and grilled meats to keep carnivores happy, but vegetarians should look elsewhere, unless the large salad bar will be enough. Excellent service, and nice views of the golf course. Dinner for two will set you back nearly $100. Reservations recommended. Credit cards: A, MC, V.

### Tio Pepe    $$$    ★★

*South Shore Road, Southampton,* ☎ *(441) 238-1897.*
*Italian cuisine.*
*Lunch: Noon–5 p.m., entrées $9–$25.*
*Dinner: 5–9:30 p.m., entrées $9–$25.*

The name is Mexican but the cuisine is decidedly Italian at this very casual place where you don't have to worry about dressing up or spending a bundle. Pizzas and pastas are the rule here, but you can also find some seafood and local dishes. During off season, Tuesdays, Wednesdays and Thursdays, dinners are half-price. Lunch hours vary—sometimes it is not offered at all during the winter—so call first. Reservations recommended. Credit cards: A, MC, V.

### Waterlot Inn    $$$    ★★★★★

*Middle Road, Southampton,* ☎ *(441) 238-0510.*
*Mediterranean cuisine.*
*Dinner: 6:30–10 p.m., entrées $24–$41.*

Dinner will set you back an arm and perhaps even a leg, but it's worth it at this splendid spot. Owned by the Southampton Princess, the Waterlot is set in 1670 manor house that was once run by a Claudia Darrell, a woman who, in 1916, was credited with saving the ship *Pollacksheilds*, which ran aground on the reefs at Elbow Beach. The captain was swept overboard, but thanks to Darrell's efforts 33 sailors—and three kittens—were saved. After enjoying a cocktail in the elegant lounge with its plush sofas, candlelit tables and antique model ships, you're escorted to your table in the lovely dining room, which overlooks a large patio and the sound. Try an appetizer such as blue point oysters or boiled half lobster tail, but be warned—each starter runs about $15. Entrées consist of selections such as Bermuda fish bouillabaisse, roasted rack of lamb, beef dishes and grilled Mediterranean vegetables. Many dishes are prepared or carved tableside, and offerings include roasted beef tenderloin and shrimp, scallops and lobster laced with permod on a bed of orzo pasta. Save room for dessert, or at least the petits fours that come with coffee. Pianist and singer Earl Darrell plays here Tuesday through Sunday as he has for the past 25 years. This is a fun place to eavesdrop on your well-heeled fellow diners. Sunday brunch to the sounds of a jazz combo is served in the summer on the patio for $28.50. Jacket and tie requested. Reservations required. Credit cards: A, DC, MC, V.

### Whaler Inn    $$$    ★★★★

*Princess Beach Club, Southampton,* ☎ *(441) 238-0076.*
*Seafood cuisine.*

RESTAURANTS

*Dinner: 6:30–9:15 p.m., prix fixe $38.*

Set on a cliff overlooking the beach at the Southampton Princess, the Whaler gets high marks for its deliciously prepared fresh fish, although the menu also includes a few meat dishes. Eat indoors or on the terrace, where the sounds of the surf make any evening romantic and the sunsets are divine. Friday nights are given over to a Louisiana Cajun Seafood Festival, complete with Dixieland band. Open only for dinner, and only during the summer season. Expect to pay around $100 for dinner for two. Reservations recommended. Credit cards: A, DC, MC, V.

## St. George's

### Carriage House $$$ ★★★★

*22 Water Street, St. George's, ☎ (441) 297-1270.*
*English cuisine.*
*Lunch: 11:30 a.m.–2:30 p.m., entrées $8–$21.*
*Dinner: 6–9:30 p.m., entrées $15–$48.*

Set in the Somers Wharf Complex overlooking the busy dock, the Carriage House serves casual lunches and more formal, candlelit dinners in an 18th-century brick mansion. Fresh Bermuda fish, carved-at-the-table prime rib and English spring lamb are among the usual offerings; be sure to inquire about the day's specials. With its carving stations and large salad bar, the popular Sunday brunch (served from noon–2:15 p.m. for $24). Features: Sunday brunch. Jacket requested. Reservations recommended. Credit cards: A, MC, V.

### Dennis's Hideaway $$$ ★★★

*Cashew City Road, St. David's, St. George's, ☎ (441) 297-0044.*
*Dinner: 7-10 p.m., prix fixe $25–$35.*

This eccentric spot is the place to come for good, home-cooked Bermudian meals dished up by Dennis Lamb and his son. The place is pretty run-down and the furnishings look like they came from Salvation Army, but no one seems to mind because the food—conch stew, fish chowder, mussel pie and other local specialties—is so fine. Many of the vegetables are grown right out from by Dennis himself. Don't worry about dressing up—Dennis's is as casual as it gets. Reservations recommended.

### Pasta Pasta $ ★★★

*York Street, St. George's, ☎ (441) 297-2927.*
*Italian cuisine.*
*Lunch: from noon, entrées $8*

There's not much atmosphere at this self-serve restaurant but the food is great and better yet, the prices are incredibly cheap by Bermuda standards. After picking up your pasta dish and sauce at the window, head upstairs to the bright and airy dining room, or get food to go and enjoy lunch in one of St. George's parks. No liquor is served. Opens at 5 p.m. on Sundays.

### Pub on the Square $$$ ★★

*3 King's Square, St. George's, ☎ (441) 297-1522.*
*English cuisine.*
*Lunch: from 11 a.m., entrées $13–$26.*
*Dinner: 5:30–10 p.m., entrées $13–$26.*

Don't expect gourmet fare at this atmospheric 1785 English-style café, but enjoy traditional pub fare and daily Bermudian specials. Din-

RESTAURANTS

ner is served until 10 p.m., though the bar stays open until the wee hours. Credit cards: A, MC, V.

**San Giorgio**                    $$                    ★★★
*Water Street, St. George's,* ☎ *(441) 297-1307.*
*Italian cuisine.*
*Lunch: Noon–2:30 p.m., entrées $9–$16.*
*Dinner: 6:30–9:30 p.m., entrées $9–$16.*
Choose from pasta, freshly rolled pizzas and antipasti choices at this unassuming and casual Italian restaurant. Located next to the Tucker House, the restaurant has the requisite red-checkered tablecloths and artwork honoring San Giorgio—a little piece of Italy right in St. George's. Good value for the money. Lunch is served Monday–Friday and dinner is served Monday–Saturday. Reservations recommended. Credit cards: MC, V.

**Wharf Tavern**                    $$$                    ★★★
*14 Water Street, St. George's,* ☎ *(441) 297-1515.*
*Seafood cuisine.*
*Lunch: from 11 p.m., entrées $5–$25.*
*Dinner: to 11 p.m., entrées $9–$25.*
Located on Somers Wharf in a 200-year-old converted warehouse, the Wharf Tavern specializes in all kinds of seafood. Try the excellent Bermuda fish cakes or, if you're in a carnivorous mood, enjoy the traditional steak and kidney pie. Frequent live music is offered during the summer, and never a cover charge. Reservations recommended. Credit cards: MC, V.

**White Horse Tavern**                    $$                    ★★★
*King's Square, St. George's,* ☎ *(441) 297-1838.*
*English cuisine.*
*Lunch: 11 a.m.–5 p.m., entrées $8–$18.*
*Dinner: 6–10 p.m., entrées $8–$20.*
Live music is featured every night during the summertime (only on weekends in the winter) at this happening spot—the city's oldest pub—that abuts the water at King's Square. You can sit inside the restaurant decorated with brick walls, green-and-white-striped tablecloths, a large bar and fireplace, and even fishing poles hanging from the ceiling. Lunch fare includes American-style burgers, English pub food such as steak and kidney pie, Bermudian fish chowder. Other all-around favorites include smoked turkey and mozzarella salad. Dinner is much the same, with the addition of lamb, pork, curry and seafood dishes. During the summer, the White House serves some 400 lunches, so you're better off coming before 11 a.m. or after 3 p.m. to avoid a long wait. At press time, the White Horse was planning to add a snack bar that will be open from 11 a.m.–1 a.m. daily; call for details. Credit cards: MC, V.

# Warwick

**Paw Paws**                    $$$                    ★★★
*87 South Road, Warwick,* ☎ *(441) 236-7459.*
*Lunch: 11 a.m.–5 p.m., entrées $7–$14.*
*Dinner: 5:30–10:30 p.m., entrées $15–$24. Closed: Tue.*
Whether you have a hankering for Bermudian or European food, you will find it in this small and charming restaurant. Dine indoors in a pretty room filled with Bermudian artwork, or out on the terrace

under bright blue umbrellas. Besides a wonderful Caesar salad, the menu offers great fish chowder, homemade lobster ravioli, vegetable quiche and mussel stew. The restaurant's name comes from a type of papaya that grows wild throughout the island. Try the signature dish, *Paw Paw Montesan*, a concoction of the fruit mixed with ground beef, cheddar cheese, onions and tomatoes. Reservations recommended. Credit cards: MC, V.

RESTAURANTS

# WHERE TO STAY

*The Princess Golf Club is a scenic test of skill as golfers battle bunkers, water hazards and unpredictable ocean winds.*

Frequent visitors to Bermuda will probably be surprised to learn there are some 75 properties on the island—a huge number considering Bermuda's small size and preponderance of residential neighborhoods. Besides the handful of major resorts, most guest accommodations are so subtly marked you could walk right by—repeatedly—and never realize what they are. The **Waterloo House**, for example, is a gorgeous enclave just a few minutes from downtown Hamilton, but it's marked only by a tiny brass sign. Across the street, the venerable **Rosedon** looks more like a private mansion than a full-fledged—and excellent—hotel.

That everything is so understated is a large part of Bermuda's great charm. You'll find no neon here, no large signs advertising low rates and waterbeds, none of the brightly lit logos of a Holiday Inn or Best Western. Most of Bermuda's properties are independent, and many have been owned and operated by the same family for decades.

It's likely to stay that way for quite some time, as the island has placed a moratorium on the construction of hotels and limited expansion of existing hotels to 10,000 beds.

But not to worry—you'll have no problem finding the right accommodation for yourself. As with anyplace, it all depends on your idea of a perfect holiday. If you're into a place where you can soak up the rays at the beach, play golf and tennis, get your nails done or splurge on a massage—or order up room service at 2 a.m.—you'll be happiest in one of the resorts. There are also many fine hotels that offer myriad services without all the hoopla and crowds associated with a resort. Many of these properties are housed in former private mansions with the trademark wooden shutters and beamed ceilings. Bermuda is famed for its many cottage colonies, which feature a main clubhouse with a dining room, lounge and bar, as well as recreational facilities such as a beach and pool. Most of the units have small kitchenettes for whipping up a snack but are not appropriate for full-time cooking. If you're interested in extensive cooking, check out the large number of housekeeping apartments and cottages. Amenities vary considerably at these spots, but most have at least a pool. Finally, Bermuda offers up a wealth of guest houses that provide spotlessly clean and comfortable accommodations for a fraction of what you'll pay elsewhere. However, you're generally on your own for meals (besides breakfast) and entertainment.

Here are a few things to consider regarding accommodations:

**Wheelchair accessibility:** Unlike the United States and its Americans with Disabilities Act, Bermuda has no law requiring accessibility. Furthermore, many properties are set on steep hills or cliffs that require a good amount of scaling stairs. When a property can accommodate wheelchairs, it is noted in the description. For more information regarding facilities for persons with disabilities, contact the Department of Tourism for a free copy of the **Access Guide to Bermuda for the Handicapped Traveller** *(43 Church Street, Hamilton HM 12, Bermuda)* or the **Society for the Advancement of Travel for the Handicapped** *(P.O. Box HM 449), Hamilton HM BX, Bermuda).*

**Meal plans:** Many hotels and resorts offer a variety of meal plans; in the high (summer) season, it is often mandatory to sign up for one. The rates quoted in this book are for European Plan, which means no meals (except for the guest houses, which, unless stated otherwise, provide breakfast). Meal plans include: MAP (Modified American Plan, breakfast and dinner), AP (American Plan, breakfast, lunch and dinner), BP (Bermuda Plan, full breakfast) and CP (Continental Plan, light breakfast). Be sure you know exactly what your options are before committing to any meal plan—you're generally locked in once you do sign up.

**Service charges:** Virtually every establishment tacks a daily service charge onto your bill, and they can add a lot to the bottom line. Except for the major resorts, which generally add on a set charge of $6 to $17 per day, the service charge is usually 10 percent of the nightly rate; some go as low as 7 percent. Paying a service charge eliminates the necessity of tipping the maid—though how many people do you know who tip the maid $10 to $25 per day? The only way around it is to stay in one of the few properties that do not levy such a tax, such as **Stonington Beach Hotel**, **Willowbank** and **Clear View Suites**.

**Hotel tax:** All room rates are subject to a 7.25 percent daily Bermuda Government Hotel Occupancy Tax.

**Energy surcharge:** Some properties charge anywhere from $1 to 4 percent of the bill per day as an energy surcharge. Fortunately, this is limited to just a handful of accommodations.

# Hotels and Resorts

Like all first-rate islands, Bermuda has a wealth of upscale resorts and hotels that cater to every whim. Virtually every resort has a pool, watersports, tennis courts, several restaurants and a beach. Dress is fairly formal at these large properties, especially for dinner. Many hotels offer much the same but may lack a beach; however, most can set you up at another property's beach, where changing facilities are provided—but you may be on your own for transportation. (Details are provided in the descriptions.)

Though the large properties are all quite fine, unless you're really into the resort atmosphere, consider staying in one of Bermuda's many venerable hotels. These historic structures give a real feel for the island that is impossible to duplicate at a large resort. They are especially worth considering in the winter months, when it's generally too cold for the beach. Hotels such as **Newstead** and **Rosedon** just ooze with charm, and many rooms are filled with antiques. Obviously, it's a personal choice, but you'll experience more of the "real" Bermuda at one of these vintage properties. Bermuda offers a reservation service at ☎ *(800) 637-4116.*

## Hamilton

**Elbow Beach Resort**          $135–$455          ★ ★ ★ ★ ★

*60 South Shore Road, Hamilton, ☎ (800) 223-7434, (441) 236-3535, FAX (441) 236-8043.*
*Single: $135–$425. Double: $135–$455.*
Set on 50 landscaped acres above a pink-sand beach, Elbow Beach (formerly a Wyndham property) is a real winner for those who like bustling resorts. It's been welcoming guests since 1908, and the management has certainly got its act down. Guest rooms are pretty and of a decent size, with wooden furnishings, desks, sofas, Italian marble

baths, armoires hiding cable TVs and large balconies. Those who can't get work out of their minds are happy to find the fax/computer hookups in each room. There are also 17 duplex cottages scattered around the grounds for extra-plush living. Facilities include a large, free-form pool, five tennis courts (two lighted), a complete health club, beauty salon, tour desk, watersports and supervised activities for the kids. Of the property's several restaurants, the Italian Cafe Lido is especially good. Each Sunday there's a fun beach party and barbecue, and there are also nightly entertainment in Spazzizzi's Bar and a pianist in the lounge. Though it's set well out of the city, Hamilton is much closer than the Sonesta or Southampton Princess—just another plus to this fine resort. 294 rooms. Credit cards: A, DC, MC, V.

### Grotto Bay Beach Hotel & Tennis Club $110–$198     ★ ★ ★ ★

*11 Blue Hole Hill, Hamilton,* ☎ *(800) 582-3190, (441) 293-8333, FAX (441) 293-2306.*
*Single: $110. Double: $110–$198.*

Colorful gardens add a peaceful feel to this 21-acre resort set on the water's edge in Hamilton Parish. Nearby are ancient caverns and grottos to be explored. The property consists of 11 three-story town houses. All rooms have an ocean view, balcony or patio, coffeemaker, and extra amenities such as a hair dryer and in-room safe. There is a swim-up bar in the pool (created from natural rock), as well as two private beaches, four tennis courts (two lighted), a fitness center, putting green, games room, complete watersports—even a croquet lawn. Parents can stash the kids in supervised programs during the summer, and rent a moped right on site. The rates include afternoon tea and continental breakfast. There's live entertainment during the high season. Explorers enjoy the twice-weekly "cave crawls" and daily cave swimming right on the premises. This resort delivers in most every way, but its relatively isolated location will make forays around the island expensive, unless you rent a moped. 201 rooms. Credit cards: A, MC, V.

## Paget

### Harmony Club          $370–$500     ★ ★ ★ ★

*South Shore Road, Paget,* ☎ *(800) 225-5843, (441) 236-3500, FAX (441) 236-2624.*
*Double: $370–$500.*

This all-inclusive resort (Bermuda's only) is located five minutes by car from Hamilton. Accommodations are in buildings reminiscent of Brittish cottages, appointed with Queen Anne furnishings, some with a patio or balcony. Features include cable TV, phone, radio, bathrobes and hair dryer. The rates include all meals and drinks in addition to a welcome bottle of champagne, a two-seat moped for the length of stay, and greens fees at the Belmont Golf Course. Guests can use the facilities at Elbow Beach for free as well. On-site amenities include daily entertainment, several restaurants, a pool, two tennis courts and a putting green. Good value at this spot, which is only open to couples—although it can be two friends, mother and daughter, and so on. In often pricey Bermuda, staying here can put your mind at rest, as you know exactly what you'll be paying and what you're getting. 71 rooms. Credit cards: A, DC, MC, V.

**Newstead**     **$160–$298**     ★★★★

*Harbour Road, Paget,* ☎ *(800) 468-4111, (441) 236-6060, FAX (441) 236-7454.*

*Single: $160–$284. Double: $216–$298.*

Newstead is a truly charming spot and a great example of a fine Bermudian home from the 1800s. The main house, painted in green with white and dark green trim, is simply lovely and contains a splendid dining room, gorgeous public rooms with games such as backgammon and chess, and several guest rooms decorated in antiques. Other accommodations are scattered around the property and run the gamut from modern poolside rooms to one-bedroom suites. The street-side rooms may be noisy, but are still quite comfortable; number 11 is especially pretty. Most have a balcony or terrace, and all come equipped with cable TV, air-conditioners and hair dryers. The property faces the sound (deepwater swimming off the dock is permissible), with great views of Hamilton right across the harbor. The ferry stops just a few yards away and whisks guests to the city in about 10 minutes. On-site facilities include a putting green, two clay tennis courts, a lovely pool punctuated with a dolphin fountain, a pleasant bar and two restaurants. There's live entertainment five nights a week in the form of a pianist or harpist; don't come expecting wild, late-night parties. Do come, however, for a dose of gracious Bermudian hospitality at its best. This is the spot to be during the yacht races, so book early. Rates include a full cooked-to-order breakfast. 49 rooms.

**Palm Reef Hotel**     **$75–$196**     ★★★

*One Harbour Road, Paget,* ☎ *(800) 221-1294, (441) 236-1000, FAX (441) 236-6392.*

*Single: $75–$160. Double: $128–$196.*

Located on the water's edge of Hamilton Harbour where the parishes of Paget and Warwick meet, this moderate hotel—Bermuda's oldest—offers pleasant guest rooms with air-conditioners, phones and radios (TV costs extra). There's a large saltwater pool on the premises, as well as a bar, two restaurants and a tennis court. Breakfast and afternoon tea are complimentary, and Hamilton is just a five-minute ferry ride away—in the hotel's private launch. 60 rooms. Credit cards: A, MC, V.

**Stonington Beach Hotel**     **$148–$356**     ★★★★

*South Shore Road, Paget,* ☎ *(800) 447-7462, (441) 236-5416, FAX: none.*

*Single: $148–$276. Double: $168–$356.*

One thing is always assured at the Stonington: great service, as the hotel is staffed by students from Bermuda's Hospitality and Culinary Institute. Located on the campus of Bermuda College with its own private beach, the hotel has a large and inviting lobby with lots of comfortable sitting areas. The guest rooms are quite pleasing, with cedar furniture, terra-cotta floors, refrigerators, radios, TV, air conditioning, ceiling fans and balcony or terrace with ocean views. Much of the hotel is negotiable by wheelchair—a plus, since Bermuda does not require accessibility by law. Facilities include a large pool, a bar and an elegant restaurant (the students whip up great fare), a lovely and well-stocked library and two all-weather tennis courts. English tea is served each afternoon, and there's frequent classical entertainment once the sun sets. The rates include a full American breakfast, and Stonington is unique in being one of the very few hotels that does not levy a service charge. No kids under three. Hamilton is 10 minutes away by taxi. 64 rooms. Credit cards: A, DC, MC, V.

### White Sands & Cottages $89–$130 ★★★

*55 White Sands Road, Paget,* ☎ *(800) 548-0547, (441) 236-2023, FAX (441) 236-2486.*

*Single: $89–$180. Double: $94–$130.*

Located on the South Shore overlooking Grape Bay Beach, this little charmer has the pretty grounds and gardens that highlight so many Bermudian properties. The attractively furnished, air-conditioned guest rooms are in the main building and in three cottages with two or three bedrooms that can be rented out to families or other large groups. All have TV, radio, phone, refrigerator and coffeemaker. There are a dining room (jacket requested after 6 p.m.), English pub-style bar, coffee shop and free-form pool on the premises. The excellent beach is a three-minute walk down the hill, while Hamilton is just two miles away—a real plus for a South Shore hotel. Besides weekly swizzle and barbecue parties, there's not much in the way of organized activities. 35 rooms. Credit cards: A, MC, V.

## Pembroke

### Rosedon $114–$244 ★★★★

*Pitts Bay Road, Hamilton, Pembroke,* ☎ *(800) 225-5567, (441) 295-1640, FAX (441) 295-5904.*

*Single: $114–$234. Double: $114–$244.*

Rosedon is an excellent choice for business travelers and others who want to be close to downtown Hamilton, which is just a five-minute walk away. The 1906 white-with-blue-trim property, located across the street from the Princess, looks more like a private mansion than a hotel, and that feel extends to the very personal and friendly service; General Manager Muriel Richardson runs a tight and professional ship. The complimentary afternoon tea, served in lovely china, is a real treat, and the weekly rum swizzle party is a hoot. On rum swizzle night, so many good hors d'ouvres are served that you can easily skip dinner. There's no restaurant on site, but you can have a hearty breakfast (included in the rates) in your room—or better yet, on the wide veranda. You also can order a simple lunch or dinner that is a real bargain by Bermuda standards or partake of the honor bar. Guest rooms in the main house are traditional but have modern amenities that include TV, refrigerators and free local phone calls. The majority of rooms are found in an addition that faces the gardens and pool. These rooms are airy and pleasantly decorated. The grounds are lush and inviting, the handiwork of a Swiss gardener who spends four months at the hotel each winter working his magic. If you long for the beach, management will take you for free—via a private taxi, no less—to the fine facilities at Elbow Beach. A peaceful little oasis right in the city, Rosedon is a real charmer to boot. 43 rooms. Credit cards: MC, V.

### Royal Palms Hotel $105–$160 ★★★

*Rosemont Avenue, Pembroke,* ☎ *(800) 678-0783, (441) 292-1854, FAX (441) 292-1946.*

*Single: $105–$140. Double: $125–$160.*

This small, family-run hotel is housed in a handsome Bermudian mansion dating to 1903. Guestrooms are spacious and individually decorated; all come equipped with air-conditioners, radio, TVs and coffeemakers, while some have kitchenettes. Dine at Ascots, a good restaurant, or enjoy a cocktail in the hotel lounge. Stroll in the gardens or take a dip in the poll. The rates include continental breakfast. Hamilton is within walking distance. 12 rooms. Credit cards: A, MC, V.

**The Princess** $150–$320 ★★★★

*76 Pitts Bay Road, Hamilton, Pembroke, ☎ (800) 223-1818, (441) 295-3000, FAX (441) 295-1914.*
*Single: $150–$320. Double: $150–$320.*

This busy hotel is just a five-minute walk from downtown, making it a logical choice for business travelers and conventioneers. The large pink building, a landmark on the city's waterfront, dates to 1884. Public areas are pretty and quite refined—this is no place to slouch about in jeans and a T-shirt. Guest rooms feature cherry wood furnishings, a couch or table and chairs, cable TV, in-room safes, as well as small and rather disappointing baths. Not all rooms offer a balcony, but each has views of the water—the better the view, the higher the rate. The Princess Club, on the sixth floor, is especially good for business travelers; the rates include a continental breakfast and evening wine and cheese in the club room. The hotel's five junior suites are large, and each offers a separate bedroom, large parlor and a good-sized bathroom.

On-site facilities include an excellent fitness center (access is complimentary), complimentary afternoon tea on Tuesdays and Thursdays, two pools, a putting green, a shopping arcade and several bars and restaurants. A private ferry shuttles guests to and from the Southampton Princess—about 25 minutes away—which has a wonderful beach, as well as 18 holes of golf and 11 all-weather tennis courts. The ferry operates only by day; it'll cost you about $25 to take a taxi there in the evening. New in 1996 were 33 mini-suites designed with the business traveler in mind. The Princess has been home to many famous guests over the years, including such diverse personalities as Mark Twain and Michael Jackson. This is the largest and most complete hotel for those who wish to be right in the city. 413 rooms. Credit cards: A, DC, MC, V.

**Waterloo House** $135–$380 ★★★★

*Pitts Bay Road, Hamilton, Pembroke, ☎ (800) 468-4100, (441) 295-4480, FAX (441) 295-2585.*
*Single: $135–$295. Double: $180–$380.*

You'd never guess this lovely spot even exists—it's marked by just a simple brass plaque. Once through the door, guests enter another world of old-style touches, including meandering pathways and pretty gardens. Located just a short stroll from downtown Hamilton, the Waterloo is set on Hamilton Harbour and dates to 1810. Guest rooms come with all the expected amenities, as well as TV on request. Some also have fireplaces. Facilities include a library, an elegant dining room, games room, and live classical music during high season. The pool is quite small but is enlivened by yellow and white striped umbrellas. Guests are free to use the beach and tennis courts at the private Coral Beach Club, but they are on their own to arrange (and pay for) transportation. With its brick walkways, gorgeous landscaping and subdued atmosphere, Waterloo is a real city oasis—but the stiff-upper-lip atmosphere may not be for everyone. 32 rooms.

## Sandys

| Willowbank | $144–$192 | ★★★ |
|---|---|---|

*Elys Harbour, Sandys,* ☎ *(800) 752-8493, (441) 234-1616, FAX: none.*
*Single: $144–$192. Double: $144–$192.*

Willowbank is open to all, but the vast majority of guests are Christians on retreat. Daily programs include optional devotion times, gospel singing, and family films. No liquor is served on the premises, though it's allowed in guest rooms. The air-conditioned accommodations are plain and simply furnished; you'll do without TV. The grounds are quite nice, with two beaches, two tennis courts, shuffleboard, a pool, the Loaves and Fishes dining room and a library. Supervised programs for kids are held during high season. Obviously, the atmosphere here is conservative, and guests are required to dress up for dinner. Willowbank is one of the few properties on the island that does not levy a service charge. 65 rooms.

## Smith's

| Palmetto Hotel & Cottages | $91–$196 | ★★★ |
|---|---|---|

*Harrington Sound Road, Flatts Village, Smith's,* ☎ *(800) 982-0026,*
*(441) 293-2323, FAX (441) 293-8761.*
*Single: $91–$120. Double: $128–$196.*

Pastel-colored cottages surround an 18th-century mansion at this comfortable property located near the Bermuda Aquarium and Zoo. Not all rooms have a sea view, but all are pleasant and come equipped with air-conditioners, phones, radios and balconies. You can get your TV fix in the main lounge. There's a very small man-made beach facing Harrington Sound; management will shuttle you for free over to the better beaches of the South Shore. Other facilities include a good restaurant, pool, moped rentals and a traditional English-style pub. The rates include breakfast. Hamilton is 10 minutes away by taxi. 42 rooms. Credit cards: A, MC, V.

## Southampton

| Pompano Beach Club | $180–$370 | ★★★★ |
|---|---|---|

*36 Pompano Beach Road, Southampton,* ☎ *(800) 343-4155, (441) 234-*
*0222, FAX (441) 234-1694.*
*Single: $180–$330. Double: $220–$370.*

The island's only American-owned and operated resort, the Pompano Beach Club has been operated by the Lamb family since its inception in 1956. All rooms have an ocean view and balcony or patio, and you'll enjoy the most wonderful Jacuzzi set on a deck overlooking the sea—perfect for sunsets! The small natural beach can disappear during high tide; two man-made beaches fill in the gap. The beaches are great for small children, as a sand bar keeps the water shallow—you can wade out 250 yards and still be only waist-deep. Guest rooms are appointed with sea-foam green carpets, Robert Allan fabrics, king beds, refrigerators, robes, irons and boards, in-room safes and pretty baths. The only thing you'll miss, perhaps, is television. On-site facilities include a lending library, exercise room, two restaurants, a bar, nightly entertainment in season, a pool, one clay tennis court and a watersports center. Golfers like this friendly spot for its proximity to the Port Royal Golf Course, which is right next door. The course's four tennis courts are also open to hotel guests. 54 rooms.

### Sonesta Beach Hotel & Spa    $130–$410    ★★★★

*South Shore Road, Southampton,* ☎ *(800) 766-3782, (441) 238-8122, FAX (441) 238-8436.*
*Single: $130–$410. Double: $130–$410.*

The best feature of this full-service resort is its sprawling grounds, which includes a large, reef-protected beach and a craggy, boulder-strewn waterfront dotted with crystal-clear tidepools. A lovely moon-gate that leads to a tiny private beach that is perfect for honeymoon-ers. Speaking of beaches, the Sonesta is the island's only resort built right on the beach (at the others, you must descend a hill to reach the sand). Guest rooms, all renovated in 1995, are nicely done in pinks and greens and include cable TV, mini-bars, iron and boards, hair dry-ers and balcony and terraces. Almost 95 percent have water views. Facilities include a new elegant lobby, two outdoor pools (one for kids), an indoor pool under a glass dome, a full dive shop, a play-ground and six tennis courts (two lit for night play). The resident ten-nis pro offers free group lessons twice a week—a nice perk. Three golf courses are within a 10-minute drive, and you can rent a moped right on the grounds. For dining, there are three restaurants and, among the lounges, a new sports bar. Perhaps the Sonesta's greatest claim to fame is its very upscale health spa, where you can work yourself into a righteous sweat, then be pampered with a massage or facial. Though first-floor rooms open right onto the beach, they can lack privacy, so you're probably better off up a flight or two. 403 rooms. Credit cards: A, DC, MC, V.

### Southampton Princess Hotel    $150–$519    ★★★★★

*101 South Shore Road, Southampton,* ☎ *(800) 223-1818, (441) 238-8000, FAX (441) 238-8968.*
*Single: $150–$469. Double: $150–$519.*

Hotels don't come much more luxurious than this. The Princess, which stands atop the highest point in Bermuda, offers fantastic views of the Great Sound, the sea and the hotel-run 18-hole, par-three golf course. Each room has a water view and balcony, and while many guests request views of the sea, the panoramics of the Great Sound and city of Hamilton are actually more picturesque (and cost less). Guest rooms are comfy, with walk-in closets, kings or two double beds, armoires, clock radios, on-demand movies, robes, irons and board and hair dryers. New are minibars and second phones with a data port. If you're feeling decadent, book one of the presidential suites, which total 2200 square feet and have two bedrooms, four full baths, a sitting room and a huge living/dining room. Or request one of the two loft suites with full kitchens. The hotel does a large busi-ness with conventions, so expect a lot of name-tag wearers.

Facilities include two large pools (one indoors), 11 all-weather tennis courts (three lit for night play), a full dive shop, health club, beauty salon, six restaurants, a disco and a large shopping arcade. Down the hill (easy to reach via shuttle bus) is the Princess Beach Club, a lovely stretch of sand featuring a bar and restaurant. Another shuttle takes guests to the Waterlot Inn, where a wonderful dining experience awaits. Guests have signing privileges at the Hamilton Princess in the city; a ferry plies between the two resorts during daylight hours.

From April to November, children 16 and under stay free and get free breakfast and dinner daily. The resort offers extensive children's activities from mid-June to mid-September, as well as Bermuda's only concierge floor, called the Newport Club, during high season. Guests on that pricier floor receive extra amenities such as private registration and check out, continental breakfast and a member-only lounge. Note that between April and mid-November, there is a mandatory meal plan for all guests.

New in 1996—and all Bermuda—was "Dolphin Quest," where six dolphins imported from Hawaii live in (relative) freedom in three acres of the sea. Guests can enter a lottery to "interact" (swim) with the creatures. The hotel promises the dolphins will not perform and that any interaction with humans will be voluntary. Princess is offering special packages that guarantee a spot in the water with the creatures; call for information. 600 rooms. Credit cards: A, DC, MC, V.

**The Reefs**                    **$220–$396**              ★ ★ ★ ★

*56 South Shore Road, Southampton,* ☎ *(800) 742-2008, FAX (441) 238-8372.*
*Single: $220–$396. Double: $220–$396.*

Each guest gets to try—on the house—Bermuda's national drink, a "Dark & Stormy," at this cliffside resort. That's just one of the small touches that makes The Reefs, located high above Christian Bay, one of the island's better choices. Most guest rooms are located in pink lanais scattered about the grounds; all have a seaview and are very nicely done with high quality rattan furnishings, refrigerators, combination baths with luxurious toiletries, robes, irons and boards, air conditioning and ceiling fans, telephones, radios and a balcony or patio. Choose from eight cottages of one to three bedrooms, all with cable TV and VCRs. Local phone calls are free, a plus for business travelers. On-site facilities include a small but pretty pool, two all-weather tennis courts, a fitness center, shuffleboard, croquet, two restaurants and a beach bar. You can snorkel right off the private beach. For a fee, guests can use the excellent spa at the nearby Sonesta. 65 rooms.

## St. George's

**Marriott's Castle Harbour Resort**      **$150–$375**      ★ ★ ★ ★

*2 South Road, St. George's,* ☎ *(800) 223-8388, (441) 293-2040, FAX (441) 293-8288.*
*Single: $150–$390. Double: $150–$375.*

Set on a hilltop overlooking Harrington Sound and Castle Harbor, this 250-landscaped-acre is the typical Marriott resort—which means most everything is done right. The views are grand, and the guest rooms feature English reproductions and all the amenities you'd expect, including irons, boards, and hair dryers. Not all rooms have balconies, though, so be sure to request one if that's important to you. The grounds include two small beaches (management will shuttle you over to a larger beach on South Shore, if you desire), well-tended gardens, three pools (one Olympic-sized), as well as an excellent, complimentary health club. Other temptations include three restaurants, nightly entertainment, complimentary afternoon tea, outdoor barbecues in the summer, complete watersports and six tennis courts. There's also an 18-hole golf course designed by Robert Trent Jones and the island's only Japanese restaurant. Resort lovers are kept happy, but note that many convention groups meet here. 402 rooms. Credit cards: A, DC, MC, V.

## Warwick

**Belmont Hotel & Golf Club**     **$105–$233**     ★ ★ ★ ★
*Middle Road, Warwick,* ☎ *(800) 225-5843, (441) 236-1301, FAX (441) 236-6867.*
*Single: $105–$187. Double: $140–$233.*
Set on a 110-acre estate overlooking the Great Sound, this resort does a fine job of keeping guests busy and happy. Take advantage of unlimited complimentary greens fees on the 18-hole, par-70 championship golf course, three all-weather, lighted tennis courts (free during daylight), and even a miniature golf course—Bermuda's only, in fact. Guest rooms are nicely done in Queen Anne-style furnishings and have cable TV, combination baths, radios and telephones. The grounds include two restaurants, a bar with entertainment, a beauty salon, business center and a large, L-shaped swimming pool with an underwater window. You're only 10 minutes by ferry to Hamilton from the Belmont's own private dock, and management will shuttle you over to the beach for free from April to November. Complimentary afternoon tea, weekly barbecue parties and supervised children's activities complete the scene. Very nice, if you don't mind having to travel to the beach. 151 rooms. Credit cards: A, DC, MC, V.

# Cottages and Apartments

Known as "housekeeping units," these accommodations are for self-sufficient travelers who like to cook their own meals (and therefore save a lot of money). Some are much like cottage colonies with lots of recreational amenities, but lack the main clubhouse. Others are quite small and have few facilities. All have a kitchen and daily maid service. Details are provided in each description.

## Devonshire

**Burch's Guest Apartments**     **$55–$90**     ★ ★
*110 North Shore Road, Devonshire,* ☎ *(441) 292-5746.*
*Single: $55. Double: $75–$90.*
Nice views of the North Shore enhance these informal apartment units. There are a small garden and pool on the grounds, and the bus stop is nearby. 10 rooms.

## Hamilton

**Clear View Suites**     **$142–$214**     ★ ★ ★
*Sandy Lane, Hamilton,* ☎ *(800) 468-9600, (441) 293-0484, FAX (441) 293-0267.*
*Single: $142–$214. Double: $156–$214.*

Travelers are accommodated in spacious one-bedroom suites with kitchen, TV, radio and phone at this waterfront spot. Situated midway between Hamilton and St. George's, the property serves breakfast in the main house (dinner only on request), and has two pools, two tennis courts and an art gallery. A public beach is just two minutes away. Clear View is among the very few properties on Bermuda that does not charge a service fee. 12 rooms.

# Paget

**Barnsdale Guest Apartments**          **$60–$145**          ★★
*Paget,* ☎ *(441) 236-0164, FAX (441) 236-4709.*
*Single: $60–$100. Double: $80–$145.*
Efficiency studios with fully equipped kitchenettes are enhanced by the pretty grounds of this family-run property. There's a pool on site, and a grocery store is within walking distance. Elbow Beach is a 10- to 15-minute hike. 7 rooms.

**Dawkins Manor**          **$50–$130**          ★★
*Paget,* ☎ *(441) 236-7419, FAX (441) 236-7088.*
*Single: $50–$190. Double: $65–$130.*
Located in a residential area, this homey property offers a housekeeping apartment and smaller rooms with kitchenettes or refrigerators. There are a pool and garden on site, and Elbow Beach is an easy five-minute walk. 7 rooms.

**Fourways Inn**          **$140–$230**          ★★★★
*One Middle Road, Paget,* ☎ *(800) 962-7654, (441) 236-6517, FAX (441) 236-5528.*
*Single: $140–$230. Double: $140–$230.*
Fourways is justifiably famous for its wonderful (and pricey) gourmet restaurant; about 10 years ago it added on five cottages with somewhat less spectacular results. The cottages are nevertheless quite lovely—all done up with marble, pastel fabrics and large, modern baths—though they lack the historical charm you'd expect considering that the main house, where the restaurant is located, dates to 1727. Each of the five cottages is configured to house a one- or two-bedroom suite or single room; all have a small kitchenette as well as a minibar, cable TV, hair dryer, bathrobes, clock radio and phone. Two have a harbor view, whereas the rest overlook the nicely manicured grounds, enhanced by the many hanging baskets of flowers. The pool is quite large, considering that it accommodates guests in just 10 rooms. The rates include a wonderful continental breakfast (killer pastries) served, along with the daily paper, to your room each morning. There is a live pianist each evening in the restaurant, and a cozy pub for more affordable lunches. The ferry to Hamilton is less than a 10-minute walk. 10 rooms. Credit cards: A, MC, V.

**Glenmar Holiday Apartments**          **$60–$90**          ★★
*Paget,* ☎ *(441) 236-2844.*
*Single: $60–$90. Double: $60–$90.*
Beaches, restaurants and shops are within close proximity of this informal property. Apartments have kitchens and air-conditioners. 5 rooms.

**Grape Bay Cottages**          **$160–$220**          ★★★
*Paget,* ☎ *(800) 637-4116, (441) 236-1194, FAX (441) 236-1662.*

*Double: $160–$220.*

Set on a bluff above a beach not far from Hamilton, this facility consists of just two cottages. Each has a full kitchen, two bedrooms, a living room with a fireplace, air conditioning, ceiling fans, telephone and radio. Maids tidy up daily, but otherwise you're on your own in this peaceful, secluded spot. This is a good place for two couples who want to share accommodations. 2 rooms.

### Greenbank & Cottages $95–$175 ★★★

*Salt Kettle, Paget, ☎ (800) 637-4116, (441) 236-3615, FAX (441) 236-2427.*
*Double: $95–$175.*

This family-run facility, just steps from the ferry (which takes you to Hamilton in five minutes), is a real charmer. There's a lovely communal parlor, with a grand piano, comfy couch and chairs, pretty floral drapes and the property's only TV in a 200-year-old Bermuda home. (You can rent a TV for your room, if you so desire.) Of the 11 units, seven face the water, while the rest have peaceful garden views. Nine have compact but fully equipped kitchens, and all have air-conditioners and telephones. The two units without kitchens get continental breakfast included in the rates. Each room is individually decorated, and some have cedar beam ceilings. Some units come equipped with twin beds, so be sure to state your preference when making a reservation. "Salt Winds" is the nicest, with a big, modern kitchen. There's no pool on site, but you can deepwater swim off the private dock. There's also a boat charter on the premises, where you can arrange for a sunset cruise or snorkel excursion. Elbow Beach is about an eight-minute ride away. This low-key property, with its brick walkways, trim gardens and green single-story cottages, is quite agreeable, and the service is caring and friendly. 11 rooms.

### Marley Beach Cottages $138–$250 ★★★★

*Paget, ☎ (800) 637-4116, (441) 236-1143, FAX (441) 236-1984.*
*Single: $138–$249. Double: $138–$250.*

Marley's is a bit more expensive than most apartment complexes on the island, but if you're into dramatic views, it's worth it. The resort sits atop a cliff and was the site for scenes from the movies "The Deep" and "Chapter Two". Each air-conditioned unit (studios and one-bedrooms) is airy, spacious and individually decorated and has a full kitchen as well as phone, TV, radio and private terrace. It's a steep walk to the three beaches down below; some find the small heated pool handier. Restaurants are nearby, and the bus stops right out front. Marley Beach will even deliver groceries if you're feeling too lazy to shop. 13 rooms. Credit cards: A, MC, V.

### Paraquet Guest Apartments $75–$145 ★★

*South Shore Road, Paget, ☎ (441) 236-5842, FAX (441) 236-1665.*
*Single: $75–$100. Double: $95–$145.*

This informal apartment building is located in a residential neighborhood close to Hamilton. Nine of the basically simple units have kitchenettes, and all feature a TV, radio, veranda and air conditioning. There's a restaurant on site, and you can walk to Elbow Beach in five minutes. 11 rooms.

### Pretty Penny $90–$125 ★★★

*7 Cobb's Hill Road, Paget,* ☎ *(800) 637-4116, (441) 236-1194, FAX (441) 236-1662.*
*Single: $90. Double: $90–$125.*

This family-run facility really is quite pretty, and is guarded by a large resident poodle. Located in a quiet residential neighborhood, the Pretty Penny is just a five-minute walk to the Salt Kettle ferry. Each unit is quite spacious and has a tiny, though cute, kitchenette, as well as a private patio, tile floors and pastel decor. Two have a fireplace at no extra charge, so be sure to request one when you reserve. There's a pool on the grounds but no restaurant, though you can walk to several, including the famous Fourways Inn. 7 rooms. Credit cards: A, MC, V.

### Valley Cottages & Apartments $65–$104 ★★

*Paget,* ☎ *(441) 236-0628, FAX (441) 236-3895.*
*Single: $65–$80. Double: $76–$104.*

It's a short walk to Elbow Beach from this informal conclave of cottages and apartments. All units have kitchens or kitchenettes, air-conditioners, phones and TV, and are quite comfortable. The bus stops just across the street, and there are a grocery store and liquor mart nearby. 9 rooms.

## Pembroke

### Hamiltonian Hotel & Island Club $74–$170 ★★★

*Pembroke,* ☎ *(800) 441-7087, (441) 295-5608, FAX (441) 295-7481.*
*Single: $74–$130. Double: $88–$170.*

Set on Langton Hill overlooking Pembroke and the city of Hamilton, this small property offers one-room suites in a garden setting. Each unit has a kitchenette equipped with refrigerator, microwave, toaster and coffeemaker. Facilities include a large pool and three tennis courts, two lit for night play. Hamilton is a 15-minute walk away. 32 rooms.

### La Casa del Masa $80–$100 ★★

*Pembroke,* ☎ *(441) 292-8726, FAX (441) 295-4447.*
*Double: $80–$100.*

Gorgeous views abound at this informal spot not far from Hamilton. Each unit has a kitchen, two double beds, TV, ceiling fan, air conditioning and telephone. There's a pool on site. 3 rooms.

### Marula Apartments $70–$150 ★★

*Mills Creek, Pembroke,* ☎ *(441) 295-2893, FAX (441) 292-3985.*
*Single: $70–$80. Double: $80–$150.*

Set on the water's edge at Mill Creek, this small property consists of a cottage and several efficiency units. There's a small pool on the grounds, but not much else in the way of diversions. Hamilton is a five-minute ride away. 5 rooms.

### Mazarine by the Sea $109–$150 ★★

*Pembroke,* ☎ *(800) 441-7087, (441) 292-1659, FAX (441) 292-6891.*
*Double: $109–$150.*

This small property is set on the water's edge on the north shore of Pembroke, but lacks a beach—though you can deepwater swim if you so desire. Each unit is air-conditioned and comes with a kitchenette; there's a pool, garden and barbecue area on the grounds. 7 rooms.

**Robin's Nest**          $95          ★★★

*10 Vale Close, Pembroke,* ☎ *(800) 223-6510, (441) 292-4347, FAX (441) 292-4347.*
*Double: $95.*

The quiet and informal accommodations at this small apartment complex are located two miles from Hamilton. Each unit has a full kitchen, air conditioning, radio, telephone, cable TV and ceiling fan. There's a nice pool on the grounds. 3 rooms.

**Rosemont**          $96–$134          ★★★

*41 Rosemont Avenue, Hamilton, Pembroke,* ☎ *(800) 367-0040, (441) 292-1055, FAX (441) 295-3913.*
*Single: $96–$134. Double: $98–$134.*

Hamilton is within walking distance of this family-owned cottage complex set in a residential area overlooking the harbor (great views). Each comfortable, self-contained unit has a fully equipped kitchenette, phone, clock-radio and color TV. The three newer penthouse suites are larger and nicer; and several rooms are wheelchair-accessible. A small pool and sun deck are located on the landscaped grounds. There's no restaurant on site, but a grocery store is nearby. This is a quiet spot, so those who like to party should look elsewhere. 37 rooms. Credit cards: MC, V.

## Sandys

**Garden House**          $92–$107          ★★★

*4 Middle Road, Sandys,* ☎ *(441) 234-1435, FAX (441) 234-3006.*
*Double: $92–$107.*

Set on three landscaped acres in a secluded location, this homey spot has self-contained studios and cottages, each with TV, full kitchens, irons and boards and hair dryers. There's no beach, but you can swim in the pool or in the deep water of the sea. Smoking is allowed outdoors only. 5 rooms.

## Smith's

**Angel's Grotto**          $95–$210          ★★★

*Smith's,* ☎ *(800) 637-4116, (441) 293-1986, FAX (441) 293-4164.*
*Single: $95–$210. Double: $95–$210.*

Located on the south shore of Harrington Sound, this small complex offers comfortable, air-conditioned units with fully equipped kitchenettes, TV, radio and one or two bedrooms. You can swim in the deep water of the sound, or stroll five minutes to the beach at John Smith's Bay. There's no pool or restaurant on site, so you're on your own for meals. 7 rooms. Credit cards: A, MC, V.

**Brightside Apartments**          $75–$85          ★★

*Flatts Village, Smith's,* ☎ *(441) 292-8410, FAX (441) 295-6968.*
*Single: $75–$85. Double: $75–$85.*

The Bermuda Aquarium, Museum and Zoo are right next to this informal apartment complex in Flatts Village. One- and two-bedroom units are equipped with kitchens, air conditioning and ceiling fans. Besides the pool, guests are on their own to amuse themselves. 11 rooms.

**Cabana Vacation Apartments**          $85–$152          ★★

*61 Verdmont Road, Smith's,* ☎ *(441) 236-6964, FAX (441) 236-1829.*
*Single: $85. Double: $84–$152.*

A 200-year-old colonial mansion houses these self-contained apartments that come with air-conditioners and full kitchens. Facilities are limited to a pool and barbecue area, but there's a grocery shop and bus stop nearby. Hamilton is 12 minutes away by car, and you can walk to the beach in the same amount of time. 7 rooms.

## Southampton

### Chance It Cottage Holiday Retreat          $75–$110          ★★★
*Southampton,* ☎ *(441) 238-0372, FAX (441) 238-8888.*
*Single: $75–$110. Double: $75–$110.*
Located high on a hill with panoramic views of the southwest coast, this agreeable spot offers apartment living for self-catering types. There's an exercise room and pool on site, and the beach and Port Royal Golf Course are within an easy walk. 5 rooms.

### Ocean Terrace          $90–$135          ★★
*Southampton,* ☎ *(441) 238-0019, FAX (441) 238-8489.*
*Single: $90–$135. Double: $90–$135.*
Located on top of Scenic Heights with splendid views, this small complex has spacious and modern units with full-size kitchens, air-conditioners, verandas, telephones and satellite TV. There's a pool on the premises, and the beach is about 10 minutes away on foot. 3 rooms.

### Sound View Cottage          $50–$75          ★★
*9 Bowe Lane, Southampton,* ☎ *(441) 238-0064.*
*Single: $50–$75. Double: $50–$75.*
Set in a residential area overlooking the Great Sound, this small property consists of a cottage housing three housekeeping apartments with kitchens. There's a pool, patio and barbecue area on the grounds, and south-shore beaches are not far. 3 rooms.

### Whale Bay Inn          $65–$110          ★★★
*Southampton,* ☎ *(441) 238-0469, FAX (441) 238-1224.*
*Single: $65–$80. Double: $80–$110.*
It's a short walk to a lovely beach from this pretty inn, which overlooks the Port Royal Golf Course. Air-conditioned apartments are nicely appointed and come complete with full kitchens, living/dining areas, separate bedrooms, TV, telephones and radio. 5 rooms.

## Warwick

### Astwood Cove          $60–$138          ★★★
*49 South Shore Road, Warwick,* ☎ *(800) 637-4116, (441) 236-0984, FAX (441) 236-1164.*
*Single: $60–$138. Double: $76–$138.*
Just a three-minute walk to the beach, this modern complex of studio apartments and suites overlooks the South Shore. Only four miles from Hamilton, the bright-white apartments have full kitchens and a balcony or terrace, and shower-baths. There's a pool on the premises and a sauna; the latter costs extra, which seems a bit petty. The landscaped grounds include a barbecue area, and there are more than a dozen restaurants within a two-mile radius. 20 rooms.

### Blue Horizons          $55–$80          ★
*93 South Road, Warwick,* ☎ *(441) 236-6350.*
*Single: $55. Double: $60–$80.*
Located about 15 minutes out of Hamilton, this informal apartment building has a moon gate, pool and snack bar on the premises. All

units are air-conditioned, and some have kitchenettes. South Shore beaches are nearby. 6 rooms.

### Clairfont Apartments      $80–$100      ★ ★

*Warwick,* ☎ *(441) 238-0149, FAX (441) 238-0149.*
*Single: $80–$100. Double: $80–$100.*

The pool and sun terrace are pleasant at this modern apartment complex, where each unit has a full kitchen and air-conditioned bedrooms. The beach is not far, and the bus stop and restaurants are within walking distance. 8 rooms.

### Longtail Cliffs      $130–$180      ★ ★ ★

*34 South Shore Road, Warwick,* ☎ *(800) 637-4116, (441) 236-2864, FAX (441) 236-5178.*
*Single: $130–$180. Double: $130–$180.*

Located on the South Shore, but without a beach of its own, this modern apartment complex doesn't look like much from the outside, but is pleasing within. Each two-bedroom, two-bath unit overlooks the ocean and has a bright and spacious feel. Some have (nonworking) fireplaces, while all boast full kitchens, cable TV, radio, telephone, living and dining areas, and air-conditioners in the bedrooms. Facilities are limited to a kidney-shaped pool, barbecue grill and coin-operated laundry. You can walk to a large public beach. The property takes its name from the longtail seagulls that nest in the adjacent cliffs; a plus for birders. 13 rooms. Credit cards: A, MC, V.

### Mermaid Beach Club      $102–$290      ★ ★

*South Shore Road, Warwick,* ☎ *(800) 441-7087, (441) 236-5031, FAX (441) 236-8784.*
*Single: $102–$290. Double: $102–$290.*

Set on the South Shore four miles from Hamilton, this informal spot has standard guest rooms as well as one- and two-bedroom suites with full kitchens. The resort has its own pretty private beach as well as a pool, bar, dive shop and restaurant. There's live entertainment during summer months. 73 rooms. Credit cards: A, MC, V.

### Sandpiper Apartments      $78–$120      ★ ★

*South Shore Road, Warwick,* ☎ *(800) 441-7087, (441) 236-7093, FAX (441) 236-3898.*
*Double: $78–$120.*

Located in a residential area not far from South Shore beaches, this casual property has studio and one-bedroom apartments equipped with kitchens, living rooms or sitting areas, cable TV and air conditioning. Amenities are restricted to a pool and Jacuzzi. Nothing too exciting, but good value for the money. 14 rooms. Credit cards: A, MC, V.

### South View Apartments      $90–$140      ★ ★

*Warwick,* ☎ *(800) 441-7087, (441) 236-5257, FAX (441) 236-3382.*
*Single: $90–$140. Double: $90–$140.*

There's little on site save a roof-top sun deck and a pretty garden, but those looking for a peaceful escape will enjoy the atmosphere at this small apartment complex. 3 rooms.

### Surf Side Beach Club      $105–$215      ★ ★ ★

*98 South Shore Road, Warwick,* ☎ *(800) 553-9990, (441) 236-7100, FAX (441) 236-9765.*
*Single: $105–$215. Double: $105–$215.*

A small private beach accents this complex of cottage-style apartments set on terraced levels. Guests are housed in large and comfortable studios or suites with full kitchens, cable TV, radios, phones and a patio or balcony with ocean views. There's two pools (one for kids), a game room, laundry and travel desk on site, but the coffee shop is open only during high season. Some rooms are wheelchair accessible. 35 rooms.

**Syl-Den Apartments**      **$75–$90**      ★★

*8 Warwickshire Road, Warwick,* ☎ *(441) 238-1834, FAX (441) 238-3205.*
*Single: $75–$90. Double: $75–$90.*
It's a 200-yard walk to the beaches of the South Shore from this modern apartment complex. If that's too far, you can laze by the small pool on the premises. 5 rooms.

**Vienna Guest Apartments**      **$70–$115**      ★★

*63 Cedar Hill, Warwick,* ☎ *(800) 637-4116, (441) 236-3300, FAX (441) 236-6100.*
*Single: $70–$105. Double: $105–$115.*
Enjoy the views from this family-run complex. Each unit has a bedroom, living room, full kitchen, ceiling fan, air-conditioner, telephone and TV. South shore beaches are within walking distance plus there's a pool on site. 6 rooms.

# Cottage Colonies

Bermuda is unique and justifiably famous for its upscale cottage colonies. Guests are housed in cottage units spread throughout the often extensive and beautifully manicured grounds. They often include small kitchenettes set up for light cooking but not heavy-duty meals. The main feature to a cottage colony is a clubhouse with a dining room, lounge and bar, where guests can congregate and get to know each other. All have a beach and/or pool, and all are quite tony.

## Devonshire

**Ariel Sands Beach Club**      **$139–$220**      ★★★★

*South Road, Devonshire,* ☎ *(800) 468-6610, (441) 236-1010, FAX: none.*
*Single: $139–$175. Double: $154–$220.*
This secluded cottage colony, where the decor of many rooms is based on Shakespeare's *The Tempest*, is on the South Shore, 2.5 miles from Hamilton. The grounds open onto a lovely private beach, where watersports can be arranged. Accommodations are on the small side but nicely done with bentwood furniture and local artwork; all have air-conditioners, radios and phones, and you can request a TV and refrigerator. Book one of the newer units, as they are much nicer than the originals (which date to 1959). The premises include a pool, restaurant, three all-weather, lighted tennis courts, and a small putting green and sand trap where golfers can practice. There are weekly barbecues and live music in season, and the public rooms, which include a library-like bar and lime-green clubhouse, are pleasant. 51 rooms.

# Paget

**Horizons & Cottages**      **$230–$700**      ★★★★

*South Road, Paget, ☎ (800) 468-0022, (441) 236-0048, FAX (441) 236-1981.*
*Single: $230–$396. Double: $327–$700.*

Set high on a hill with sweeping vistas, this is a truly lovely spot for the well-heeled crowd, who are kept pampered and happy. Guests are accommodated in the main house or in the cottages that dot the 25-acre estate. All units are beautifully and individually decorated and have extra touches like a trouser press, safes, bathrobes, fresh flowers and a private balcony or terrace (you can get a TV on request). Most of the spacious and luxurious cottages have a kitchen and fireplace, as well. The inviting parlor in the 18th-century manor house—a perfect example of fine Bermudian architecture—has hardwood floors, a huge fireplace with a grand mantle, Oriental rugs and splendid antiques. The candlelit restaurant is a favorite of local movers and shakers, and the food is divine. The property features a nine-hole "mashie" golf course, pretty pool, putting green and three all-weather tennis courts. There's no beach right here, but guests can easily walk to one at the private Coral Beach Club. Horizons has been managed by the same family since 1928, and the attention to detail shows. 50 rooms.

**Sky Top Cottages**      **$68–$125**      ★★★

*65 South Shore Road, Paget, ☎ (441) 236-7984, FAX: none.*
*Single: $68–$113. Double: $75–$125.*

Breathtaking views abound from this friendly apartment complex, where the beaches down below are just five minutes away. The grounds are quite lovely, too, with sloping lawns, a citrus grove and flower-lined walkways. The air-conditioned cottages come in studios and one-bedroom apartments. Each cottage has English-style decor and is individually decorated. All but two have kitchens, but you'll have to rent a TV if you can't do without. There are no facilities on site, but Hamilton is reached via taxi in 10 minutes. Excellent value. 11 rooms. Credit cards: MC, V.

# Sandys

**Cambridge Beaches**      **$209–$550**      ★★★★★

*30 Kings Point Road, Sandys, ☎ (800) 468-7300, (441) 234-0331, FAX (441) 234-0331.*
*Single: $209–$520. Double: $230–$550.*

Cottage colonies don't come much better than here at Cambridge Beaches, set on 25 acres on a peninsula surrounded by water. The grounds are gorgeous and so are the accommodations, with many cottages furnished in antiques and equipped with such extras as bidets, fireplaces and whirlpools. You can choose from a standard cottage (no ocean view) to one that's 300 years old. The property features a posh health spa where—for an extra fee—you can exercise or simply be pampered with a facial or massage in one of four treatment rooms. The resort sports five private beaches (many with private coves) as well as a formal restaurant, cocktail lounges and a reading room where high tea is served daily. The full-service marina enables you to participate in everything from scuba excursions to kayak trips—or perhaps rent a Boston whaler. For more recreation, try the putting green, three tennis courts (one lit for night play), pool or croquet lawn. Though the locale, on Bermuda's western tip, is far from Hamilton, Cambridge Beaches is quite close to the attractions and shopping at the Royal Naval Dockyard. Those wanting to venture into the city are accommodated three times a week via private ferry during the high season; the rest of the year management will pay for the token for the commercial ferry. During summer, the live entertainment includes indoor and outdoor dancing and cruises under the stars. The prices are high, all meals are included in the rates, and you can dine at several properties such as Pompano Beach and The Reefs, so you're not always stuck on site. Children under 5 must be accompanied by a nurse or nanny. 75 rooms.

| **Lantana** | **$180–$240** | ★ ★ ★ ★ ★ |

*Sandys,* ☎ *(800) 468-3733, (441) 234-0141, FAX (441) 234-2562. Single: $180–$300. Double: $210–$240.*

Set on its own private beach overlooking the Great Sound, Lantana is among Bermuda's most exclusive cottage colonies. Once a 22 acre onion farm, the property has been landscaped into wonderful gardens filled with a riot of blooms and lifelike bronze sculptures made by local artist Desmond Fountain. The luxurious lodgings are in suites, all lovingly decorated in pastel colors and with large, modern baths. Standard amenities include refrigerators, irons, hair dryers and private patios or balconies; some cottages also sport fireplaces. The six cottages are spacious and have kitchens; one has its own pool. The breathtaking grounds include two all-weather tennis courts (with a resident pro on hand), a pool, a putting green, croquet and shuffleboard, as well as two bars and two restaurants. The small, man-made beach has pink sand, and all watersports await, including a certified windsurfing school. The ferry ride to Hamilton takes a half-hour. Rates in the winter include all meals. 65 rooms.

## Smith's

| **Pink Beach Club & Cottages** | **$190–$385** | ★ ★ ★ ★ |

*South Road, Smith's,* ☎ *(800) 355-6161, (441) 293-1666, FAX: none. Single: $190–$355. Double: $180–$385.*

True to its name, the two beaches are pink at this very nice complex of cottages set on 18 landscaped acres. The cottages—pink as well— have single rooms or one- and two-bedroom suites. All are spacious and nicely done in maple furniture with modern amenities such as hair dryers, TV and trouser presses; the only drawback is that some rooms are on the dark side and could use more sunlight. There's a tennis pro on hand to give pointers on the resort's two all-weather courts, as well as a saltwater pool and many watersports. The menu changes daily in the fine dining room, while breakfast (included in the rates) is served right to your room each morning. There's live entertainment seven nights a week from April to November, weekly swizzle parties and a dinner dance on Fridays. For duffers both the Mid Ocean Club and Castle Harbour Golf Club are nearby. This is Bermuda's largest cottage colony and the service is excellent—you'll especially enjoy the cooked-to-order breakfast prepared by a maid in your own kitchenette each morning. 81 rooms. Credit cards: MC, V.

## Southampton

**Munro Beach Cottages**            **$102–$168**              ★★

*Whitney Bay, Southampton,* ☎ *(441) 234-1175, FAX (441) 234-3528.*
*Single: $102–$168. Double: $102–$168.*
This secluded complex offers eight duplex cottages with two units
apiece. Each is air-conditioned and is equipped with full kitchen,
phone, radio and TV. A small, private beach is down the hill, and the
Port Royal Golf Course is right next door. One extra-nice feature:
grocery delivery at no extra charge. 16 rooms.

## St. George's

**St. George's Club**               **$165–$550**            ★★★★

*Rose Hill, St. George's,* ☎ *(441) 297-1200, FAX (441) 297-8003.*
*Single: $165–$450. Double: $165–$550.*
Set on 18 manicured acres within walking distance of downtown St.
George's, this cottage colony is a time-share property that also
accommodates one-time vacationers. Guests are housed in one- and
two-bedroom air-conditioned cottages that are quite spacious and
come equipped with full kitchens, fine china and crystal, a living
room, dining room, cable TV and private balcony or terrace with
expansive views. All units have modern baths, some come with large
whirlpool tubs. For recreation, there's an 18-hole Robert Trent
Jones-designed golf course (guests get reduced rates and good tee
times), a putting green, three pools, three all-weather tennis courts
(two lit for night play) and a free shuttle to a nearby beach. A conve-
nience store is on hand for those who want to do their own cooking;
otherwise you can dine at one of the resort's two restaurants or in picturesque St. George's. 69 rooms. Credit cards: A, DC, MC, V.

# Guest Houses

Most of the island's guest houses are in old Bermudian mansions, with the trademark pastel colors, wooden shutters and
high, beamed ceilings. A few are on the waterfront or have a
pool. All are relatively informal and very clean. Unless stated in
the description, all offer either a light of full breakfast, but you're
on your own for other meals. Some have a communal kitchen,
where guests can prepare a light snack. The owners of such properties take great pride in their lodgings and can be a great source
of insider's information, so be sure to take advantage of their
willingness to suggest attractions and restaurants.

## Paget

**Little Pomander Guest House**       **$80–$114**             ★★★

*Hamilton Harbour, Paget,* ☎ *(441) 236-7635, FAX (980) 236-8332.*
*Single: $80–$115. Double: $80–$114.*
This small charmer consists of two Bermudian cottages set on the
waterfront of Hamilton Harbour, making it an easy walk into town.
Accommodations consist of three self-contained units and five guest
rooms, all with cable TV, refrigerator, microwave oven, air-conditioner and radio. All are very nicely decorated and pleasant. There's
also a communal grill for warm-weather barbecues. No meals are

served besides breakfast (complimentary to those in the guest rooms), and while the property lacks a pool, guests can use the tennis courts at the Pomander Tennis Club across the street for free. 8 rooms. Credit cards: A, MC, V.

### Loughlands Guest House　　　　$55–$118　　　　★★★
*79 South Road, Paget, ☎ (441) 236-1253, FAX: none.*
*Single: $55–$75. Double: $76–$118.*
Set in a stately 1920 mansion, this property is enhanced by its choice and varied collection of antiques that grace the public rooms—including a 100-year-old grandfather clock and a splendid Victorian chest. The guest rooms are nicely done as well and very comfortable; they come equipped with a radio, air-conditioner and coffeemaker. A handful lack a private bath. Breakfast is served in a gracious colonial-style room; you're on your own for other meals. The spacious grounds include a large pool and tennis court—features not often found at guest houses. You can walk to Elbow Beach in 10 minutes. 25 rooms.

### Que Sera　　　　$45–$80　　　　★★
*Paget, ☎ (441) 236-1998.*
*Single: $45–$50. Double: $80.*
This small guest house is close to the Botanical Gardens, and its own grounds are lovely as well, with a large pool and patio for catching the rays. Each room is air-conditioned and has a TV and radio. One also has a fireplace and several have kitchens. No breakfast is served. 3 rooms.

## Pembroke

### Canada Villa　　　　$50–$90　　　　★★
*Pembroke, ☎ (441) 292-0419, FAX (441) 296-1128.*
*Single: $50–$70. Double: $70–$90.*
This old Bermuda home offers informal accommodations close to Hamilton. Each room is air-conditioned and has a ceiling fan and clock radio, but no TV. Continental breakfast is served, and guests are welcome to use the kitchen whenever the mood strikes. There's a pool on site. 5 rooms.

### Edgehill Manor　　　　$50–$104　　　　★★★
*Rosemont Avenue, Hamilton, Pembroke, ☎ (441) 295-7124, FAX (441) 295-3850.*
*Single: $50–$72. Double: $82–$104.*
This pleasant, friendly house is within walking distance of Hamilton's shops and restaurants. The vintage Bermuda home accommodates guests in individually decorated and air-conditioned rooms that feature French Provincial furnishings and colorful fabrics. Each room has a TV and radio, two have kitchenettes and most sport a private terrace or patio. The grounds, which are done up in semi-tropical gardens, feature a swimming pool. Guests can take advantage of the buffet-style breakfast and afternoon tea, but otherwise are on their own for meals. 9 rooms.

### Fordham Hall　　　　$70–$105　　　　★★
*Pitts Bay Road, Pembroke, ☎ (800) 537-4163, (441) 295-1551, FAX (441) 295-3906.*
*Single: $70–$90. Double: $90–$105.*

You can easily walk to Hamilton from this informal guest house set on a hill with great views of the harbor. Dating to 1886, the house has a glass-enclosed porch where you can enjoy continental breakfast (included in the rates.) There's also a spacious, but rather sparsely furnished, living room where guests can while away the hours. Rooms are small and plain, but very clean. Ceiling fans do the job in lieu of air-conditioners. All rooms lack TV and phones. This spot is quite homey—even the sign reminding guests to check out by 11 a.m. is done in needlepoint! 12 rooms.

**Hi-Roy** $56–$98 ★★

*22 Princess Estate Road, Pembroke, ☎ (441) 292-0808.*
*Single: $56. Double: $98.*

This cozy guest house offers great value, with the rates that include both breakfast and dinner. All rooms have private baths, satellite TV and air-conditioners. This family-run spot is a favorite with younger vacation travelers. Owner Everard Jones is a great jazz lover, and will happily share his collection with guests. 6 rooms.

**Oxford House** $105–$138 ★★★

*Woodbourne Avenue, Hamilton, Pembroke, ☎ (800) 548-7758, (441) 295-0503, FAX: none.*
*Single: $105–$118. Double: $125–$138.*

If you want to be close to Hamilton but not spend a fortune on the more upscale hotels, this place is for you. Built in 1938, the family-owned house has large, comfortable and individually decorated rooms—each named for one of Bermuda's parishes—that come equipped with a coffeemaker, TV, radio, phone and air-conditioner. There's a small lending library on the site, and breakfast is served in a charming room. 12 rooms.

**Pleasant View Guest House** $50–$110 ★★

*Princess Estate, Pembroke, ☎ (441) 292-4520.*
*Single: $50–$60. Double: $80–$110.*

There is indeed a fine view from this comfortable guest house just off North Shore Road. Bedrooms are large and airy and come equipped with air-conditioners, ceiling fans, cable TV, clock radio and telephone; some also sport refrigerators. There's a pool and lounge on the premises, and breakfast is a treat. 6 rooms.

## Southampton

**Greene's Guest House** $90–$100 ★★★

*71 Middle Road, Southampton, ☎ (441) 238-0834, FAX (441) 238-8980.*
*Single: $90. Double: $100.*

Lovely views of the Great Sound at this comfortable guest house just five minutes from the beach. Each room has a private bath, air-conditioner, refrigerator, coffeemaker, TV, VCR, radio and telephone. There's a pool on site, as well as a game room, common sitting room, and an honor bar with pretty sea views. Continental breakfast is included in the rates. 6 rooms. Credit cards: A, MC, V.

**Pillar-Ville Guest House** $30–$90 ★★

*Southampton, ☎ (441) 238-0445, FAX (441) 238-0489.*
*Single: $30–$50. Double: $60–$90.*

WHERE TO STAY

This family-run guest house is a great choice for those who want a Southampton address without paying Southampton prices. Located between the Southampton Princess and the Sonesta, the small property is painted an outrageous shade of turquoise. It's a short but steep walk down to a private beach with lounge chairs. The largest unit is a self-contained cottage with a full kitchen, two bedrooms, two baths, fireplace, ceiling fans and air conditioning, but the plastic covering all the furniture keeps it from living up to its full potential. All rooms are clean and have fans, air-conditioners, small kitchens and cable TV. Watch out for owner/manager Vivian Wilson, who—with a twinkle in his eye—will be sure to ask you to spell your name backwards! Most rooms can be had for $55–$90, making this spot an excellent deal. 7 rooms.

**Royal Heights Guest House**      **$90–$125**      ★★★

*Lighthouse Hill, Southampton,* ☎ *(441) 238-0043, FAX (441) 238-8445.*

*Single: $90–$100. Double: $100–$125.*

Russel and Jean Richardson treats their guests like, well, royalty at this clean and casual guest house. Set high on a hill, this complex offers lovely views, and the guest rooms quite nice. All are air-conditioned and have refrigerators, TV, clock radios and balconies. Room number 3 is the largest and most popular. Rates include continental breakfast, and there's a nice pool on site. The beach is not far, but save some energy for the steep walk back. Also within an easy walk are Gibbs lighthouse and the bars and restaurants of the Southampton Princess. 6 rooms. Credit cards: MC, V.

# St. George's

**Hillcrest Guest House**      **$50–$120**      ★★

*1 Nea's Alley, St. George's,* ☎ *(441) 297-1630, FAX (441) 297-1908.*

*Single: $50. Double: $84–$120.*

This 19th-century Bermuda home is an easy stroll from St. George's and its many historic attractions. Though the guest rooms are rather disappointing after you see the eclectic splendor of the antique-filled public spaces, all rooms are clean and comfy. Rooms have air-conditioners, but lack amenities such as telephones or TV, though you will find clock radios. There are no facilities on site, though you can keep things cold in the communal refrigerator. Note that breakfast is not served. 11 rooms.

# NIGHTLIFE

*Frog & Onion Pub is the island's most happening bar. Daily specials are named for famous old English pubs.*

While Bermuda is not generally associated with the swinging nightlife of a San Juan or Nassau, it does offer its share of fun once the sun goes down. Virtually every major hotel and resort has a complimentary weekly **swizzle party** when the manager fetes guests with hors d'oeuvres and the famed swizzle rum drink. During the summer, most properties provide an assortment of evening entertainment, everything from sedate chamber music to rollicking theme shows. During the rest of the year, however, you'll generally have to venture off site to find much nightlife. Obviously, most of the action takes place in the city of Hamilton (Pembroke Parish), which has a slew of **English-style pubs** and a small handful of **nightclubs** for those seeking the disco beat. You can get away without paying a cover charge in the winter, but expect to fork out at least $15 per person to get into a club in the high season.

Besides the spots listed below, young locals hang out at **Robin Hood**, **MR Onions**, **Flanigans** and the **New Captain's Lounge**, all detailed in the restaurant section. The **Cock & Feather** has frequent live music and is a great place to while away the hours with Bermudians, especially if you get into the spirit of buying $1 bingo cards (similar to an instant lottery ticket) as so many here do. Another popular spot for the after-work crowd is the **Hog Penny**, whose small bar brims with English-style charm.

On other parts of the island, **Henry VIII**, in Southampton, has a lively bar scene with frequent year-round live entertainment, while in Hamilton Parish, the **Swizzle Inn** draws young rowdies who splash graffiti on the walls and tack up their business cards for posterity. Over at Dockyard, make tracks for the **Frog & Onion**, a happening pub with pinball machines, pool tables and the requisite dart board. In St. George's, similar merriment takes place at the **White Horse**, which has live music every night during summertime as well as karaoke for those who dare.

As any visitor soon notices, Bermudians tend to dress quite nicely, even at ye olde neighborhood bar. The rule of thumb is "smart casual," which means at least a collared shirt on men and preferably a jacket, especially in the summertime. Too-revealing clothes are considered more smutty than sexy here, so save that see-through blouse for Las Vegas—it just won't go over in Bermuda.

### Casey's Lounge ★★

*25 Queen Street, Hamilton, Bermuda, ☎ (441) 293-9549.*
*Hours: 10 a.m.–10 p.m.*
This spot is rather a dive, but locals like it, and, according to the bartender, "Tourists don't know what they're missing." The only decor is a large stuffed blue marlin and portraits of past owners on the walls, but the jukebox is great, with lots of selections from the late 1920s and up. Casual clothes do just fine here.

### Clay House Inn ★★★★

*North Shore Road, Bermuda, ☎ (441) 292-3193.*
Once an important jazz club that still occasionally features big-name performers, the Clay House now offers a wide variety of entertainment. A calypso revue, with the requisite limbo dancers, fire eaters and steel bands, takes place each Monday through Wednesday. A good time is had by all, including lots of cruise ship passengers during the summer. The cover charge of $25 includes two drinks. Tourists are scarce the rest of the week, when the club features local blues and jazz bands; the cover charge is usually around $10.

### Club 21 ★★★

*Royal Naval Dockyard, Bermuda, ☎ (441) 234-2721.*
*Hours: Varies.*
This spot provides the only dancing on this side of the island, and frequently features great live jazz. A good place for those not up to the long drive into Hamilton. Hours and days open vary, as does the cover charge, so call first.

### Cock and Feather ★★★

*8 Front Street, Hamilton, Bermuda, ☎ (441) 295-2263.*
Live entertainment is presented nightly during high season at this local's hangout, where you can sit inside or out on the pleasant ter-

race. The place is usually hopping, even when there is no band, and lots of folks get into the spirit of playing $1 bingo cards. For more details on this spot, see "Restaurants."

### Gazebo Lounge

*Hamilton Princess Hotel, Hamilton, Bermuda,* ☎ *(441) 295-3000.*
During high season, the Gazebo is given over to a rollicking calypso revue that costs about $30. In the winter, a local theater group presents four decent plays (generally comedies or musicals) in repertory every Thursday, Friday and Saturday. That costs $25, with a dinner package available for $54. Call ahead for a schedule.

### Henry VIII

*South Shore Road, Bermuda,* ☎ *(441) 238-1977.*
This Olde England-themed restaurant also attracts a fair amount of locals and tourists who hang out in the atmospheric pub or in the back room, where live bands play and/or comedians slay the crowd.

### Hubie's Bar

*52 Angle Street, Hamilton, Bermuda,* ☎ *(441) 293-9287.*
*Hours: 10 a.m.–10 p.m.*
Eubie's is located "back 'o town" in a not especially desirable neighborhood when drug deals go down, so take a cab. This is the place to be on Friday nights, when an immensely talented jazz band keeps the joint rockin'—but only until 10 p.m., alas, when owner Hubie Brown turns on the lights and people file out in a remarkably orderly manner. Despite the basic decor, the locals who frequent this spot dress to the nines—expect to see lots of impeccably attired men and women shaking it on the dance floor. The rest of the week, this is a quiet local's place and nothing special, but don't miss the scene Friday nights.

### Neptune Club

*Southampton Princess, Bermuda,* ☎ *(441) 238-2555.*
*Hours: 9 p.m.–1 a.m.*
Jimmy Keys is once again at the keyboard at the Neptune Club, the Southampton Princess' nightspot. Keys puts on a fun and entertaining show, impersonating—quite impressively—everyone from Elton John to Willie Nelson to Ray Charles to Bob Marley. He plays from early March to New Year's Eve; the club is dark in January and February. Occasionally during the summer, another comedian or entertainer fills in when Keys is off, so call ahead. Doors open at 9 p.m.; the show starts at 9:30 p.m. and the club stays open until 1 a.m. General admission: $5.

### Oasis Nightclub ★★★★

*Front Street, Hamilton, Bermuda,* ☎ *(441) 292-4978.*
*Hours: 9 p.m.–3 a.m.*
Located atop the Emporium Building—reached via a glass elevator—Oasis usually draws a younger crowd than The Club, and the place stays swinging till 3 a.m. The large warehouse-style, high-tech club features mainly disco and top 40 dance music; in the adjacent Back Room Bar, you can rock to local bands or partake in "laser karaoke." Among the locals who frequent this spot are some of Bermuda's gay population. General admission: $15.

### The Club

*Bermudiana Road, Hamilton, Bermuda,* ☎ *(441) 295-6693.*

*Hours: 10 p.m.–3 a.m.*

The Club, located atop the Little Venice Restaurant, rocks to 3 a.m. and attracts a good mixture of locals and tourists. It's quite unassuming for a disco, with a small bar, pretty shuttered windows, lots of brass and mirrors, and art deco touches—but you'll still find the requisite light show on the small dance floor. A friendly spot and a good place to kick up your heels. Admission is free if you dine at Little Venice, the Harbourfront or La Trattoria. General admission: $15.

# BERMUDA FOR ADVENTURERS

*Sailboat tours are a fun way to view the island's miles of pink, sandy beaches and coral reefs.*

An upscale destination like Bermuda doesn't often conjure up images of adventure travel and, in fact, a vacation here is a far cry from jungle-trekking through Belize or a safari in deep Africa. That's not to say, however, that those with a travel bent toward testing their endurance will be left without challenges on the island.

## Scuba Diving

Bermuda is rightly known for its excellent scuba diving, thanks to the more than 600 square miles of reef that surround it. Those very shallow reefs that terrorized long-ago sailors are today a diver's joy. The treacherous reefs have claimed more than 350 ships, some as far back as the 1500s, whose remains lie in a watery grave ready for divers to explore. Bermuda's fringing reef is also home to hundreds of fish species, including most of those found in the Caribbean as well as a few species known only in these waters. Expect to spot hogfish, jacks, parrot fish, trumpetfish, grasbys, grouper, porcupine fish, wrasse, damselfish, squirrelfish, sergeant majors, moray eels, arrow crabs, spiny lobsters, triggerfish and even octopus and sea turtles.

Diving to inspect shipwrecks is especially popular (see "Sports and Recreation" for a list of the most visited), and reef diving can be equally spectacular. The colorful reefs are especially dramatic along the South Shore and in the North Rock areas. These so-called "boiler reefs" take their name from the white foam caused by swells breaking over their surface.

Visibility is usually quite good, especially the farther out you go; it averages 100 feet. The diving season runs from mid-March through November, with a few ships taking divers out as late as Christmas and beyond. Water temperatures are comfortable in the mid-80s from June through September, so an eighth-inch shorty or even just a T-shirt will keep you warm. But during April, May, September and October, plan on donning a full quarter-inch wetsuit and hood.

Snorkelers also have much to see. Among the better sites are Tobacco Bay, a public beach at the edge of St. George's; John Smith's Bay on South Shore, where solid reefs await just 50 yards offshore; Elbow Beach on the east end of South Shore, where the reef begins 10 yard offshore and continues out for more than a mile, and Achilles Bay, located on Bermuda's eastern tip near Fort St. Catherine, where visibility averages between 60 and 80 feet.

For a list of dive shops that can provide everything from instruction to night dives, see "Sports and Recreation."

## Helmet Diving

Helmet diving is not exactly a life-threatening activity—and it's also incredibly easy—but it's uniqueness makes it worthy of a mention in this section. After a boat ride to an underwater "garden," passengers climb down a ladder until about chest-deep in the water. There, they don a large brass helmet into which oxygen is continuously pumped, making it easy to breathe normally, while walking about the ocean floor at a depth of some 10 to 15 feet. You can hand-feed the snappers, sergeant majors, angelfish, hogfish and coneys that make the area home. It's a great way for nonswimmers, eyeglass-wearers and children to explore the underwater world—without even getting their hair wet. The season runs from May through October, and two operators offer helmet dives of about a half-hour. See "Sports and Recreation" for details.

# Parasailing

If your idea of a good time is dangling high in the air while being pulled along by a motorboat, then you've got to try parasailing in Bermuda, where the views are as exhilarating as the experience itself. Parasailing is offered at Southampton Princess, Marriott's Castle Harbour, St. George's ParaSail and the Royal Naval Dockyard's Skyrider. It costs about $50 per ride.

# Kite-skiing

If regular water-skiing (available throughout the island) isn't daring enough for you, try kite-skiing, in which you can reach speeds as high as 50 m.p.h. via the wind power that comes from a large kite that helps pull you along on water-skis. The same company, **Kiteski Bermuda** (☎ *[441] 293-1968* or *[441] 234-8768*) also offers a "flying water-ski" called the armchair, a sit-down water-ski that rides above the water on a hydrofoil.

# Windsurfing

Bermuda's constant breezes make for a windsurfer's paradise; the best places to zip along the shoreline are at Elbow Beach, Great Sound, Shelly Bay, Harrington Sound and Somerset Long Bay. Beginners will be happiest—and safest—along the placid surf at Castle Harbour and Mangrove Bay. Plan on spending about $20 to rent a board for an hour and about $35 for an hour-long lesson. (See "Sports and Recreation" for places to rent equipment.)

# Jet-skiing

They are loud, kill your knees and are somewhat obnoxious to those on the beach, but that doesn't stop disciples of jet skis from extolling the thrills of a motorized zip through the surf. You can rent the skis (at about $80 per hour) at Royal Naval Dockyard's **Club Wet 'n' Wild** (☎ *[441] 234-2426*).

# Bicycling

Even experienced bikers will find cycling in Bermuda a constant challenge. The island is very hilly, the roads are exceedingly narrow, the wind can be overwhelming, and traffic is everpresent. If all that is not enough to stop you, you'll find several places to rent bicycles (called push or pedal bikes to differentiate them from the more popular motorized scooters, or mopeds) around the island.

*Cycling by the beach is a favorite activity of locals and tourists.*

The best place to cycle is along the Railway Trail (see "Attractions"), which is open only to pedestrians and cyclists. South Shore Road offers excellent views and some nice, flat terrain, but you'll be fighting traffic most of the way. While Bermudians are a polite lot who rarely toot their horns (in fact, it's illegal unless absolutely necessary), don't forget that you'll be sharing the roadways with many hapless tourists trying to negotiate their motorized scooters. The bottom line: Only experienced bikers should attempt exploring Bermuda via cycle, and it is definitely not recommended for preteen children.

Prices for bicycles are generally about $15 per day—much cheaper than for the motorized versions, but then again, they're a lot more work. Three- and 10-speed bikes can usually be rented at the island's many motorized scooter shops, but call first to make sure. For cycling tours around the island, contact **Pedal Pushers** *(Royal Naval Dockyard,* ☎ *[441] 234-2241).*

# BEACHES

*Bermuda's uncrowded beaches are inviting all year round.*

Though they are generally on the small side, Bermuda's beaches are especially picturesque, surrounded in most cases by jagged rocks great for tidepooling, with large boulders just offshore jutting up from the ocean floor. The island's best beaches lie along the South Shore, where the sand has a pink hue (the result of minuscule pieces of coral mixed in with the granules of sand) and the surf is gentle due to the ever-present barrier reefs. All pubic beaches are free.

**Horseshoe Bay Beach** (South Shore Road, Southampton) is the island's most famous beach—and rightfully so. The public strand is a glorious crescent and has restrooms and a snack bar. This is a favorite local's spot. Behind Horseshoe Bay is scenic South Shore Park, with sandy trails and rolling sand dunes just perfect for a leisurely hike. This is one of Bermuda's two beaches with a lifeguard on duty in the summertime—a good thing, as the undertow can be strong.

The other lifeguard is stationed at **John Smith's Bay** (South Road, Smith's), that parish's only public beach. A new picnic area is frequently visited by a mobile van selling food and drink, and the beach is accessible to people with disabilities.

**Astwood Park** (Warwick) is noted for its sweeping views of the South Shore. The pretty sandy cove offers up good snorkeling.

Though the stretch at **Elbow Beach Hotel** (off South Road, Paget) is private, visitors can pay a small fee (about $4) and get a towel and access to a changing room. You can also rent a lounge chair or umbrella. There's a restaurant on site for light lunches and snacks. The adjacent **Elbow Beach** is public but tends to get overly crowded, especially on the weekends.

Bermuda's longest strand is **Warwick Long Bay** (South Road, Southampton), a half-mile-long beach with gentle surf. Another scenic spot is West Whale Bay Park, also in Southampton, where the snorkeling is great and the small beach's isolation (it's accessible only by foot) makes it perfect for lovers. Nearby is the 19th-century Old West Whale Bay Fort, now mostly overgrown with vegetation.

*Family/Charles Island Beach is a favorite spot for watersports.*

Over on the north shore, the waters of **Somerset Long Bay** (Cambridge Road, Sandys) are calm, making it especially suitable for nonswimmers and children. The quarter-mile-long beach is surrounded by parkland.

In St. George's, **Tobacco Bay Beach** (Coot Pond Road) is a small, coral cove with changing rooms, a snack bar and watersports equipment for rent. **Clarence Cove** (North Shore and Spanish Point roads, Pembroke), located within Admiralty House Park, is a small crescent that is nearly landlocked. Its sea caves are great for snorkeling, and the lush park makes a nice backdrop. Just to the west is **Spanish Point Park**, where you can easily swim to a small island right off the beach.

One of the island's few beaches with trees is at **Shelly Bay** (North Shore Road, Hamilton), a favorite spot for families for its shallow water and large playground complete with jungle gym, slides and swings. Those without children will probably be happier elsewhere, however, as this spot is often filled with the sounds of shrieking tots.

BEACHES

# GOLF

*Winston Churchill, Babe Ruth and President Bush have tested their golf skills at Mid-Ocean Golf Club.*

Golf is nearly as Bermudian as Bermuda shorts, and the island has eight golf courses, an astounding number for such a small place. While Bermuda is known for its high prices, greens fees here are surprisingly reasonable—many excellent courses fetch under $60 for 18 holes of play, and the one nine-hole course lets you go around twice at no extra charge, save cart rental. Furthermore, many hotels offer money-saving golf packages that are well worth investigating.

Of Bermuda's eight courses, six are open to the public. (However, your hotel may be able to get you into the private **Mid Ocean Club** and **Riddles Bay Country Club**). All accept MasterCard and Visa. All courses enforce a dress code that requires shirts with collar and sleeves and Bermuda-length shorts or long pants. Jeans, cut-offs and gym shorts are prohibited. Greens reseeding usually takes place from late September to early November, so be sure to inquire about conditions during that time.

The new **Bermuda Golf Academy** (near the Southampton Princess and Rort Royal Golf Course, Middle Road, Southampton, ☎ *[441] 236-1629*), is a great place to practice before hitting the links. The facility has a 300-yard driving range with 50 covered

**WEST END**

# GOLFER'S GUIDE TO BERMUDA

Bermuda has more golf acreage per square mile than anywhere else in the world. The challenging golf courses designed by Robert Trent Jones, Charles Banks and Charles Blair MacDonald boast a hazard few others can claim—stunning panoramic vistas at every hole. November through March is considered the prime golfing season.

## PORT ROYAL GOLF COURSE

The famous 15th hole of this government-run course is near the picturesque old Whale Bay Battery. This par-71, 6565-yd. Robert Trent Jones course is enjoyably hilly and pleasantly rural. Well-trapped greens and bunkered fairways conspire with striking views and a lush setting against an impressive score card. Rated the best links in Bermuda, more than 50,000 rounds are played here each year.

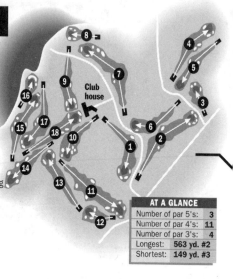

### AT A GLANCE

| | |
|---|---|
| Number of par 5's: | 3 |
| Number of par 4's: | 11 |
| Number of par 3's: | 4 |
| Longest: | 563 yd. #2 |
| Shortest: | 149 yd. #3 |

## PRINCESS GOLF CLUB

Plan to use every club in your bag on this par-54, 2684-yd. scenic test of skill. In addition to elevated tees, strategically placed bunkers and water hazards, the breathtaking views and unpredictable breezes off the Atlantic add unwanted strokes to your game on this executive course.

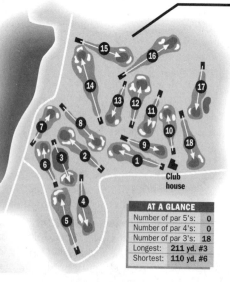

### AT A GLANCE

| | |
|---|---|
| Number of par 5's: | 0 |
| Number of par 4's: | 0 |
| Number of par 3's: | 18 |
| Longest: | 211 yd. #3 |
| Shortest: | 110 yd. #6 |

GOLF

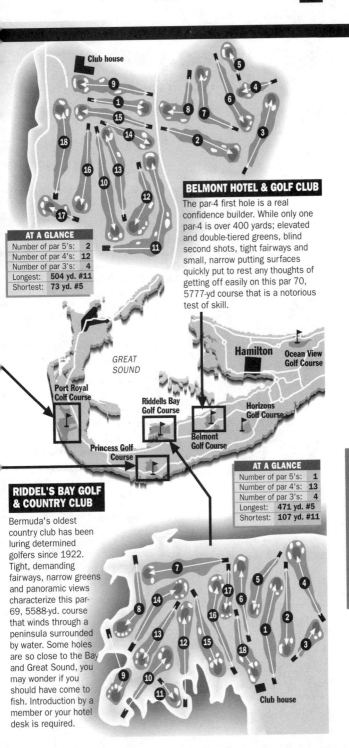

**Club house**

**BELMONT HOTEL & GOLF CLUB**

The par-4 first hole is a real confidence builder. While only one par-4 is over 400 yards; elevated and double-tiered greens, blind second shots, tight fairways and small, narrow putting surfaces quickly put to rest any thoughts of getting off easily on this par 70, 5777-yd course that is a notorious test of skill.

**AT A GLANCE**

| | |
|---|---|
| Number of par 5's: | 2 |
| Number of par 4's: | 12 |
| Number of par 3's: | 4 |
| Longest: | 504 yd. #11 |
| Shortest: | 73 yd. #5 |

*GREAT SOUND*

**Hamilton**

**Ocean View Golf Course**

**Port Royal Golf Course**

**Riddells Bay Golf Course**

**Horizons Golf Course**

**Belmont Golf Course**

**Princess Golf Course**

**RIDDEL'S BAY GOLF & COUNTRY CLUB**

Bermuda's oldest country club has been luring determined golfers since 1922. Tight, demanding fairways, narrow greens and panoramic views characterize this par-69, 5588-yd. course that winds through a peninsula surrounded by water. Some holes are so close to the Bay and Great Sound, you may wonder if you should have come to fish. Introduction by a member or your hotel desk is required.

**AT A GLANCE**

| | |
|---|---|
| Number of par 5's: | 1 |
| Number of par 4's: | 13 |
| Number of par 3's: | 4 |
| Longest: | 471 yd. #5 |
| Shortest: | 107 yd. #11 |

**Club house**

**GOLF**

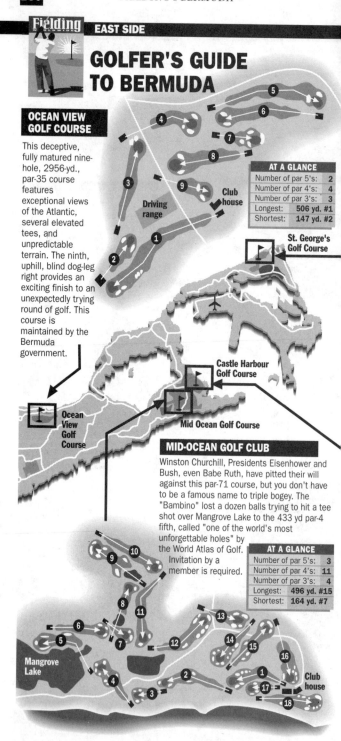

**Fielding**

**EAST SIDE**

# GOLFER'S GUIDE TO BERMUDA

## OCEAN VIEW GOLF COURSE

This deceptive, fully matured nine-hole, 2956-yd., par-35 course features exceptional views of the Atlantic, several elevated tees, and unpredictable terrain. The ninth, uphill, blind dog-leg right provides an exciting finish to an unexpectedly trying round of golf. This course is maintained by the Bermuda government.

| AT A GLANCE | |
|---|---|
| Number of par 5's: | 2 |
| Number of par 4's: | 4 |
| Number of par 3's: | 3 |
| Longest: | 506 yd. #1 |
| Shortest: | 147 yd. #2 |

Driving range

Club house

St. George's Golf Course

Castle Harbour Golf Course

Ocean View Golf Course

Mid Ocean Golf Course

## MID-OCEAN GOLF CLUB

Winston Churchill, Presidents Eisenhower and Bush, even Babe Ruth, have pitted their will against this par-71 course, but you don't have to be a famous name to triple bogey. The "Bambino" lost a dozen balls trying to hit a tee shot over Mangrove Lake to the 433 yd par-4 fifth, called "one of the world's most unforgettable holes" by the World Atlas of Golf. Invitation by a member is required.

| AT A GLANCE | |
|---|---|
| Number of par 5's: | 3 |
| Number of par 4's: | 11 |
| Number of par 3's: | 4 |
| Longest: | 496 yd. #15 |
| Shortest: | 164 yd. #7 |

Mangrove Lake

Club house

GOLF

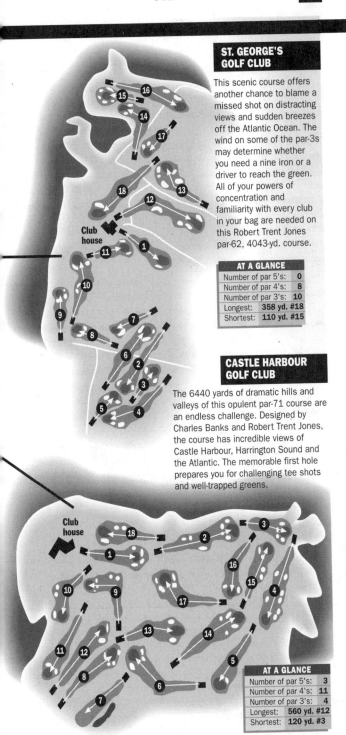

## ST. GEORGE'S GOLF CLUB

This scenic course offers another chance to blame a missed shot on distracting views and sudden breezes off the Atlantic Ocean. The wind on some of the par-3s may determine whether you need a nine iron or a driver to reach the green. All of your powers of concentration and familiarity with every club in your bag are needed on this Robert Trent Jones par-62, 4043-yd. course.

### AT A GLANCE

| | |
|---|---|
| Number of par 5's: | 0 |
| Number of par 4's: | 8 |
| Number of par 3's: | 10 |
| Longest: | 358 yd. #18 |
| Shortest: | 110 yd. #15 |

## CASTLE HARBOUR GOLF CLUB

The 6440 yards of dramatic hills and valleys of this opulent par-71 course are an endless challenge. Designed by Charles Banks and Robert Trent Jones, the course has incredible views of Castle Harbour, Harrington Sound and the Atlantic. The memorable first hole prepares you for challenging tee shots and well-trapped greens.

### AT A GLANCE

| | |
|---|---|
| Number of par 5's: | 3 |
| Number of par 4's: | 11 |
| Number of par 3's: | 4 |
| Longest: | 560 yd. #12 |
| Shortest: | 120 yd. #3 |

GOLF

bays, an 18-hole practice green, target greens, a chipping bunker and teaching professionals. It's open daily from 7:30 a.m. to 10:30 p.m.

While golfing is a year-round activity on the island, it's especially pleasurable from October to March, when the temperatures are cooler, the humidity lower and the courses less crowded. A number of tournaments during that period keep things hopping. The popular **Bermuda International Open Golf Championship**, which takes place each October at Port Royal, is open to male professionals and amateurs with a handicap under 10. The professional purse is $35,000; for details, call Port Royal at ☎ *(441) 234-0974.* In late October, the **Bermuda Masters International Golf Classic** is designed for male and female players of all skill levels and features a celebrity host. The tournament, held at Port Royal, Castle Harbour and Belmont, is part of a package that includes accommodations and three rounds of golf; call Elegant Vacations ☎ *(800) 451-4398.*

In January, the **Bermuda Senior Golf Classic** is open to both men and women. The weeklong event includes sightseeing and cocktail parties; call ☎ *(441) 297-8148.* Another popular event is **Bermuda Valentine's Mixed Foursomes Invitational Golf Tournament**, in February, which includes six nights' accommodation, four rounds of golf, parties and entertainment. Call ☎ *(441) 297-8148.* Also in February, the **Bermuda Amateur Golf Festival** attracts hundreds of tourists with its variety of tournaments for men, women and couples. Call Robustelli Sports Marketing International at ☎ *(203) 352-0545.* Finally, the **Bermuda Easter Lily Invitational Pro-Am Golf Tournament for Ladies**, held each spring, is limited to 25 teams, each consisting of one lady golf professional and three lady amateurs. Contact ☎ *(441) 297-8148.*

For more information on golfing in Bermuda, contact the **Bermuda Golf Association** at *Box HM 433, Hamilton HM BM, Bermuda;* ☎ *(441) 238-1367.*

### Belmont Golf Club

*Belmont Road, Bermuda,* ☎ *(441) 236-1301.*

Eighteen holes; par 70; 5777 yards. Belmont is one of Bermuda's easiest courses—which is hard to believe when you get through the first two straightforward holes (and keep in mind that "easy" is a relative term on this island of links). The rest of the course is filled with doglegs and other blinds; the 11th hole is a killer, with its severe dogleg and blind tee shot. While only one par-four hole exceeds 400 yards, the links' many elevated and double-tiered greens, tight fairways, blind second shots and small and narrow putting surfaces make it challenging. Expect slow play—especially on the weekends—and a fair number of curse words from players new to the course. Greens fees are $57 (free for guests of the hotel), and gas carts are mandatory). Green Fees are $18 for nine holes, $36 for 18. Clubs rent for $25.

*Castle Harbour Golf Club features dramatic hills and valleys.*

### Castle Harbour Golf Club

*Marriott's Castle Harbour, Bermuda,* ☎ *(441) 293-2040.*
Eighteen holes; par 71; 6440 yards. This Resort Championship
course, designed by Charles Banks and Robert Trent Jones, is noted
for its hilly terrain, constant wind and elevated greens. The views are
breathtaking—and so is the difficulty level of the 18th hole, considered the hardest on the island. This is one of the island's most expensive courses, but it shows in the meticulous grounds and fine greens.
Greens fees are $90 from Jan. 3–Nov. 11 ($52 after 4:30 p.m.) and
$60 the rest of the year. Clubs rent for $25. Gas carts (mandatory) are
$40 ($32 after 4:30 p.m.), and shoes rent for $6.

### Mid Ocean Golf Club

*Tucker's Town, Bermuda,* ☎ *(441) 293-0330.*
Eighteen holes; par 71; 6547 yards. You'll need a club member to get
you into this splendid private course, but it's well worth the trouble
to play what is considered to be one of the world's best. (Your hotel
may also be able to get you in.) Greens fees are the highest on the
island (unless you're lucky enough to come with a member), but playing Mid Ocean is a thrill for avid duffers. The grounds are simply
beautiful and perfectly maintained, the views mesmerizing. The
course is classic in that it rewards for good shots and penalizes for bad
ones—this is not the spot for novices. It's been played by the likes of
Winston Churchill, Dwight Eisenhower, George Bush and Babe
Ruth, who lost a dozen balls trying to hit a tee shot over Mangrove
Lake to the fifth hole, called "one of the world's unforgettable holes"
by the *World Atlas of Golf.* Greens fees are $120 ($50 when playing
with a member), and clubs rent for $12. Caddies get $25 per bag.

### Ocean View Golf Course

*North Shore Road, Bermuda,* ☎ *(441) 295-6500.*
Nine holes; par 35; 2965 yards. True to the name, this government-
owned course (formerly the only place blacks could play) provides
pretty sea views and lovely vistas of the island's north shore. Unpredictable, hilly terrain and frequent wind make this course more challenging than it may first appear. A much needed $3 million
renovation in 1994 returned Ocean View to its former glory. Greens

GOLF

fees are \$28 (\$14 after 3:34 p.m.); you can go around twice at no extra cost. Gas carts cost \$30 (18 holes) or \$15 (nine holes). Pull carts are \$5 and clubs rent for \$15.

*Port Royal Golf Course is near the picturesque Whale Bay Battery.*

### Port Royal Golf Course

*Off Middle Road, Bermuda,* ☎ *(441) 295-6500.*

Eighteen holes; par 71; 6565 yards. Robert Trent Jones designed a winner with Port Royal, one of the island's most scenic and lush courses. It's also one of Bermuda's most popular, with some 50,000 rounds played here each year. Owned and operated by the Bermuda Government, the course is considered one of the world's best public links. The course is relatively flat (though hillier on the back nine), has many elevated tees and, like most of Bermuda's courses, can be constantly buffeted by winds. The 15th hole is especially picturesque—if it looks familiar, you've probably seen it somewhere in an ad for Bermuda or in a golf magazine. Because it is so popular and reasonably priced, the course is not always in tip-top condition. Greens fees are \$55 (cheaper after 4 p.m.); inquire about a five-day package that costs \$220 for Monday-Friday play. Gas carts are \$30 (18 holes) or \$15 (nine holes); pull carts go for \$8. Clubs rent for \$20 and shoes for \$10.

### Princess Golf Club

*Southampton Princess Resort, Bermuda,* ☎ *(441) 238-0446.*

Eighteen holes; par 54; 2684 yards. This short course, which serves as the "front lawn" of the Southampton Princess, averages just 2.5 hours' playing time and requires skillful work with irons. The terrain is remarkably steep and hilly—you'll want to spring for a gas cart unless you're in super shape. The views are lovely (if you ignore the high-rise hotel), and elevated tees, numerous bunkers, lots of water and winds sweeping off the sea keep things challenging. The greens are kept as they should be—nice and green, thanks to a good irrigation system. Greens fees are \$36 (\$32 for Princess guests); you can buy five rounds for \$144 or \$128 (hotel guests). Gas carts go for \$30 (\$28 for hotel guests); pull carts are \$6. Clubs rent for \$15 and shoes for \$6.

GOLF

## Riddells Bay Golf & Country Club

*Riddell's Bay Road, Bermuda,* ☎ *(441) 238-1060.*
Eighteen holes; par 69; 5588 yards. Considered the elder statesman
of Bermuda golf, the private Riddells Bay has been challenging duffers
since 1922. The course winds along a narrow peninsula (only 600
yards at its widest) and has Bermuda's trademark tight fairways and
small, narrow greens, though the terrain is relatively flat. Visitors must
be introduced by a member or the management of their hotel. Greens
fees are $48 weekdays, $60 Saturdays, Sundays and holidays (less if
you play with a member). Gas carts are $35; pull carts are $5. Clubs
rent for $13.

*Golfers at St. George's Golf Club have to contend with distracting
ocean views.*

## St. George's Golf Club

*1 Park Road, Bermuda,* ☎ *(441) 295-6500.*
Robert Trent Jones designed this scenic course, built in 1985 and
Bermuda's newest. The views of the ocean are splendid, but this is the
island's windiest course and that often makes golfers crazy, especially
when it comes to choosing the right club. Though the course is short,
the ever-present wind keeps play long and challenging, and the greens
are often slick from the salt air. Greens fees are a bargain at $38, and
a five-day package costs just $150 for weekday play. Gas carts cost
$30; pull carts, $56. Clubs rent for $16.

GOLF

# SHOPPING

*The Royal Naval Dockyard's market offers many unique gifts.*

Shopping is a great pleasure in Bermuda, where the stores are elegant, the service courteous and professional, and the goods of high quality. The dark lining around this silver cloud is that prices are generally quite high, despite there being no sales tax. While bargains can be found on luxury items, such as cashmere, imported fragrances, china, crystal and decorative figurines, these are still high-ticket goods no matter how you slice the cake.

Prices are cheaper by some 20 to 30 percent than in the United States on the above-mentioned items from manufacturers including Baccarat, Wedgewood, Royal Doulton, Belleck, Aynsley and Llardo. Perfumes from the likes of Gucci, Chanel, Yves Saint Laurent and other designers are about 25 to 30 percent lower than in the United States—and remember, the price you see is the price you pay, as there is no sales tax. However, keep in mind that you can only bring $400 worth of merchandise back into the United States duty-free, with the exception of Bermuda-made goods and antiques more than 100 years old. So, if you're buying a complete set of china, be sure to factor in the customs duty (10 percent up to $1000 worth of goods) to make sure you're truly saving money. With U.S. department stores in the habit of offering frequent sales, you may do just as well at home.

Many items are shockingly expensive, such as film, camera batteries and cigarettes (nearly $5 per pack), so you're best off stocking up on these items before you hit the island. Even a decent T-shirt that attests to your visit will run at least $20. On the other hand, as a collector of refrigerator magnets, I was astounded to find nearly all priced at only $2—and they were quite nice, at that. Prices are virtually the same throughout the island, so don't bother comparison-shopping.

Some made-in-Bermuda items to look out for (and which are identified by a sticker) include Bermuda Gold liqueur, made by Somers Distillers; Black Seal Rum by Gosling's; beers by Bermuda Triangle Brewing; and Barritt's Bermuda Stone Ginger Beer, a soft drink that mixes well with gin, vodka and sweet red wine. For a memento of the spicy concoctions used to enhance Bermuda fish chowder and drinks, bring home some of Outbridge's Sherry Peppers, Pepper Jellies, Vinegar Pepper and Sherry Rum Pepper, which you'll easily find in most gift shops. You can pick up one-of-a-kind fragrances made right on the island at both Bermuda Perfumery and Royal Lyme Ltd., while island-roasted java—which has its own alluring scent—can be found at Rock Island Coffee. Finally, handcrafted Bermuda cedar, pieces of which you'll see in many fine hotels and restaurants, can be found throughout the island; **Yankee Store** in the city of Hamilton (☎ *[441] 295-2570)* has an especially good selection.

Stores are generally open from 9 a.m. to 5 p.m. Monday through Saturday, and most are closed on Sundays and public holidays. Some shops in Hamilton stay open until 9 p.m. on Friday evenings from late November to Christmas Eve, and also stay open late and on Sunday during the high season when cruise ships are in port. If you have your heart set on shopping on a Sunday, head for the Royal Naval Dockyard, where the shops are open from 10 a.m. to 5 p.m.

The island has three department stores—**A.S. Cooper & Sons** (☎ *[441] 295-3961)*, **H.A. & E. Smith** (☎ *[441] 295-2288)* and **Trimingham Brothers** (☎ *[441] 295-1183)*, all headquartered on Front Street, with smaller branches throughout the island. The three also have small outlets in the posher hotels, with prices exactly the same as in Hamilton. These family-owned stores, which date to the 19th century, are a true delight, with their traditional wooden showcases and accents, beamed ceilings and artfully arranged upscale goods.

If you're interested in art, Bermuda delivers with plenty of galleries. In St. Georges, **Carole Holding** *(Somers Wharf, Water Street,* ☎ *[441] 297-1373)*, has a gallery that sells her pastoral watercolors. If they look vaguely familiar, it's probably because you've noticed her work on the walls of your hotel guest room—she's a popular commercial artist. Also in St. George's, the **Bridge House Gallery** *(1 Bridge Street,* ☎ *[441] 297-8211)* features prints and originals by more than a dozen local artists, as well as cedar work, ceramic cottages, banana and gombey dolls and other island-produced crafts, plus small antiques. The Bridge House, built in 1700, is a classic example of early Bermudian architecture and is now run under the auspices of the **Bermuda National Trust**—which has its own good gift shop in Paget *at the corner of The Lane and Pomander Road* (☎ *[441] 236-6483).*

The splendid works of Desmond Fountain, whose lifelike bronze statues grace many a park and hotel on the island, can be seen at the **Sculpture Gallery in the Southampton Princess Hotel** (☎ *[441] 238-8840)* or at the **artist's studio** by appointment only (☎ *[441] 292-3955)*—but be prepared to a drop an arm and a leg for one of his bronze ones.

**The Windjammer Gallery**, which deals exclusively with living artists, has two shops in Hamilton *(89 Reid Street,* ☎ *[441] 292-7861* and *95 Front Street,* ☎ *[441] 292-5878)* that offer a wide selection of original and foreign art as well as prints and limited editions.

**The Art House Gallery** *(South Shore Road, Paget West,* ☎ *[441] 236-6746)* has a good array of original watercolors, oils and signed color lithographs by Joan Forbes, whose pastel-colored renderings of the island are a delight. Also on hand are the lovely cards and books of Bermudian Dana Cooper. Her *My Bermuda ABC* and *My Bermuda 123* make wonderful gifts for children.

Renowned local artist Michael Swan has a gallery in the **Clocktower Mall at the Royal Naval Dockyard** (☎ *[441] 234-3128)* that displays his attractive local scenes, created with an airbrush on acrylic. He also creates T-shirts that are a far cut above the standard offerings. Finally, don't miss the **Bermuda Society of the Arts Gallery in City Hall** *(Church Street, Hamilton,* ☎ *[441] 292-3824)*, where varied works by local artists are on display and sale. And for more locally made goods, check out the Royal Naval Dockyard, where artisans are at work in the **Craft Market** (☎ *[441] 234-3208)* and at **Island Pottery** (☎ *[441] 234-3361)*.

The Royal Naval Dockyard is an especially good place to come on a Sunday, as all stores here are open, in contrast to most of the rest of the island. The Clocktower Centre is a lovely shopping mall with lots of interesting specialty stores. Among the more offbeat are the **Hall of Names** (☎ *[441] 234-3410)*, where $15 buys the history of your surname and family coat of arms from a database of 400,000 European and British names. At **Admiral's Locker** (☎ *[441] 234-3835)*, they sell very imaginative decorative items, predominately nautically themed, and Third World arts and crafts at fairly reasonable prices. Across the way, **Victoriana** (☎ *[441] 234-1392)* has a good selection of small an-

tiques, including vintage ink wells and bottles as well as Victorian memorabilia. For handcrafted Bermuda items, try **Bermuda
Gombey Trader** (☎ *[441] 234-2845)*, where they offer up island-
made Bermuda and Caribbean souvenirs and special jams, mar-
malades, honeys and chutneys. Bermuda tea towels, tablecloths
and the like are at **Dockyard Linens** (☎ *[441] 234-3871)*, while
the **Ships Inn Book Gallery** (☎ *[441] 234-2807)* is a tiny shop with
good deals on used books.

The city of Hamilton has a kaleidoscope of boutiques catering
to every whim. Linens can be found at the **Irish Linen Shop** *(31
Front Street West,* ☎ *[441] 295-4089)*, where they have a huge
assortment of tablecloths, napkins, hankies and the like. **Pegasus**
*(Pitts Bay Road,* ☎ *[441] 295-2900)* is a charming and cluttered
shop next to Bacardi Rum that sells hand-painted house signs,
lots of Winnie the Pooh memorabilia and antique maps and
prints. **International Imports** *(Par-la-Ville Road,* ☎ *[441] 292-
1661)* urges tourists to "shop where the chefs shop" and backs
that up with a great selection of upscale cookware and accesso-
ries. Inquire about the frequently offered one-day cooking classes. At **William Bluck & Co.** *(Front Street,* ☎ *[441] 295-5367)*, they
have a nice selection of hand-painted flowerpots as well as imported decorative items from the traditional to the funky. Nearby, the giant **Phoenix Drug Store** *(Reid Street,* ☎ *[441] 295-3838)*
has all you need in the way of medicines and sundries, including
junk food, an ATM machine and a bookstore on the second
floor. Other highlights of Hamilton: **Bermuda Bookstore** *(Queen
Street,* ☎ *[441] 295-3698)*, with a great selection of best-sellers
and books on the island; **Bermuda Coin & Stamp** *(49 Old Cellar
Lane,* ☎ *[441] 295-5503)*, with the world's largest collection of
Bermuda philatelic materials and coins and **True Reflections** *(54
Court Street,* ☎ *[441] 295-9424)*, with exotic fabrics, sarongs,
and other arts and crafts celebrating ethnic culture.

# FIELDING'S CHOICE

*Quaint house signs surrounded by flowers lead to cottages.*

## Best Resort

**Southampton Princess, Southampton**

All you could want in a resort is here at the sprawling Princess, including 18 holes of golf, indoor and outdoor pools, a divine beach club, 11 tennis courts, plus rooms and guest privileges at the sister property in Hamilton.

## Best Large Hotel

### Hamilton Princess, City of Hamilton

The atmosphere can be a bit, well, stodgy, but it only serves to complement the polished woods and brass, impeccable service and hall (literally) of fame where pictures of famous and well-heeled guests reside. Perfect for business travelers and the well-heeled, though families will be more comfortable in less genteel surroundings.

## Best Small Hotels

### Newstead, Paget

It looks more like a private mansion than a hotel at this upscale hotel, and in fact the main manor house dates to the 1800s. Choose from antique-filled rooms to modern suites, though the gorgeous public areas are so well-appointed you'll inevitably spend lots of time there, soaking up the views of the city.

### Rosedon, City of Hamilton

Located just across the street from the Princess, Rosedon harks back to an earlier, gracious era—apparent in the fine breakfast or afternoon tea served on the wide veranda. The grounds bring to mind a botanical garden, while the service is both personable and professional.

### Waterloo House, City of Hamilton

Walk through the small entryway and it's like stepping into a secret garden, with winding pathways, flowering blooms and discreet patios. This Relais et Chateaux property is steps from the city center.

## Best Cottage Colonies

### Cambridge Beaches, Sandys

The readers of *Conde Nast Traveler* have named Cambridge Beaches Bermuda's best resort, and we agree. The six beautiful pink-sand beaches are just the icing on the cake at this impeccable spot, where a spiffy health spa, complimentary ferry, varied watersports, tennis courts, full-scale marina and lovely accommodations keep guests sated.

### Horizons & Cottages, Paget

Romance seems to ooze from every corner of this chic resort, where each cottage has its own special feel. If you can drag yourself outside, a nine-hole golf course, three tennis courts and beach club await.

## Best Apartments & Cottages

### Greenbank & Cottages, Paget

There's something tremendously appealing about this small, family-run site that borders Hamilton Harbour. Accommodations are simple but comfortable, and the on-site watersport facility is a big plus.

### Pretty Penny, Paget

Tucked away in a residential neighborhood on grounds well-maintained for privacy, Petty Penny is a good choice for charming rooms and personable service.

## Best Low-Cost Property

### Salt Kettle House, Paget

Book early if you want to spend your holiday at Salt Kettle; repeat guests fill the place up year after year. Though the lodging is simple, guests can enjoy the more lavish surroundings in two well-appointed lounges.

## Best Expensive Restaurants

### Fourways Inn, Paget

You're sure to swoon at the surroundings as you enter the large and lovely dining room at this famed spot, and the food won't disappoint, either. Vegetarians delight in the many imaginative dishes cooked *sans* meat.

### Waterlot Inn, Southampton

Antiques, candlelight, tableside preparations and professional service make Waterlot a winner. Earl Darnell has been playing the piano and crooning old standards for the past 25 years at this delightful spot.

# Best Moderate-Price Restaurants

### Harbourfront, City of Hamilton

Overlooking Front Street with dining either out on the patio or inside the pretty dining room, this popular restaurant offers up everything from Italian specialties to fresh sushi.

### Tuscany, City of Hamilton

Though it's actually fairly new, the decor at this Italian restaurant makes it look vintage, with the traditional beamed ceiling, brick walls and a lovely mural. Wonderful pizza, as well as the standard fish, meat and pasta dishes.

### Frog & Onion Pub, Sandys

A great place for an informal lunch or dinner, this atmospheric spot—with its huge fireplace, thick stone walls and happening pub—is a perfect extension of historical ambience at the Royal Naval Dockyard.

# Best Inexpensive Restaurants

### The Wok, City of Hamilton

The scores of downtown workers who flock here for a take-out lunch are onto something: The Wok serves up tasty and affordable Chinese specialties that won't put too big a dent in your pocketbook.

### Pasta Pasta, St. George's

Your eyes will probably be bigger than your stomach as you order up a tasty Italian meal at this no-frills cafe that, as the name suggests, specializes in reasonably priced Italian dishes.

### Lighthouse Tea Room, Southampton

If you can ignore the tacky signs hanging everywhere reminding you to buy a souvenir mug and book early for Mother's Day, you'll enjoy the traditional English sandwiches and pastries available.

## Best Pubs

### Hog Penny, City of Hamilton

Bermuda's best-known pub has earned its fame; it's about as English as you can get, in both atmosphere and cuisine—without crossing the sea. Tourists and locals commingle happily at the dark, friendly bar.

**Cock & Feather, City of Hamilton**

Locals hang out here as much to eat and drink as to play "bingo cards," an instant-lottery-style game of chance that's hard to resist.

**Henry VIII, Southampton**

If you don't mind the Olde English theme carried out to an extreme, you'll enjoy the friendly, boisterous atmosphere at this large Tudor-style restaurant and bar.

## Best Discos

**The Club, City of Hamilton**

It looks more like a library than a disco here, but that doesn't stop patrons from dancing away the night at this small, upscale club.

**Club Oasis, City of Hamilton**

A younger and rowdier scene than at The Club, Oasis also draws a fair number of Bermuda's gay population.

## Best Views

**Gibbs Hill Lighthouse, Southampton**

You don't even have to climb the 185 (spiral, no less) steps to enjoy the views from atop Gibbs Hill, but the view at the top is worth the sweat.

**The City of Hamilton from Newstead Hotel, Paget**

Best seen from the window-lined dining room, Hamilton's lovely Front Street beckons across the harbor.

## Best Attraction

**Royal Naval Dockyard, Sandys**

It may sound kitschy, but all is done just right at this large attraction on Bermuda's easternmost tip. Besides the requisite shopping, there are craft displays, art exhibits, a handful of good restaurants and the excellent Maritime Museum.

## Best Nature Activities

### Crystal Caves, Hamilton

Caverns are hardly the first thing that come to mind when thinking of Bermuda, which makes a walk through this beautiful limestone cave all the more a delightful surprise.

### Railway Trail

The train is long gone, but the trail—which stretches virtually along the entire northern coast—has been loving maintained for hikers and bikers.

## Most Romantic Spots

### The Ferry at Night

You don't have to be rich to take a moonlight cruise—just hop aboard the ferry and snuggle your loved one as you glide past the waterfront hotels and mansions of the harbour.

### Secluded Beach Coves Along South Shore

It's easy to find a stretch of sand just big enough for two along the South Shore. There's an especially pretty one past the moon gate at the Sonesta Resort.

### Front Street via Hansom Cab

Sure it's corny, but don't let that stop you from snuggling under a blanket while a graceful horse clip-clops you along the scenic thoroughfare.

# CRUISING TO BERMUDA

## By Shirley Slater and Harry Basch

Several major cruise lines sail to Bermuda in the balmy spring and summer months with most departing from New York or Boston and a few from Florida and the Carolinas. (The waters of the North Atlantic are less turbulent April through October.) Some cruise vessels stop in Bermuda on the way to or from the Caribbean, but these stops are often very brief and may not allow you enough time to see the entire island. Ports of call include Hamilton, King's Wharf and St. George's. Getting around the island is easy if you rent a moped or bike, and there is frequent bus service to nearby towns. (Buses are clean, uncrowded and service is excellent.) A taxi tour is another great way to see the island. Drivers are friendly, accommodating and eager to share the legends and lore of Bermuda. Shore excursions often include beach tours, island tours, glass-bottom boat rides, and nightclub shows. Golf and tennis packages at the resorts can also be arranged. Shoppers in Hamilton will find good buys on Louis Vuitton luggage, Irish crystal, English bone china, straw bags and fragrances. Royal Naval Dockyard shops feature local crafts, fashions and food products. St. George's is known for its art gallery, small boutiques and the replica of the ship *Deliverance*. The stocks and ducking stools at the 17th century pillory on the square, once used for punishment, now provide photo opportunities for grinning tourists.

The following directory is a guide to the major cruise lines and ships offering cruise vacations to Bermuda. Prices and ship itineraries change frequently and lower price discounts apply in late summer, so be sure to check prices with the individual lines for the dates you plan to travel.

# Celebrity Cruises, Inc.

5201 Blue Lagoon Drive, Miami, FL 33126
☎ (305) 262-8322, (800) 437-3111

*A passenger volunteer assists executive chef Walter Lauer in a cooking demonstration aboard the Meridian.*

## History ........................

The Greek-based Chandris Group, founded in 1915, began passenger service in 1922 with the 300-ton *Chimara*, and by 1939 had grown to a 12-ship family-owned cargo and passenger line. In the post-World War II years, the company acquired a number of famous cruise liners, most of which have been retired. Under the Fantasy label, the company operates the *Amerikanis* but has retired the *Britanis*.

In April 1989, Chandris formed Celebrity Cruises with the intention of creating an upscale division with a premium cruise product. The *Meridian*, a massive makeover of the classic liner *Galileo Galeilei*, debuted in April 1990, followed the next month by the all-new *Horizon*. In April 1992, sister ship *Zenith* followed.

In October of that same year, Chandris formed a joint venture with Overseas Shipholding Group (OSG), a large publicly-held bulk-shipping company, and entered into the next expansion phase, ordering three 70,000-ton ships to be constructed by Joseph L. Meyer in Papenburg, Germany. The first of these, the innovative *Century*, debuted at the end of 1995, followed in the fall of 1996 by sister ship *Galaxy*.

—Chandris introduced the fly/cruise concept in the Mediterranean in the early 1960s.

—Pioneered fly/cruise packages in the Caribbean in 1966.

—Celebrity pioneered affiliations with land-based experts from London's three-star Michelin restaurateur Michel Roux to Sony Corporation of America to create innovative onboard products and programs.

## Concept . . . . . . . . . . . . . . . . . . . . . . . . . . . . .

Celebrity from its beginning has aimed at presenting the highest possible quality for the best price, and offers luxury service and exceptional food with a very solid value for the money spent. These stylish ships illustrate the decade's new values—luxury without ostentation, family vacations that don't just cater to the kids and close-to-home getaways that provide pure pleasure.

*Celebrity's celebrity came in part from its exceptionally good food, created and supervised by Guide Michelin three-star chef Michel Roux; here, a whimsical touch adorns a buffet dish at lunchtime.*

## Signatures . . . . . . . . . . . . . . . . . . . . . . . . . .

Perhaps the single best-known feature of this fleet is its superlative cuisine, created and supervised by London master chef Michel Roux, a longtime *Guide Michelin* three-star chef, who takes a hands-on approach, popping in for surprise visits to the ships, training shipboard chefs in his own kitchens and sending key supervisory personnel for regular culinary check-ups.

## Gimmicks . . . . . . . . . . . . . . . . . . . . . . . . . . .

The Mr. and Mrs. icebreaker game. At the beginning of each cruise, a man and a woman on board are chosen to represent Mr. and Mrs. (*Horizon, Zenith, Meridian, Century*). During the cruise, passengers are encouraged to ask individuals if they're the Mr. and Mrs. selected, and the first to find them gets a prize. In the meantime, everyone gets acquainted. Anyone for musical chairs?

## Who's the Competition. . . . . . . . . . . . . . . . .

In its brief six years of service, Celebrity has managed to virtually create a class of its own by providing a product priced competitively with Princess and Holland America but with a level of food, and sometimes service, that approaches Crystal Cruises. Previously, the line limited its itineraries to Caribbean and Bermuda sailings, but has expanded to include Alaska and Panama Canal sailings, and very likely will enter the Mediterranean in 1998 with its mid-sized *Meridian*, oldest vessel in the fleet.

## Who's Aboard. . . . . . . . . . . . . . . . . . . . . .

Young to middle-aged couples, families with children, and, aboard the *Meridian* on certain early-season Bermuda sailings from southeastern ports, groups of senior citizens from Florida retirement communities who request early sitting dinners that start at 5:30 instead the normal 6 or 6:30 p.m. In winter season, Celebrity attracts some European and French Canadian passengers as well. Although the line is only six years old, it has many frequent cruisers with double-digit sailings.

## Who Should Go. . . . . . . . . . . . . . . . . . . . .

Anyone looking for a good value for the money; discriminating foodies who will find very little if anything to complain about; families with children; couples of all ages. When the line was first introduced in 1990, Al Wallack, then Celebrity's senior vice president for marketing and passenger services, had several suggestions: "People who are joining country clubs but not necessarily the most expensive or exclusive country club on the block;" passengers of the former Home Lines and Sitmar ships who did not merge into Princess and who like "ships that look like ships, ships that have a European quality."

## Who Should Not Go . . . . . . . . . . . . . . . . . . .

Anyone who calls for catsup with everything or after perusing the menu asks the waiter, "But where's the surf and turf?"

## The Lifestyle . . . . . . . . . . . . . . . . . . . . . .

Upscale without being pretentious, sleek and fashionable without being glitzy, the Celebrity ships offer a very comfortable seven-day cruise that is outstanding in the areas of food, service and surroundings. Evenings aboard are fairly dressy, with jacket and tie for men requested on both formal and informal nights; only casual nights suggest a sports shirt without jacket. Meals are served at assigned tables in two seatings.

Book a suite and you get all-day butler service; take the kids along during holiday and summer sailings and you'll find well-trained youth counselors on board. Ladies looking for a dancing partner will find social hosts on many sailings.

Evenings the ships present musical production shows and variety shows (except when they are docked in Bermuda, which does not permit professional entertainment other than live music on cruise ships in port), recent feature films, and duos or trios playing for dancing or listening in small lounges around the ships. Daytimes bring popular culinary demonstrations by the executive chef, arts and crafts lessons, trapshooting, napkin folding, golf putting, lectures on finance or current affairs, a trivia quiz, basketball, exercise classes and bingo.

## Wardrobe . . . . . . . . . . . . . . . . . . . . . . . . . .

A seven-night cruise normally schedules two formal nights, in which the line suggests "both men and women may prefer more dressy attire, such as an evening gown for women and a tuxedo or dress suit for men." In our experience aboard the line's ships, a cocktail dress or dressy pants suit for women and a dark suit or blazer with tie will be acceptable. There is also a tuxedo rental service aboard the *Zenith*.

Two nights are designated informal, and men are asked to wear a jacket and tie, women a suit or dress, and three casual nights when a sport shirt and slacks are acceptable for men, dresses or pantsuits for women.

Daytime wear is casual, with good walking shoes a must. Bermuda-bound passengers in spring and fall should take a jacket or sweater, hat or scarf, for going ashore; there's often a cool breeze blowing.

## Bill of Fare . . . . . . . . . . . . . . . . . . . . . . .A+

Celebrity's executive chef, Vienna-born Walter Lauer, who goes from one ship to another constantly checking quality, describes it as "creating something new, where you can't cook everything in advance. Here there is the chance to do something new, more of the high standards in cuisine." One example: All the stock for soups is made from scratch on board rather than using prepared bases as many cruise kitchens do.

*A rolling cart of wines available by the glass serves the buffet restaurants.*

Lauer's mentor, Michel Roux, says, "The most important thing is to have a very good quality product and to rely on cooking skill more than the richness of the product." Fresh ingredients cooked to order figure prominently, and the menus are changed every six months.

Basically, the idea of serving simple but sophisticated dishes prepared from fresh ingredients as close as possible to serving time was revolutionary in the basic banquet/hotel catering kitchens of big cruise ships. But it succeeds splendidly. Usually if we find two or three dishes a meal that tempt us we're happy, but we could cheerfully order one of everything straight down the menu on these ships.

For lunch you might find a vegetable pizza or minestrone to start, then a main-dish salad of romaine with Mediterranean tabouli, hummus and pita bread garnished with garlic chicken; a piperade omelet with ham, tomatoes, peppers and onions; broiled ocean perch; roasted chicken with Provencale potatoes; spaghetti with fresh tomato sauce; grilled calf's liver with bacon and onions.

Dinner could begin with New England clam chowder or a pasta tossed with cilantro, oregano, ancho chile and fresh cream; a low-fat version of coquilles Saint-Jacques on vegetable tagliatelle; a pan-seared darne of salmon; roast lamb with garlic, thyme, fresh mint and olive oil with country roasted potatoes; broiled lobster tail or prime rib of beef. The dessert menu always includes one lean and light suggestion, along with fruit and cheese, pastries, ice creams and sorbets and a plate of showcase sweets presented to each table by the waiter, who describes them in mouth-watering detail. Full vegetarian menus are offered at every lunch and dinner.

A substantial 24-hour room service menu, gala midnight buffets, barbecues on deck, continental breakfast in bed, late morning bouillon and afternoon tea are other meal options during a typical cruise.

Lunchtime buffets are reminiscent of Impressionist paintings, with displays of fresh fruits and vegetables, woven baked baskets holding bread and wonderfully crunchy homemade breadsticks, fresh and crisp salads, a huge display of fresh vegetables, a rolling cart of wines by the glass, cold and hot main dishes and plenty of desserts.

*A variety of entertainment from production musicals to, as here, classical string quartets in the* Horizon's *Centrum.*

## Showtime . . . . . . . . . . . . . . . . . . . . . . .A

The production musical shows have a lot of verve and are well-performed and well-costumed; they follow the usual musical revue formats with salutes to Broadway and/or Hollywood, but with fresh looks at vintage shows like "Hair" and "Jesus Christ Superstar." Variety performers, musical soloists and duos and a Caribbean band round out the evening entertainment. Daytimes are chock-a-block with games, movies, lectures and exercise classes. The new *Century* and *Galaxy* introduce still more technological marvels from rooms with "video wallpaper" to a nightly light-and-sound spectacular.

## Discounts . . . . . . . . . . . . . . . . . . . . . . . .

Special advance purchase fares save up to 45 percent for passengers who book well ahead of time; ask a travel agent for details.

# Horizon ★★★★★

# Zenith ★★★★★

The *Horizon* and *Zenith* are very similar sister ships, with a few modifications on the interior of the *Zenith*—an expanded health club, a much larger forward observation lounge and 10 more passenger cabins (including two additional suites), giving her a higher gross registry tonnage than the *Horizon*. The children's playroom was moved to a higher deck on the *Zenith*, and the topmost deck's Mast Bar eliminated, along with Fantasia, the teen center ice cream and juice bar, which is replaced by a meeting room on the *Zenith*. The *Zenith* also has warmer colors and more woodwork in its decor.

Because most of the cabins aboard are modular design, insides and outsides are virtually identical in size (around 176 square feet) and furnishings, with the cabin's deck position determining the price.

The Brochure Says

"Attention to detail...you notice it the minute you come on board."

### Translation

The care and attention to detail goes beyond the design and decor into every part of the service. At a second seating luncheon our waiter was removing the cover plate when he noticed a tiny spot on the tablecloth underneath it and, horrified, immediately began apologizing profusely as he removed all the tableware, tore off the offending linen and snapped on a new cloth, then reset the entire table. When we tried to make a joke about it, he said, "No, this is very serious, and this is my mistake; I'm terribly sorry."

## Cabins & Costs

### Fantasy Suites: ............................... A-

*Average Price: $3999 plus low cost airfare add-on.*

The two top suites, called Royal Suites on the *Zenith* and Presidential Suites on the *Horizon*, are 510 square feet with separate sitting room (the one we like has caramel leather sofas and chairs), glass dining table with four chairs, wood and marble counter, TV set and big windows; the bedroom has twin or king-sized beds, walk-in closet with generous storage space and built-in safe, and a second TV set. The marble bathroom is not large but does have a Jacuzzi bathtub. And there's butler service, hot cabin breakfasts if you wish, fresh fruit replenished daily and a welcome bottle of champagne.

### Small Splurges: ............................... A-

*Average Price: $2499 plus low cost airfare add-on.*

Deluxe suites, 18 on the *Horizon* and 20 on the *Zenith*, have two lower beds or a king-sized bed, sitting area with two chairs or loveseat and chair, glass table, large window and small TV, as well as a long marble-topped desk/dresser with chair. The bathroom is very like the one in the bigger suites (see "Fantasy Suites" above). Perks: Butler service, terrycloth robes, hot breakfasts served in-cabin, fresh fruit, a welcome bottle of champagne.

### Suitable Standards: ............................ B

*Average Price: $1399 plus low cost airfare add-on.*

Most standard cabins measure 176 square feet and have two lower beds or a double, two chairs, table, window, large built-in desk/dresser, TV set and bath with shower. Four outside wheelchair-accessible cabins on each ship have generous bedroom and bathroom space for turning, a big shower with fold-down seat, extra-wide doors and ramp access over the low bathroom sill.

### Bottom Bunks: ................................ B

*Average Price: $1249 plus low cost airfare add-on.*

The cheapest insides are also 176 square feet with two lower beds or a double, two chairs, table, TV, wide dresser and bath with tile shower and white Corian self-sink and counter. A vertical strip of mirror on the wall where a window would be lightens and brightens the space. Some have third and fourth fold-down upper bunks.

## Where She Goes

In summer, *Zenith* sails from New York on seven-day cruises to Bermuda, calling at Hamilton and St. George's.

### The Bottom Line

When the line was first introduced, executives were careful not to over-hype the new product and bombard the public with extravagant promises. Instead, they let the product speak for itself, and it did—in volumes. Early passengers commented that they had not expected so much for the price, and Celebrity's reputation grew quickly among knowledgeable cruise passengers looking for a good buy.

After sailing aboard all the line's ships, we find very little to criticize, other than the captain's formal parties with their tepid, watery, premixed cocktails; and we often wish, in dining rooms aboard other ships, we had one of Celebrity's menus facing us instead.

### Fielding's Five

#### Five Great Spaces

1. The shipshape navy-and-white nautical observation lounges high atop the ships and forward, America's Cup on the *Horizon* and Fleet Bar on the *Zenith*. Lots of wood and brass trim and snappy blue chairs with white piping around the edges.

2. The self-service cafe, with two indoor and one outdoor buffet line with an inviting array of dishes at breakfast and lunch, waiters on hand to carry passengers' trays to the tables, and a rolling wine cart of vintages available by the glass at lunchtime. The floors are wood and tile, the seats a pretty floral pattern.

3. Harry's Tavern, named for former company president Harry Haralambopoulos, is a small Greek taverna decorated with a mural depicting a Mexican fountain splashing under Greek trees occupied by South American parrots on a Tuscan hillside.

4. The elegant Rainbow Room on the *Zenith*, with its cabaret/night-club ambience, wood-toned walls, gently curved bar, raised seating areas and blue leaf-patterned upholstery.

5. The show lounge offers optimum sightlines in most areas, with seven different seating levels on the two decks facing the large raised stage; multimedia projections and high-tech lighting design enhances the well-costumed shows.

#### Five Good Reasons to Book These Ships

1. Because the *Horizon* may very well be the best restaurant on the seas this summer.

2. Because they represent perhaps the best value for the money in the whole world of cruising.

3. Because they take service seriously (see "Translation").

4. Because there's an excellent health center where you can work off the calories.

5. Because the whole family can experience a top quality cruise experience without mortgaging the farm.

### Five Things You Won't Find On Board

1. Hot breakfasts served in standard cabins; you only get it in suites.

2. Private verandas.

3. Permission to bring your own alcoholic beverages aboard for cabin consumption; the brochure spells this out as unpermissable. You're expected to buy your drinks on board. (Other cruise lines permit passengers to use personal supplies while in the privacy of their cabins.)

4. A hungry passenger.

5. A cinema. Movies are shown daily on the cabin television.

# Meridian      ★★★★

This smooth-sailing former ocean liner has a 29-foot draft and a top cruising speed of 24.5 knots, so it's one of the fastest ships at sea. The deck crew scrubs down the teak early every morning, when determined early-morning walkers do their mile or two if they don't mind working their way through the water and suds.

The *Meridian* has a longer, sleeker line than the newer *Horizon* and *Zenith*, with the dining room on a middle deck amidships and the show rooms and lounges one deck above. The topmost decks house the skylight suites, swimming pool and whirlpool spas and a self-service cafe that doubles as a late-night disco.

**The Brochure Says**

"The decor: inviting and perfectly understated. Put simply, you feel right at home. Except at home, you don't have a steward bringing you whatever you need, whenever you need it."

### Translation

Rather than setting out to astonish, Celebrity works quietly, training its staff to serve meals or make cabins in precisely the same way time after time after time. A most recent sailing five years after the first one found all the details we had admired from the beginning still in place, still being done exactly the same way, down to the presentation of various breakfast teas in a wooden chest.

## Fantasy Suites: ............................. B+

*Average Price: $2439 plus low cost airfare add-on.*

Eight romantic Skylight Suites on the top deck let you look up at the night sky. The sitting area is beside floor-to-ceiling windows with sofa, two chairs, coffee table and a long built-in wood dresser/desk with 16 drawers. Two lower beds or one double, a wide nightstand with three drawers and a big cabinet/console, plus a closet with four doors opening to full- and half-length hanging sections, shelves and a safe, can stow plenty of wardrobe for a week—even for Ivana Trump. The bath, just barely big enough, is marble with a spa tub. Occupants of suites have the use of terrycloth bathrobes during the cruise, fresh fruit daily, a complimentary bottle of champagne as well as the services of the butler, on our cruise happy Herbert from Honduras.

## Small Splurges: ............................. B+

*Average Price: $1339 plus low cost airfare add-on.*

A pair of category Two deluxe junior suites on Atlantic Deck are as large as the top-ranked Skylight Suites, and represent a best buy (on our cruise, one of them was occupied by two cabin-savvy travel agents). You'll find a sitting area, two lower beds, two chairs, a big closet, lots of storage shelves, mini-refrigerator and bathroom with tub.

## Suitable Standards: ............................ C

*Average Price: $1099 plus low cost airfare add-on.*

Category seven outside cabins are on Caribbean Deck, one deck below the dining room, with a choice of twin beds or a double bed (have your travel agent specify which you want when booking), desk/dresser with five drawers, and bath with shower. Some of the vintage bathroom fixtures and mirrors—including a round chrome porthole-shaped mirror and a big mirror on a stand—date from the *Galileo*. All cabins have hair dryers, complimentary toiletries, bottles of mineral water, TV sets and most have safes. Cabins on Europa, Caribbean and Bermuda Decks have portholes rather than windows.

## Bottom Bunks: ............................. C+

*Average Price: $949 plus low cost airfare add-on.*

The lowest-priced category 14 inside cabins offer double beds or upper and lower berths, with two dressers, plenty of storage. There are only six of them.

## Where She Goes

In summer, the *Meridian* sails to Bermuda on round-trip seven-night cruises from New York, spending three days docked at Kings Wharf on the island's eastern tip by the newly-restored Royal Dockyard complex of shops, restaurants, museums and movie theaters.

## The Bottom Line

Because of the ship's deep draft (29 feet), the *Meridian* is relegated to Bermuda's only deepwater port at Kings Wharf, some distance from the capital of Hamilton, which is 30 minutes away by tender, 50 minutes away by taxi. Cabins aboard are fairly spacious and the food, as we have said before, is excellent. When the ship is full, however, the dining room gets a little crowded, with less space between tables than on the line's new ships.

A nice additional touch: In the suites, daily lunch and dinner menus, along with wine lists, are delivered in mid-morning.

## Fielding's Five

### Five Favorite Places

1.  The Rendez-Vous Lounge always seems to be full of happy passengers comfortably ensconced in coral tub chairs at little marble tables to wait for dinner one deck below, to dance to a duo alternating rock'n roll, Big Band favorites or'50s pop like "Blue Moon"—hey, a keyboard synthesizer helps—or watching a cooking demonstration or playing team trivia.

2.  The Marina Cafe makes a pretty set-up out of buffet lunch, with an arrangement of wine bottles and grapes and a huge display of fresh vegetables at the entrance, then a chef in a crisp white toque carving a roast, plus salads, cold cuts and vegetables decorated with carved characters created from squash and onions, along with half a dozen hot dishes and a dessert table of sweets, including sugar-free pastries.

3.  A two-level cinema that plays recent films on a reasonable schedule that lets someone who's missed everything since "Forrest Gump" play catch-up.

4.  Two glass-enclosed promenade deck areas called Palm Court are divided into smoking areas on one side and nonsmoking on the opposite, with bamboo chairs and marble-topped tables, perfect for needlepoint, reading, playing Scrabble or having a quiet chat.

5.  Interlude Bar, a great hideaway with pretty peach chairs and comfortable leather barstools, just the spot for a tête-à-tête.

### Five Good Reasons to Book These Ships

1.  The food, the food, the food, the food, the food!

2.  The best martini at sea (from Franco in the Rendez-Vous Lounge).

3.  A smooth and even ride in seas that can sometimes get rough.

**4.** A fresh and delightful production show called "Fifty Years of Broadway."

**5.** A courteous and caring crew from the captain on down.

## Five Things You Won't Find On Board

**1.** An empty dance floor.

**2.** A lot of passengers springing for the caviar, Russian vodka and champagne specials in the Zodiac Lounge—at least not on our sailing.

**3.** A glass of champagne on the tray of pre-mixed cocktails at the captain's welcome-aboard party.

**4.** A stale breadstick—they're always crisp and freshly baked.

**5.** An empty seat during the cooking demonstration (free samples are dispensed afterward), as with this "Filet Mignon Celebrity" demonstrated by executive chef Walter Lauer:

Four 8-ounce filet mignon steaks

3 oz olive oil

3 finely chopped shallots

2 TB peeled, seeded and cubed fresh tomato

8 black olives, chopped

2 TB green peppercorns

5 ounces heavy cream

2 ounces cognac (optional)

8 ounces brown veal stock

1 TB chopped fresh basil

Season the steaks with freshly ground black pepper and salt, then sauté in a hot pan with olive oil until cooked to taste. Remove steaks from pan and keep warm. Add shallots to pan and sauté until light brown. Add tomato cubes, black olives and green peppercorns and heat, then flame with cognac (optional). Add veal stock and cream, and cook down to reduce by half. Finish the sauce by adding the chopped basil, season to taste, and serve steaks with sauce to four.

# CUNARD

555 Fifth Avenue, New York, NY 10017-2453
☎ (212) 880-7500, (800) 221-4770

*Cunard made headlines in 1994 when it acquired not only the posh* Royal Viking Sun *with its swim-up bar on pool deck but all rights to the prestigious Royal Viking brand name and its subsidiary labels.*

## History . . . . . . . . . . . . . . . . . . . . . . . . .

"I want a plain but comfortable boat, not the least unnecessary expense for show," Samuel Cunard instructed the Scottish shipyard that built his 1154-ton wooden paddlewheel steamer *Britannia* in 1840. And when it set out on its maiden voyage from Liverpool to Halifax and Boston on July 4, with 63 passengers, 93 crew members and a cow to supply fresh milk on the voyage, the conservative businessman from Nova Scotia was more concerned about his cargo—he had a lucrative contract to carry Her Majesty's mails and dispatches across the Atlantic twice a month—than his passengers.

That same year, Cunard quadrupled his fleet, eventually cutting down crossings from the usual six weeks of that era to two weeks.

In its 157-year history, Cunard has operated more than 190 ships, including the famous *Queen Mary* and *Queen Elizabeth*, who saluted each other in the midAtlantic as their paths crossed. They transported 4000 people a week between the United States and United Kingdom.

In the late 19th and early 20th centuries, the Cunarders carried hundreds of thousands of immigrants from Europe to the United States, and during World War II carried troops to and from Great Britain.

*Cunard's* **Mauretania** *is remembered today with a striking 16-foot model displayed aboard the* **QE2** *complete with lighted portholes.*

But the 1920s and 1930s were the heyday of ocean liners. Cunard's legendary *Mauretania* with its four red-and-black stacks and lavish wood-paneled, plaster-ceilinged public rooms, ruled the waves through the twenties. The *Queen Mary* was star from the '30s to the waning days of transatlantic crossings in the '60s, with guests such as the Duke and Duchess of Windsor, in perpetual, glittering exile with their 75 suitcases and 70 trunks; Noel Coward; Rex Harrison; Rita Hayworth; Richard Burton and Elizabeth Taylor.

Samuel Cunard would probably not be surprised at the size and diversity of his company's present fleet—seven seagoing ships ranging from the 1814-passenger *QE2* to the deluxe little 116-passenger *Sea Goddess* ships—but he would probably be astonished to find that people book passage by sea not by necessity but for the sheer pleasure of traveling slowly, emulating those shadowy companions of another day who enjoyed an infinite supply of the one travel luxury we lack—time.

—First company to take passengers on regularly scheduled transatlantic departures (*Britannia*, 1840).

—Introduced the first passenger ship to be lit by electricity (*Servia*, c. 1881).

—Introduced the first twin-screw ocean liner (*Campania*, 1893).

—Introduced the first steam turbine engines in a passenger liner (*Carmania*, 1905),

—Introduced the first gymnasium and health center aboard a ship (*Franconia*, 1911).

—Introduced the first indoor swimming pool on a ship (*Aquitania*, 1914).

—First cruise line to introduce an around-the-world cruise (*Laconia*, 1922).

—Held the record from 1940 to 1996 for the largest passenger ship ever built (*Queen Elizabeth*, 1940).

—The only cruise company to sail regularly-scheduled transatlantic service year-round (*Queen Elizabeth 2*).

## Concept . . . . . . . . . . . . . . . . . . . . . . . . . . .

In the wide diversity of Cunard ships, the flagship *Queen Elizabeth 2* stands alone, providing an around-the-world cruise, regular transatlantic crossings and warm-water cruises.

The highly rated *Royal Viking Sun* and the prestigious *Vistafjord* offer very good quality food, service and accommodations at sea for the most demanding and sophisticated travelers.

Cunard's ultra-deluxe little *Sea Goddess* ships are among our very favorite vessels, because they give passengers the sense of sailing on their own private yachts.

In the mid-sized, moderately priced range are two classic ships, the sparkling new *Cunard Dynasty*, making shorter cruises to popular destinations and the beloved, if somewhat vintage, *Cunard Countess*, which cheerfully cruises year-round with some interesting island ports of call.

## Signatures . . . . . . . . . . . . . . . . . . . . . . . . .

The distinctive red-and-black funnel that has characterized Cunard ships since the *Britannia* in 1840 has not been affixed to the *Royal Viking Sun* and the pair of *Sea Goddess* ships. The *Sun* retains the red RVL sea eagle, and the *Sea Goddess* ships carry a golden goddess.

The dark hull of the *QE2* is a modern-day version of the standard Cunard North Atlantic black as opposed to the white hulls more typical of cruise ships.

The Cunard lion, rampant, wearing a crown and holding a globe in his paws, first appeared in 1880 when the company went public; according to ship historian John Maxtone-Graham, rival sailors disparagingly called it "the monkey wi' the nut."

*Serving caviar and champagne in the surf is an eye-catching Sea Goddess tradition; here, passengers and crew wading at Jost van Dyke in the British Virgin Islands.*

## Gimmicks . . . . . . . . . . . . . . . . . . . . . . . . . .

Serving caviar from the blue two-kilo tins is a trademark/ gimmick aboard the *Sea Goddess* ships, where it adorns the serve-yourself appetizer table at cocktail time and is fetched ashore by waiters in black tie and swim trunks on beaches in the Caribbean.

## Who's the Competition . . . . . . . . . . . . . . . . .

A unique vessel, the *Queen Elizabeth 2* has no real competition except herself, because of the intense love/hate relationship her passengers accord this most famous and most misunderstood vessel. They complain about signs of aging or inconveniences aboard the ship, then scream when things are changed. Every other year like clockwork, when the ship comes out of drydock in late autumn, something or other on board doesn't work. They complain to each other, rage to the media and threaten lawsuits—then book passage again the next time they're going to take a cruise.

Cunard's purchase of the *Royal Viking Sun* eliminated much of the direct competition facing *Vistafjord*; now the pair competes with the Crystal ships. *Sea Goddess*, almost always mentioned in the same breath with *Seabourn*, is really more like Radisson Seven Seas' *Song of Flower* or the Silversea ships since the admittedly-steep fares include all the beverage service on board, still an optional extra with Seabourn.

## Who's Aboard . . . . . . . . . . . . . . . . . . . . . . .

Perhaps the broadest possible spectrum of passengers is aboard one of the short segments of the *QE2's* world cruise, everyone from the very rich penthouse passengers to the Miss Marples in the *Mauretania* dining room, who are signed up for the full cruise, and the transients taking a segment, a mix of middle-aged, middle-income couples and upscale singles and families. The Panama Canal transit and the transpacific segment between Los Angeles and Honolulu always sell out.

Older couples and singles, most of them North Americans with an upper-range income, are typically aboard *Royal Viking Sun* while the *Vistafjord* usually draws a more cosmopolitan and slightly younger crowd, a mix of North Americans, British and Germans.

*Sea Goddess* attracts almost exclusively couples who have money or want people to think they do and who may or may not be married.

## Who Should Go. . . . . . . . . . . . . . . . . . . . . . .

Families with children aged two to eight will find *QE2* a good ship because of its nursery overseen by two professional British nannies and a special high tea (which correctly used means a light supper, not English-style afternoon tea) for kids at 5:30.

Anyone who loves luxury and can afford it should book one of the *Sea Goddess* ships to be pampered with caviar and champagne around the clock as if it's your own private yacht. And aging baby boomers who've done well in business should reward themselves by sampling the *Royal Viking Sun* or *Vistafjord* to see if that's how they want to vacation when they retire.

## Who Should Not Go . . . . . . . . . . . . . . . . . .

It's interesting that with most cruise lines, the crossover from one ship to another is easily made, even with a size disparity, as with Princess Cruises' mid-sized *Pacific Princess* versus the very large *Regal Princess*. But with the Cunarders, things are different. It's impossible to visualize a *Sea Goddess* passenger going over to the *Cunard Countess*, or even a *QE2* penthouse passenger who dines in the Queens Grill switching to the first seating in that ship's Mauretania restaurant. So when it comes to Cunard, "Who should not go on which ships?" is the real question, which will be addressed under the individual ships.

## Wardrobe. . . . . . . . . . . . . . . . . . . . . . . . . .

Except for the *Cunard Countess* and *Cunard Dynasty*, which are termed "informal cruising," the Cunard ships call for a fairly dressy wardrobe. Day wear aboard the ships is smart casual or "country club" garb. On informal nights, especially on the *Royal Viking Sun*, some of the men wear madras jackets with bright linen pants in what we think of as a preppy or southeastern resort look.

## Bill of Fare . . . . . . . . . . . . . . . . . . . A+ to B

Since the food on the *Queen Elizabeth 2* varies according to which restaurant room you're assigned, we'll discuss and rate that ship's food under its "Cabins and Costs" section.

The *Royal Viking Sun* and *Vistafjord* have good to excellent cuisine, with some dishes cooked to order and a pleasurable range of choices, including the option to order special meals. Wine lists are outstanding on both ships. *Sea Goddess* cuisine and service have always been superlative, even their deck buffet dishes. *Cunard Dynasty* and *Cunard Countess* serve a varied menu of popular Continental and international dishes in the dining rooms, along with buffet breakfasts and lunches in the deck cafe.

## Showtime . . . . . . . . . . . . . . . . . . . . . . B+

Cunard entertainment, while hewing to a general pattern, varies according to the size of the ship's show lounge facilities. The classic stars—*Royal Viking Sun* and *Vistafjord*—follow a traditional format of musical production shows and variety acts by magicians, ventriloquists, puppeteers and comedians, as well as audience participation game shows like Liars Club and Team Trivia. There's usually a dance team (yes, Velez and Yolanda live!) who perform on variety nights and teach dance classes during the daytime to groups or in optional private lessons. On the *Sea Goddess* ships, entertainment consists primarily of the passengers socializing with each other or dining alone in their suites, so except for a musical group that plays nightly for dancing, or a late-night cabaret artist, there is usually not much happening.

The *QE2* presents a full range of entertainment with gala balls, famous lecturers and entertainers, notable orchestras and big bands, authors signing their books and karaoke nights in the pub.

The entertainment aboard the mid-sized *Cunard Dynasty* and *Cunard Countess* also presents production shows and variety acts, but usually on a somewhat smaller scale.

## Discounts . . . . . . . . . . . . . . . . . . . . . . . .

Cunard gives a 20 percent early booking discount to passengers who book and place a deposit on a cabin 120 days before sailing.

# Queen Elizabeth 2

# ★★★★★/★★★★

The *QE2* is the only vessel reviewed in this guide that carries a dual rating—five stars for its Grill Room class, meaning passengers booked in cabins that are assigned to dine in the Queens, Britannia and Princess Grills in categories Q1 through P2, and four stars for the rest of the ship, which includes the Caronia and the Mauretania Dining Room cabins.

Built as a two-class turbine steamer in Brown's Clydebank yard in 1967 and 1968, the *QE2* set out on its maiden voyage to the Canary Islands December 23, 1968, prior to the official delivery of the vessel to the line. A fault developed in the turbines along the way and the ship was returned to the builder. Since the passenger accommodations were still unfinished, Cunard refused to accept delivery of the ship on the planned date of January 1, 1969, and the ship made its actual maiden voyage May 2, 1969, from Southampton to New York.

The classic ocean liner retooled its engines from steam turbine to diesel in 1987, and some of the crew say the plumbing has never worked right since. The most massive renovation since the engine retooling took place was in late 1994, when 850 bathrooms were remodeled and most of the public rooms and deck spaces changed and/or relocated—"cosmetically the biggest renovation ever done to the *QE2*," according to Captain John Burton-Hall—and set up a howl from unhappy passengers who complained of unfurnished cabins, bad plumbing and "exploding toilets" which reverberated throughout the world media for a month.

Life aboard the *QE2* could be compared to living in a self-contained seagoing city with its own post office and city hall (the bureau), its own police force (on-board security, both uniformed and plainclothes), its own public library with a fulltime professional librarian, its own pub, five restaurants, a movie theater, a shopping mall, a travel agency (shore excursions and tour office), eight bars, a bookstore, a computer center, casino, photo shop, florist, daily newspapers, gymnasium, spa, beauty salon, barber shop, 40-car garage, kennel, hospital with operating room, a private club (Samuel Cunard Key Club), casino, laundromat, video rental shop, a sports center and bank. Even the staff demeanor is more serious and businesslike than on a cruise ship.

"Everywhere she goes, in every corner of the globe, *Queen Elizabeth 2* creates excitement."

### Translation

They got a lot of press in 1994-95, so everybody in the world knows the *QE* was refurbished again. Actually, the renovations are obligatory because of the ship's status as a troop carrier; every two years it has to be taken out of commission to carry out government-required surveys. As Captain Burton-Hall says, "We're like a 747, really, we have to be up and running all the time." The 1996 renovations dramatically reconfigured the ship.

## Fantasy Suites: . . . . . . . . . . . . . . . . . . . . . . . . . . . . . . A

*Average Price: $1940; low cost airfare add-on.*

Any of the 31 penthouse suites except #8184 (the only one without a private veranda) would do well, although some of them overlook lifeboats as well as the sea. Each has lounge chairs and table in the veranda, king-sized bed, sofa and two chairs, built-in desk/dresser, good storage space, mini-refrigerator, safe and bathroom with toilet, bidet, deep tub and double sinks. You'll dine in the elegant Queens Grill with its own private cocktail lounge on treats like fresh grilled Dover sole, fresh lobster and fresh foie gras by request, and from the breakfast menu, shirred eggs with caviar and cream, along with a rolling cart of more than a dozen different kinds of marmalade.

## Small Splurges: . . . . . . . . . . . . . . . . . . . . . . . . . . . . A

*Average Price: $1420; low cost airfare add-on.*

Ultra-deluxe outside cabins in category P1 are spacious and comfortable, nicely furnished in rich dark blue and beige fabrics, with sofa and chairs, a long desk/dresser in wood, a big walk-in closet, a bath with tub, mini-refrigerator and terrycloth robes, plus plenty of storage space. You dine in the Princess Grill, a red candybox of a room with small tables and an intimate atmosphere. Both the Princess and Britannia Grills have recently improved menus and food preparation.

# Suitable Standards: .......................... C+

*Average Price: $1290; low cost airfare add-on.*

Standard outside cabins in the C categories are not identical or even similar, and the size is the luck of the draw. But all are refurbished with attractive fabrics and colors and a renovated bathroom. Figure on twin beds and, in Category C4, a shower instead of those lovely long, deep tubs. You'll dine in the Caronia restaurant after cocktails, if you like, in the Crystal Bar, which serves the Princess Grill, Britannia Grill and Caronia. We found the food and service in the Caronia better than we recall from the old Columbia first-class restaurant although the room itself is less dramatic.

# Bottom Bunks: ............................... C

*Average Price: $970; low cost airfare add-on.*

A cabin with two lower beds and bath with shower located amidships on a lower deck is the least expensive cabin for two; remember that *QE2* also has a number of single cabins. You'll dine in the Mauretania restaurant. All the dining rooms on the ship carry the same basic menus, but the service, quality of preparation and availability of special order dishes may vary from one to another. The Mauretania features single meal seatings following the November 1996 refit.

## Where She Goes

The *QE2* sets out in early January every year on her around-the-world cruise, usually sailing from New York to Los Angeles, then on to the Pacific and Asia, Australia, India, Southern Africa, South America and the Caribbean. The rest of the year the ship makes a series of transatlantic crossings between the U.S. and U.K., interspersed with warm-water cruises to Bermuda and the Caribbean.

## The Bottom Line

While her newest scheduled renovation reduces the number of berths, the *QE2* will never be a perfect luxury cruise ship because she serves too diverse a group of passenger types and nationalities to offer one consistent across-the-board product. Her entertainment is ambitious, particularly with renowned lecturers and soloists from the world of politics, media, music, theater and film, but the musical production shows still leave something to be desired, primarily because there's no venue devoted exclusively to them. Two decks of advanced spa areas, including a full thalassotherepy area, plus an indoor pool, make the ship a good destination for fitness- oriented travelers no matter what the climate in the area cruised. "We're looking for the over-40s professional people who know the meaning of quality service, style, people who want the best, whether it's in food or entertainment or sheer relaxation," says cruise director Brian Price. But despite the frequent intrusion of "cruise" activities, the ship retains the atmosphere of a transatlantic liner with places to go and things to do rather than the aimless fun-and-games ambience of a pure cruise ship.

### Five Big Changes On the Ship

1. The Cunard history and artifacts exhibits along the Heritage Trail, with a four-panel mural of Cunard history in the Midships Lobby, a striking 16-foot model of the 1906 *Mauretania* with lights glowing from each porthole, and menus and silver serving pieces from the much-loved 1948 *Caronia*, nicknamed the Green Goddess for her unusual green livery.

2. The Golden Lion Pub, with its friendly publican drawing pints and half-pints of Carlsberg lager or Tetley bitter.

3. The greatly-enlarged Lido self-service buffet restaurant, which replaces an indoor/outdoor pool area that was rarely used; it has a sliding glass dome roof, pale wood floors and neon cove lighting and can seat 500 passengers at a time for breakfast, lunch, children's high tea and midnight buffet. A stairway leads down to the Pavilion, a new glassed-in casual buffet adjacent to the pool deck serving early continental breakfast and lunchtime hot dogs, hamburgers, steak sandwiches and vegetarian specials.

4. The former Midships Bar has been replaced by the elegant little Chart Room, an intimate lounge where singer/pianists perform sophisticated music of Porter and Gershwin.

5. The already excellent library has been expanded into two rooms, one staffed with a professional librarian who checks out books and videotapes to passengers free of charge, the other a bookshop that sells volumes about ships and the sea plus an ever-changing collection of books written by lecturers sailing aboard.

### Five Off-the-Wall Things to Do

1. Try and find the dog kennels.

2. Try and find the nursery.

3. If you're dining in the Queens Grill, make a special dinner order of bubble and squeak or baked beans on toast.

4. Go to karaoke night at the pub and see if you can sing "Moon River" without hitting a single note on key. (It isn't easy, but a dear little English lady in a Miss Marple frock did it one night when we were aboard.)

5. Enter the table tennis competition against the keen British and Australian players.

### Good Reasons to Book This Ship

1. Because she's the *QE2* and there's no other ship in the world like her.

2. To earn Cruise Miles (like frequent flyer miles) for discounts or future free cruises.

3. To walk through the wonderful self-guided Heritage Trail chock-a-block with 150 years of Cunard artifacts and history; it's riveting for anyone who loves ships.

### Five Things You Won't Find On Board

1. A little entrance stage into the first-class dining room like there used to be, since the first class and tourist class eateries changed places.

2. The private lounge that used to distinguish the Princess Grill; now everyone has before-dinner drinks in the large Crystal Bar.

3. That indoor swimming pool under the sliding dome roof has gone; in its place, a 500-seat buffet restaurant that one disgruntled passenger said "looks like a big cafeteria." Funny, that's exactly what it's supposed to be. Anyhow, there's another indoor pool in the spa down on Deck 7.

4. Access to all the bars and lounges; one is a private key club for world cruise passengers only, another the Queens Grill bar, accessible only to passengers who dine in the Queens Grill.

5. A dinky little dance band—the *QE2* prides itself on its 15-piece dance orchestra.

CUNARD LINE

**MAJESTY** ®

CRUISE LINE

*901 South America Way, Miami, FL 33102*
☎ *(305) 530-8900, (800) 645-8111*

## History . . . . . . . . . . . . . . . . . . . . . . .

Majesty Cruise Line, an upscale spin-off of Miami-based Dolphin Cruise Line, inaugurated its $220 million, 1056-passenger *Royal Majesty* in July 1992 when it was christened in New York by actress/singer Liza Minelli. The new line came up with some fresh ideas, including a totally non-smoking dining room and a number of nonsmoking cabins and was built in less time than normal because the hull had already been completed for a ship that was never finished at Kvaerner-Masa Yard in Finland.

—The first Miami-based ship in the mini-cruise market to split itineraries between the Bahamas and Mexico, so a passenger could book two back-to-back cruises with different itineraries (1993).

## Concept . . . . . . . . . . . . . . . . . . . . . . .

After years of sailing the popular *Dolphin IV* from Miami on three- and four-day budget cruises, Dolphin Cruise Line decided to start up a sister company to operate a new, upscale ship offering to an increasingly younger market cruises that were elegant but still affordable, with an emphasis on hospitality and service.

## Signatures . . . . . . . . . . . . . . . . . . . . . .

The distinctive crown logo is visible on the ship's super-structure.

The most attention-getting detail about *Royal Majesty* is the nonsmoking rule—no smoking in the dining room, show lounge or in 132 designated cabins, 25 percent of the total.

"It's a unique selling point," commented one of the travel agents on the inaugural sailing. "A few clients out there among the smokers won't like it, but for every one of them you lose, you'll pick up three others that are thrilled to be in a dining room without any smoking."

# Gimmicks . . . . . . . . . . . . . . . . . . . . .

The Hanna-Barbera costumed characters aboard are equally popular with kids and adults, and when they appear, which they do frequently, video and still cameras pop up all over the ship as loved ones run to be photographed with Fred and Barney.

# Who's the Competition . . . . . . . . . . . . . . .

One prominent travel agent said he did not see that the *Royal Majesty* was competing with Carnival's *Fantasy* in the three-day market but that it would compete with RCCL's *Nordic Empress*. In the seven-day Bermuda market, it does compete head-to-head with Celebrity's *Meridian* and *Horizon*.

# Who's Aboard . . . . . . . . . . . . . . . . . . . .

Younger couples and singles, a lot of families with small children on holidays and, in summer, around 200 non-U.S. citizens from Canada, Latin America and the United Kingdom are on each cruise. Also in summer, on the Bermuda sailings, a number of yuppie couples and as many as 300 children. In winter, many of the cruisers are older Florida residents, but once spring and summer arrive, the ship fills with yuppies, singles, couples and families with kids.

# Who Should Go . . . . . . . . . . . . . . . . . . . .

It's a good ship for seniors because it's not too large, has a warm atmosphere and a caring cruise staff. Children love the Hanna-Barbera characters, of course, and families have enough options to be together when they wish or apart and still have a good time. But it's also a happy hunting ground for single guys looking for great-looking, single, thirty-something women.

# Who Should Not Go . . . . . . . . . . . . . . . . . .

Dowager veterans of the world cruise, and anyone who would be a party-pooper with a lot of families with children, yuppies and singles having a really great time.

# The Life-style . . . . . . . . . . . . . . . . . . . .

It's a young, active ship with exercise classes such as tai chi, aerobics and stretch-and-tone scheduled before 9 a.m., plus quiz, Scrabble and ping pong competitions, dance and golf lessons, ice-carving demonstrations and art auctions. A Medieval Royal Fest with knights and jesters, face painting and fun and games is held on board during most cruises. A Club Nautica watersports program provides optional shore excursions with deep-sea fishing, snorkeling, scuba and sailing. Besides the daily program for adults, children are issued their own colorful activities booklets with Fred Flintstone on the cover. Particularly during spring and fall, *Royal Maj-*

*esty* will have conference and incentive groups on board wearing badges and going to meetings in the ship's conference rooms.

# Wardrobe.........................

Because there are usually a number of first-time cruisers aboard, some of them group and incentive travelers, dress codes are not as strictly adhered to as on some ships. But the line does observe two formal nights when men are asked to wear "proper attire," and two semi-formal nights that usually call for jacket and tie. Casual-dress evenings call for resort-wear rather than shorts, T-shirts or jeans.

# Bill of Fare...................... B+

In the dining room, dinner menus usually offer a choice of four or five main dishes, say, Cornish game hen, steak, veal, grilled fish and a vegetarian pasta dish. A choice of three or four appetizers, two soups, two salads and a range of desserts presented at the table fills out the menu.

The buffet breakfasts are copious, with ready-made omelets, scrambled eggs, bacon, sausage, ham, potatoes, herring, smoked salmon, bagels, fruits, cereals and all kinds of freshly made pastries.

A "Light at Sea" menu lists calories, cholesterol and sodium count (but not fat grams). We tried the low-calorie pita pockets with chicken, cucumber, tomatoes and onions that were delicious. Other lunchtime options that day were a California frittata, sautéed ling cod, mignons of turkey supreme Cacciatore, braised round of beef, plus an onion, tomato and white bean salad garnished with black olives.

One of our favorite food venues on board is the Piazza San Marco out on deck, serving pizza, hot dogs, ribs, hamburgers, french fries and ice cream, along with optional wine, beer and soda on ice. Steps away are tables with umbrellas and red-checkered cloths, like an Italian sidewalk cafe with a big stretched canvas canopy overhead in a sort of Sydney Opera House sail shape. (OK, like an Australian sidewalk cafe then.)

Dining room service is friendly and generally efficient, except for the open-seating breakfasts. One morning every order delivered to our table of six was confused. There's also 24-hour room service with cold plates, desserts, coffee tea or milk.

# Showtime....................... B+

Royal Majesty presents live theatrical productions such as "Star-Spangled Girl" and "Murder at the Howard Johnson's" during each cruise by a resident acting company. A Medieval Feast highlights one evening during each cruise, and a "Big Chill"'50s and'60s party, karaoke sing-alongs, fun and games with the cruise staff and some musical production and variety shows round out the programs.

## Discounts . . . . . . . . . . . . . . . . . . . . . . .

The AdvanSaver promises that the earlier you book, the more you'll save.

# Royal Majesty  ★★★★

It's an elegant ship with some of the most distinctive fabrics and carpeting we've seen anywhere, along with a generous use of wood that lends a warm ambiance.

Cabins are located on six of the nine passenger decks, with a top deck sunning area, below which is the Majesty Deck pool and spa area. Deck 5, the Countess Deck, is where most of the public rooms are located, starting from the forward observation deck and lounge and moving back through a series of small rooms that double as meeting areas when a conference is on board and bars, card rooms and such when there's no group. Amidships is the Crossroads lobby area, directly below the casino, and the dining room is aft. The show room is conveniently located one deck above the dining room, making it an easy progression from dinner to entertainment.

The Brochure Says

"From the beginning a ship designed for conferences."

### Translation

We met a lady in the elevator who was wearing a name tag on her bathing suit.

# Fantasy Suites: ............................... A

*Average Price: $1899 plus airfare.*

Two royal suites are the top digs aboard, two large separate rooms with floor-to-ceiling bay view windows, a living room with paisley sofa, coffee table, two chairs, glass dining table with four chairs and long built-in granite counter, and a bedroom with queen-sized bed, covered in a paisley print bedspread, nightstands, desk/dresser with chair, TV/VCR, minibar, safe, hair dryer, ironing board, bathrobes and 24-hour butler service. There's also a marble bath with long tub and a big walk-in closet/dressing room with good hanging storage.

# Small Splurges: ............................... A

*Average Price: $859 plus airfare.*

The 14 deluxe suites have twins or queen-sized beds, a granite-topped built-in desk and dresser with blue tweed chair, a granite-topped nightstand with four drawers, a big window in the bedroom side and a sliding fabric panel in strips of beige fabric that can be pulled across the room to separate the bedroom from the sitting area. The latter has a large sofa and two chairs, plus a wood-and-glass coffee table. A built-in wood console has TV/VCR and underneath is a wooden cabinet with glassware and minibar. In the marble bathroom is a tub, sink with marble counter and big mirror with good makeup lights, a built-in hair dryer, shower over the tub and complimentary toiletries. There is a glass bay window in the sitting area, and the artwork in the cabin consists of three pleasant watercolors. You also get 24-hour butler service in these suites.

# Suitable Standards: .......................... B

*Average Price: $719 plus airfare.*

The outside standard cabins are very attractive because of the elegant fabrics used throughout the ship. These are crisp brick red, apple green and black plaids with a smaller patterned carpet in the same colors. You can request queen-sized, double or twin beds, and also get a picture window, color TV, safe, hair dryer, ironing board (ingeniously built into a dresser drawer) and signature kimonos for use during the cruise. The bath is adequately sized with shower only, and there's also a pair of nightstands with drawers, a desk/dresser with chair and a closet with two full-length hanging spaces and one half-length hanging space with four drawers under, quite adequate for a week's cruise. Four cabins are designated wheelchair-accessible.

# Bottom Bunks: ............................... B

*Average Price: $649 plus airfare.*

Even the lowest-priced inside doubles have two lower beds, and a handsome mirror wall where the window would be successfully presents the illusion of light and space, brightening the room inside. There's a nightstand with drawers, a desk/dresser with chair, bath with shower only, adequate closet and wall-hung TV set. Some of these cabins have upper berths as well.

## Where She Goes

The ship sails from Boston for seven-night roundtrip sailings to Bermuda during the summer.

## The Bottom Line

This is a classy ship and the prices are right. The deck sunbathing areas are a bit small and can be crowded when the ship is jam-packed full, as it was on an Easter weekend last spring when we were aboard, along with some 200 children.

The *Royal Majesty* is one of the rare new ships that offers a full promenade around the ship for inveterate walkers and joggers. Rubberized red matting covers the entire deck, with a special track laid out in green in the center; five laps around is a mile.

It's a good vessel for fitness-conscious people, with plenty of exercise options on board and ashore, including walking tours with cruise staff members. The only thing that surprises us is, for a ship with such an active nonsmoking policy, there are an awful lot of smokers aboard and it's hard to get completely away from the smell of it in the corridors, even when you book a smokefree cabin, eat in a smokefree dining room and watch the show in a smokefree lounge.

## Fielding's Five

### Five Special Places

1.  The dining room, one of the first nonsmoking cruise dining rooms at sea in 1992, now one of many, has lights bright enough to see but not flat cafeteria lighting, and there is enough sound baffle on the ceiling to reduce the room noise a bit.

2.  Body Wave, the really hot gym on board with every imaginable kind of equipment, plus an adjacent exercise room with wood floor, windows, mirrors, barre and sauna.

3.  Royal Fireworks, where a resident theater company performs two one-act comedies each cruise, with two-seat sofas and swivel chairs in autumn leaf tones, a wood parquet dance floor and bandstand, and elegant blond-burled wood-covered walls.

4.  Royal Observatory, with striped red-and-black tub chairs, antique ship models and drawings, a curved wood bar with brass rail and curved glass walls facing forward.

5.  The Polo Club, one of the most sophisticated bars at sea, low key, with excellent music, whether a late-morning jazz session with some of the musicians from the ship's orchestra or a cocktail-hour classical guitarist playing music you can hear and converse over at the same time.

MAJESTY CRUISE LINE

## Good Reasons to Book This Ship

1. To take an Elvis birthday theme cruise.

2. To cruise with Fred Flintstone, Barney Rubble, Yogi Bear and George Jetson—all Hanna-Barbera characters licensed to Majesty.

3. To take a Pro-Am Golf Classic Cruise.

4. Safety and security are taken very seriously on board; in addition to our boarding passes, we are required to show photo IDs to reboard the ship, and the lifeboat drill is one of the most thorough at sea, which starts indoors with indoctrination and putting on lifejackets, then moves outside in orderly rows so that passengers end up lined up on boat deck with men in the back, women in front of them, and women with children in the very front.

## Five Things You Won't Find On Board

1. The chance for someone in your family to eat up a fortune in the tempting but expensive minibar; it cannot be opened until authorized by the cabin occupants and unlocked by the cabin steward.

2. A delay getting back your laundry and dry cleaning; same-day service is provided.

3. A child under 2 or not potty-trained accepted into the Little Prince playroom, which has a kiddies' pool, child-scaled furniture and toys, a slide that ends in a pool of bright plastic balls, a rope-climbing area and some white wall panels waiting to be decorated with crayons.

4. A moment of silence in the serene-looking Crossroads lobby with its white piano, white marble floor and potted palms, because just above in the open atrium is the Winners Circle Casino with slot machines constantly ringing and pinging.

5. A self-service laundry.

MAJESTY CRUISE LINE

# NORWEGIAN
## CRUISE LINE

95 Merrick Way, Coral Gables, FL 33134
☎ (305) 445-0866, (800) 327-7030

*The sports bar on the* **Windward** *underscores NCL's emphasis on active and theme cruises.*

## History . . . . . . . . . . . . . . . . . . . . . . .

Norwegian Caribbean Lines was founded in 1966 by Knut Kloster and Ted Arison (see Carnival Cruises, History, above) to create casual, one-class cruising in the Caribbean in contrast to the more formal, class-oriented tradition of world cruises and transatlantic crossings. That partnership soon broke up, however, leaving Kloster to begin a rapid expansion of the line while Arison went off to found Carnival Cruise Lines.

NCL's first ship was the *Sunward*, but the fleet soon grew to include the *Starward* (1968), *Skyward* (1969), *Southward* (1971) and, also in 1971, a replacement for the original *Sunward* called *Sunward II* (the former *Cunard Adventurer*).

But the real coup came in 1979 when the Kloster family bought French Line's *France*, which had been laid up in Le Havre for five years, made a major rebuilding to convert the former ocean liner into a cruise ship and renamed her *Norway*. From her debut in 1980, she was the flagship of the line, and the other four vessels came to be called "the white ships" for their white hulls that contrasted sharply with the dark blue hull of the *Norway*. (All the original "white ships" have been retired from the fleet, the last in September, 1995.)

In 1984, Kloster Cruise Limited, the parent company of Norwegian Cruise Line, bought Royal Viking Line, promising to make minimal changes to the highly respected company. Two years later, Kloster changed the Norwegian registry of the RVL ships to Bahamian, then a year after that closed down the long-time San Francisco headquarters and moved the entire operation to Florida.

In 1987, the former Norwegian Caribbean Lines changed its name to Norwegian Cruise Line with an eye to long-range marketing of Alaska, Bermuda and European cruises, and in 1989 acquired San Francisco-based Royal Cruise Line. This time, however, Kloster left the company in San Francisco with most of its executive roster intact.

The dismantling and sale of RVL happened in the summer of 1994, with the flagship *Royal Viking Sun* and the Royal Viking name, logo, past passenger list and general goodwill sold to Cunard, who promptly (but only briefly) named their new division Cunard Royal Viking Line (see Cunard, above). The *Royal Viking Queen* was soon transferred over to Royal Cruise Line and renamed the *Queen Odyssey*. Two earlier RVL ships, *Royal Viking Star* and *Royal Viking Sea*, also went to Royal to become *Star Odyssey* and *Royal Odyssey*.

In 1996, Royal Cruise Line was dismantled, the *Crown Odyssey* becoming NCL's *Norwegian Crown*, the *Queen Odyssey* becoming *Seabourn Legend* and the *Star Odyssey* becoming the *Black Watch* for Fred Olson Lines.

In the late 1980s, Knut Kloster began taking a less active role in the company in order to pursue his dream of building the world's biggest passenger ship, the 250,000-ton, 5600-passenger *Phoenix World City*. Despite its detractors who say the project's dead, the giant ship may still be a viable possibility, pending funding.

—The first three- and four-day cruises to the Bahamas incorporating a private island beach day.

—First line to restage hit Broadway musicals aboard cruise ships; the *Norway*'s first production was "My Fair Lady."

—The official cruise line of the National Basketball Association, the Basketball Hall of Fame and the National Football League Players Association; NCL presents a number of sports theme cruises throughout the year.

—First cruise line to broadcast live NFL and NBA games live aboard its ships.

# Signatures . . . . . . . . . . . . . . . . . . . . . . . .

Theme cruises—especially the annual *Norway* jazz festival, now in its 14th year, and the sports theme cruises which are aboard all the ships.

The "Dive-In" program—the first and perhaps most successful of the watersports packages found on cruise ships combines onboard instruction and equipment rentals with shore excursions to snorkel and dive spots. A Sports Afloat T-shirt is given to participants in designated activities who accrue seven tickets by the end of the cruise.

# Gimmicks . . . . . . . . . . . . . . . . . . . . . .

The line's award-winning advertising campaign built around a sexy young couple who look like they might star in lingerie or perfume ads and the slogan, "It's different out here." The campaign itself is great, but it could be argued they're barking up the wrong mast, because we've never seen that couple on an NCL ship.

# Who's the Competition . . . . . . . . . . . . . . . .

The main competitors in all its cruising areas (now that Carnival has entered Alaska) are the ships owned by Kloster's old nemesis Arison and the rapidly-growing Royal Caribbean Cruise Line. The *Norway*, unique in the otherwise modern fleet because of her history as the famous ocean liner *France*, should be competing with other classic ships like the *Rotterdam* and the *Queen Elizabeth 2*, but with a year-round, seven-day Caribbean itinerary and the same food and entertainment as the rest of the NCL fleet, she doesn't.

# Who's Aboard . . . . . . . . . . . . . . . . . . . . .

A lot of sports-oriented young couples from the heartland; yuppies and baby boomers; jazz fans for two weeks every autumn on the *Norway*; people who want to see a Broadway show without actually having to set foot in Times Square.

# Who Should Go . . . . . . . . . . . . . . . . . . . . .

Young couples and singles looking for a first-time cruise; music fans who'll enjoy not only the two-week annual jazz festival but the annual blues festival and two country music festivals; TV quiz show fans to take the annual "Wheel of Fortune" cruise; comedy aficionados for the summer comedy cruise; rock'n rollers for the '50s and '60s cruise; Big Band devotees for the November sentimental journey; and fitness buffs for the annual fitness and beauty cruise each fall aboard the *Norway*.

Young families who will appreciate NCL's "Kids Crew" program for kids 3 to 17, with special kids-only activities onboard and ashore. They're divided into four different age groups: Junior Sailors, 3–5; First Mates, 6–8; Navigators, 9–12; and teens, 13–17.

## Who Should Not Go

Longtime cruise veterans looking to check out a new line, senior singles, and urban sophisticates who've "been there, done that."

## The Lifestyle

"Elegant, yes; stuffy, never," was the way they described themselves a couple of years ago, and it's fairly apt. NCL's ships offer traditional cruising, with themed sailings (see Who Should Go, above), international themed dinners several times a sailing, live calypso music on deck, and something going on around the ship every minute. Not long after boarding, passengers are offered free spa demonstrations, free casino lessons, a rundown on the children's program for the week, a free sports and fitness orientation, dive-in snorkeling presentation and as many as three singles parties—one each at 8 p.m. for college-aged spring break celebrants and over-30 singles (a Big Band dancing session is usually scheduled at the same time for the over-50s set), plus a third at 11:30 for any singles that couldn't find a friend at the first two parties.

In other words, you'll stay busy aboard—and that's before the dozen or so shore excursions offered in each port of call!

## Wardrobe

NCL calls for less stringent dress codes than its competitors, good news for guys who hate to wear ties. A seven-day cruise usually calls for two formal outfits, two informal outfits and a "costume" for a theme country/western or Caribbean night if you wish. Short cruises schedule one formal night and two informal nights. Formal garb is described by NCL as "cocktail dresses or gowns for the ladies and the men wear a jacket and tie or tuxedo." On informal nights, "just about anything but shorts is fine." For daytimes, take along some exercise clothing, bathing suits, shorts, T-shirts and sandals, plus light cotton clothes and walking shoes for going ashore. NCL also reminds passengers not worry about clothes—if they forget something, they can buy anything they need in the shipboard shops.

# Bill of Fare . . . . . . . . . . . . . . . . . . . . . B

The food is big-ship cruise fare with some new cutting-edge options.

The dinner menu usually provides five appetizers, three soups, two salads, a pasta and four main dishes, one of which is fish, along with a full vegetarian menu offered nightly. There are four desserts plus ice cream and fruit, and low fat, low calorie dishes are indicated on the menus with an asterisk. Dinners are served in two assigned seatings at assigned tables, with first seating at 6:30 p.m. and second seating at 8:30 p.m.

A welcome-aboard buffet is typical of lunchtime self-service offerings—a make-your-own taco table and a vegetarian buffet with hot and cold selections, plus carved roast beef, turkey goulash with rice and pre-cooked hamburgers, along with a dessert table and separate beverage service area.

An alternative restaurant called Le Bistro, on board the *Norway, Seaward, Dreamward* and *Windward*, requires an advance reservation and a tip to the waiter but makes no surcharge for the food. The menu, described as "South-Beach style" by the Miami-based line (meaning Miami Beach's trendy art deco district), offers for starters a Norwegian seafood medley, escargots, French onion soup or clam chowder, three salads including Caesar and a warm spinach, then a vegetable main course, two pastas and three main dishes—chicken Provençale, pepper steak Madagascar and veal medallions with a wine/herb sauce and polenta. Dessert choices include a warm apple tart, a chocolate dessert and a selection of fruit and cheese.

# Showtime . . . . . . . . . . . . . . . . . . . . . . A

NCL was the first cruise line to create a buzz about its onboard entertainment, presenting shipboard versions of popular Broadway shows from "My Fair Lady" to the relatively current "The Will Rogers Follies" and the popular revival "Grease." In addition to the Broadway shows, each ship presents a song-and-dance Sea Legs revue as well as variety performers on other evenings.

Also aboard: Q and A sessions with sports stars, several different lounges offering live music for dancing, art auctions, games, dance lessons, and pop psychology lectures about astrology or fashion colors.

# Discounts. . . . . . . . . . . . . . . . . . . . . . . .

Early booking discounts knock off as much as 15 percent of the cruise price.

Children under 2 sail free; a maximum of two adults and two children per cabin is the limit for this offer.

# Dreamward ★★★★★

How do you make a big ship look like a little ship? The answer is clearly illustrated aboard NCL's new *Dreamward*, a ship that carries 1246 passengers but offers so many intimate spaces it actually seems cozy. There are no soaring atriums or double-decker dining rooms; instead, three separate dining rooms that seat from 190 to 282 passengers appear to have more smaller tables seating two to four than big ones seating six to eight. Instead of a vast self-service buffet area, the ship has incorporated quick pick-up breakfasts and lunches into a small snack bar adjacent to the Sports Bar & Grill, with a continental breakfast and lunchtime hot dogs and hamburgers. Salads, desserts and beverages are laid out buffet-style. Many areas, including some of the dining rooms and deck sunbathing spots, have been terraced to give an illusion of smaller space but with more privacy.

### The Brochure Says

"No matter where you choose to go, you are certain to have a lot of fun getting there: full-court basketball, a jogging track and fitness center, golf driving nets, outdoor hot tubs, a two-story casino, a Sports Bar & Grill with ESPN, NFL and NBA games beamed in live, dozens of top-notch entertainers—they're all here, just waiting for you."

### Translation

We're ready for the young and the restless, and double-dare anyone to get bored aboard.

### Cabins & Costs

Fantasy Suites: . . . . . . . . . . . . . . . . . . . . . . . . . . . . . . . A

*Average Price: $1338 plus low cost airfare add-on.*

Top digs are six 350-square-foot grand deluxe suites with concierge service, all facing forward on three different decks for a captain's-eye view of the world. The living room is sumptuously furnished with a brocade sofa and three chairs, a long desk and dresser with eight drawers and glass coffee table. In the bedroom, you can choose either twin or queen-sized beds. The bathroom has tub and shower, and additional perks include a mini-refrigerator and a private safe.

## Small Splurges: . . . . . . . . . . . . . . . . . . . . . . . . . . . . . B

*Average Price: $1149 plus low cost airfare add-on.*
Penthouses with private balconies are 175 square feet inside plus a veranda that is large enough for two chairs and a table. A separate sitting area with love seat and chairs, floor-to-ceiling windows, twin or queen-sized bed, private safe, TV set, mini-refrigerator and concierge service are included.

## Suitable Standards: . . . . . . . . . . . . . . . . . . . . . . . . . B

*Average Price: $989 plus low cost airfare add-on.*
Standard outside staterooms are virtually identical in size (160 square feet) and furnishings—sitting area and twin or queen-sized bed, TV set, built-in cabinetry—with the price varying according to deck location. "I'd advise clients to book one of the lower-category outsides," one travel agent told us, "because the differences in deck and amenities isn't that much." Accordingly, we'd recommend the D category outsides; get any lower on the totem pole and you're facing partial or full obstruction from hanging lifeboats. Six wheelchair-accessible cabins have shower seat and hand rails plus spacious turn-around room and no sills to impede the wheels.

## Bottom Bunks: . . . . . . . . . . . . . . . . . . . . . . . . . . . . C

*Average Price: $799 plus low cost airfare add-on.*
The lowest-priced cabins aboard are category J inside double cabins with two lower beds in 150 square feet of space. Needless to say, you shouldn't expect a sitting area with sofa.

### Where She Goes

The *Dreamward* spends summers in Bermuda with seven-day sailings every Saturday from New York, spending one full day and night in St. George's, then repositioning to Hamilton for two-and-a-half days there.

### The Bottom Line

This is a very special ship, stylish enough for frequent travelers but accessible to first-time cruisers as well. It offers everything an active young passenger might wish without appearing intimidatingly huge. While the cheaper cabins are not as spacious as you might wish, they're a lot bigger than many NCL cabins used to be. And the fact that this vessel returns to the human scale in contrast to the awesome new megaships is a great plus.

### Five Fabulous Places

1. The sunbathing deck, not acres of astroturf lined with sunbathers sprawled everywhere, but lounge chairs arranged in a series of teak terraces separated by low wooden planters filled with clipped box-woods, rather like an amphitheater.

2. Sports and Sky Decks include two golf driving areas, Ping-Pong tables in an enclosed alcove, a volleyball-basketball court and shuffleboard on rubberized mats, plus a full fitness center with sauna and massage.

3. The big forward Observation Lounge doubles as a late-night disco with marble dance floor and a pair of electronic route maps that show the ship's itineraries.

4. Le Bistro, originally a fourth dining room, has turned into a 76-seat specialty restaurant with no surcharge, only a request for advance reservations and a tip for the waiter afterwards. It's a good place for a quiet dinner for two, perhaps celebrating a romantic occasion, or a place to get together with other new friends.

5. The 150-seat Sun Terrace dining room, three levels set high atop the ship and aft, facing a wall of windows to the sea, and one deck below, The Terraces, 282 seats on several levels that also overlook the sea through an expanse of glass with a huge undersea mural on the back wall.

### Four Good Reasons to Book This Ship

1. To meet jocks, both professional and amateur.

2. To luxuriate aboard a ship that was designed especially for new, younger cruise passengers who want everything a shoreside resort can offer, including an oceanfront room.

3. The Sports Bar & Grill, which brings in live sports telecasts from around the world daily on big-screen TV sets, with small snack bars not far away in a quiet corner if you want a hot dog with your beer or soda.

4. To venture aboard a young-minded ship beyond the Caribbean into Alaska or Bermuda.

### Five Things You Won't Find On Board

1. A single cabin.

2. A self-service laundry.

3. Anyone wearing shorts in the dining room after 6 p.m.

4. A giant atrium with revolving sculpture.

5. A lavish lunchtime deck buffet.

# ⚓ROYAL CARIBBEAN

*1050 Caribbean Way, Miami, FL 33132*
☎ *(305) 539-6000, (800) 327-6700*

*The signature Viking Crown Lounge and RCCL logo.*

## History . . . . . . . . . . . . . . . . . . . . . . . . .

In 1969, three Norwegian shipping companies, I.M. Skaugen, Gotaas Larsen and Anders Wilhelmsen, founded RCCL for the purpose of offering year-round seven and 14-day cruises out of Miami. Now owned by Wilhelmsen and the Hyatt Hotels' Pritzger family of Chicago, Royal Caribbean Cruises Ltd. is a publicly traded company on the New York Stock Exchange.

The spring 1996 delivery of the *Splendour of the Seas* brought the line's total to 10 vessels. Just past its 25th anniversary, RCCL is definitely one a handful of major players in the cruise industry.

—First cruise line to commission three new ships expressly for the Caribbean cruise market, *Song of Norway* (1970), *Nordic Prince* (1971) and *Sun Viking* (1972).

191

—First cruise line to "stretch" a ship, cutting it in half and dropping in a new midsection, then putting it back together (*Song of Norway*, 1978).

—First cruise line to commission a specially designed ship for three- and four-day cruises (*Nordic Empress*, 1990).

—First seagoing, 18-hole miniature golf course (on *Legend of the Seas*, 1995).

—First cruise line to open shoreside hospitality centers in popular ports where passengers can leave packages, make phone calls, bone up on local shopping or sightseeing, get a cold drink and use toilet facilities (1995).

## Concept.............................

Consistency is the key word here. RCCL aims to provide a cruise experience to mainstream, middle-of-the-road passengers that is consistent in style, quality and pricing, with a majority of the ships following a consistent year-round schedule. Rod McLeod, head of sales and marketing, calls it "the doughnut factor" from a travel agent who once commented that what he liked best about RCCL was that all the doughnuts on all the line's ships taste exactly the same.

## Signatures........................

RCCL ships are easily recognized at a distance because of the Viking Crown Lounge, a cantilevered round glass-walled bar and observation lounge high atop the ships projecting from or encircling the ship's funnel; company president Edward Stephan dreamed it up after seeing the Seattle Space Needle.

Lounges, bars and restaurants on board are named for Broadway musicals and operettas, sometimes with unintentionally funny results, as with the *Sun Viking's* Annie Get Your Gun Lounge. (That's also a musical that few of today's RCCL passengers would remember.)

## Gimmicks.........................

ShipShape Dollars, given out each time a passenger participates in an exercise or sports activity; with six you get egg roll. Actually, you get egg-yolk yellow T-shirts proclaiming the wearer ShipShape. Passengers compete wildly for them and proudly wear them for years afterward aboard cruise ships of competing lines.

## Who's the Competition.................

RCCL competes directly with Carnival and Norwegian Cruise Line for passengers, but it also vies price-wise with more upscale lines like Celebrity and Princess. The line's new megaliners have brought in a more glitzy sheen, with flashy gaming rooms created by a Nevada casino designer instead of a ship designer. The company has also gone head-to-head with Carnival in the mini-cruise market, pitting its ladylike *Nordic Empress* against the neon-throbbing *Fantasy* and glow-in-the-dark *Ecstasy.*

# Who's Aboard......................

All-American couples from the heartland between 40 and 60, with new clothes, new cameras and nice manners; families with fairly well-behaved children; two or three 30-something couples traveling together; born-to-shop types who find the line's newer ships with their mall-like galleries familiar and comforting; clean-cut young couples on their honeymoons; single 20-somethings on holiday sharing an inexpensive inside cabin, more often females than males.

Statistically, the median age is a relatively low 42, with a household income from $40,000 to $75,000. One-fourth are repeat passengers, half are first-time cruisers. More Europeans, Australians and Latin Americans are also gravitating to the line.

# Who Should Go......................

These are ideal ships for first-time cruisers because the staff and the signage instruct and inform without appearing to lecture, putting everyone at ease right away. Also for honeymooners, fitness freaks (except on the *Sun Viking* and *Song of Norway,* which don't have gyms), sunbathers, big families on a reunion and stressed-out couples who want some time together in a resort atmosphere. Baby Boomers and their juniors 25 to 45 years old will always be warmly welcomed: RCCL wants YOU!

# Who Should Not Go .................

Dowager veterans of the world cruise.

Small ship enthusiasts.

Anyone who dislikes regimentation.

# The Lifestyle ......................

RCCL's ships follow a traditional cruise pattern, with specified dress codes for evening, and two meal seatings in the dining room at assigned tables for a minimum of four and a maximum of eight or 10; very few if any tables for two are available. A daylong program of games, activities and entertainment on board is supplemented by shore excursions that emphasize sightseeing, golf and watersports.

# Wardrobe......................

RCCL makes it easy for passengers by spelling out dress-code guidelines in the brochure. A four-day cruise has two casual nights where sport shirts and slacks are suggested for men, at least one formal night where women wear cocktail dress or evening gowns and men wear suits and ties or tuxedos, and may have a theme night where passengers don'50s or country/western garb if they wish. During the daytime, comfortable casual clothing—jogging outfits, shorts or slacks, T-shirts, bathing suits and coverups—is appropriate on deck but sometimes not in the dining room.

## Bill of Fare . . . . . . . . . . . . . . . . . . . . . . . . B+

Non-threatening, special-occasion food is produced by an affiliated catering company on a rotating set menu that is similar but not identical on the different ships. There's a wide variety and good range of choices, and the preparation is capable if not inspired. Dinner includes seven appetizers (four of them juices), three soups, two salads, five main dishes and six desserts (three of them ice creams). On a typical day main dishes may include crabmeat cannelloni, sole Madagascar, pork loin *au jus*, roast duckling and sirloin steak. In addition, a nightly vegetarian menu, a kids' menu and a ShipShape low-fat, low-calorie menu are offered.

Our very favorite from the latter seems tailored to The Ladies Who Lunch—it starts with a shrimp cocktail without sauce, then consomme, hearts of lettuce salad with carrot curls and fat-free dressing, followed by poached fish and vegetables, then rich, sugary Key Lime Pie with a whopping 12 grams of fat per slice.

Room service is limited to breakfast and cold snacks such as sandwiches, salads and fruit-and-cheese plates. Breakfast and lunch buffets are served in a self-service cafeteria with hot and cold dishes available, and early morning coffee, afternoon tea and midnight buffets fill out the legendary eight-meals-a-day format.

Captain Sealy's menu for kids includes fish sticks, peanut butter and jelly sandwiches, tuna fish, pizza, hamburgers and macaroni and cheese, plus chocolate "ship" cookies. On a recent sailing aboard the *Splendour of the Seas*, we felt the food preparation and presentation had greatly improved.

## Showtime . . . . . . . . . . . . . . . . . . . . . . . A/C

The major production shows produced by the line, complete with Broadway-style playbills and computerized light cues, are sensational on the bigger ships with their state-of-the-art technical facilities. Unfortunately, on the smaller vessels, the shows still come out of the under-inspired and overworked south Florida production companies and suffer from make-do stagecraft and poor sightlines. Passengers entertain each other at karaoke nights, masquerade parades and passenger talent shows, and pack appropriate garb for country/western night and'50s and'60s rock'n roll night.

# Discounts. . . . . . . . . . . . . . . . . . . . . . . . .

Booking six months in advance earns discounts of 10 to 20 percent off the brochure rate.

# Song of America ★★★

Unlike this ship's many fervent fans, we dismissed her as Nordic high-tech razzle-dazzle when she was new because of her popsicle interior colors, but in a more recent renovation, some of the original orange cabin furnishings have been muted to beige tones and the former grape-and-raspberry upholstery in the Can Can Lounge and Guys & Dolls Lounge has quieted down as well. It's been some time since the Schooner Bar was introduced and the outdated cinema removed (now that the cabins have color TV sets for video movies) in favor of a conference and meeting area and expanded casino. The soundproofing has been beefed up since the early days as well.

Traditionalists like the long sleek lines compared to today's shoebox shapes, and sunbathers find plenty of room to stretch out on the expansive Compass and Sun Decks. For nightlife, the ship has three spacious lounges for shows, music and dancing, plus the smaller Schooner piano bar.

**The Brochure Says**

"We'll do everything, so you have the option of doing nothing. We'll clean up your room (twice a day), cook for you (six times a day), entertain you and take you to far-away places with strange-sounding names."

### Translation

A cruise is an easy vacation, because you buy everything in a neat package, even your round-trip airfare and transfers. You have a cabin steward who cleans your cabin twice a day, replacing towels and refilling the ice bucket, and you can eat every couple of hours if you concentrate. Best of all, your cruise ship takes you to exotic spots like Bermuda where the inhabitants speak English and welcome U.S. dollars.

## Cabins & Costs

### Fantasy Suites: .............................. B

*Average Price: $3173; low cost airfare add-on.*

The Owner's Suite, #7000, on Promenade Deck, is double the size of the deluxe outside suites, with sitting area with sofa, chairs and coffee table; mini-refrigerator, color TV, twin beds and an optional third berth, wide desk/dresser, three picture windows and bathroom with tub. On the down side, you're overlooking a public deck area from your picture windows.

### Small Splurges: .............................. C+

*Average Price: $1203; low cost airfare add-on.*

A deluxe suite in B category, not as lavish space-wise as the Owner's Suite, but comfortable enough, with sofa, chairs, desk/dresser, color TV, separate sleeping area with twin beds and big window, and bath with tub.

### Suitable Standards: .......................... C-

*Average Price: $1188; low cost airfare add-on.*

The modular cabin design means all standards are virtually identical, with the category and price difference reflected in the deck location. The H category A deck outside doubles have two lower beds (one sofa/daybed and one fold-up twin) except for cabins 3207–3210, 3147–3150 and 3013–3018, all of which have twin beds that can be put together into a queen-sized bed. Most of these also have a pull-down third berth. All have bathrooms with shower only.

### Bottom Bunks: .............................. C

*Average Price: $1049; low cost airfare add-on.*

The B Deck inside doubles in the forward part of the ship, Q category, are the lowest-priced accommodations. Each has two lower beds that can be put together to make a queen-sized bed, a bath with shower, wall-mounted color TV set and a desk/dresser with stool.

## Where She Goes

In summer, *Song of America* sails to Bermuda from New York every Sunday, and spends one day in St. George's, then two-and-a-half days in Hamilton.

## The Bottom Line

This long, sleek beauty is one of only three classic non-mega-sized ships remaining in the rapidly-growing RCCL fleet, and it has retained its popularity over the years, with some loyals claiming as many as two dozen sailings aboard since its debut.

Because the cabins are on the small side (around 120 square feet for standard doubles), the passenger space ratio is a modest 26.8, but deck areas and lounges are spacious and comfortable, and warm-weather cruisers shouldn't have to spend too much time in their rooms.

Anyone sensitive to cigarette smoke may find, as we do, that although the Viking Crown Lounge with its expansive (and unopenable) glass windows offers dramatic sea and sunset views, it also retains the smell of smoke despite the line's zealous attempts to clean and freshen the air.

**Fielding's Five**

### Five Special Spots

1. The cozy Schooner Bar, just the right size on this ship compared to the bigger version aboard the megaliners.

2. The Sun Walk that overlooks the amidships pool deck, which allows you to get in your daily mile or two while checking out the scenic sunbathers below.

3. The 360-degree view from the Viking Crown Lounge, the first one for the line that was wrapped completely around the stack instead of just part of it.

4. The Oriental Terrace and Ambassador Room, two narrower dining ells that branch off the big Madame Butterfly dining room on both port and starboard sides.

5. The Mast Bar on Compass Deck with its 14 barstools that overlook the onboard action.

# INDEX

# Order Your Guide to Travel and Adventure

| Title | Price | Title | Price |
|---|---|---|---|
| Fielding's Alaska Cruises and the Inside Passage | $18.95 | Fielding's London Agenda | $14.95 |
| Fielding's The Amazon | $16.95 | Fielding's Los Angeles | $16.95 |
| Fielding's Asia's Top Dive Sites | $19.95 | Fielding's Malaysia & Singapore | $16.95 |
| Fielding's Australia | $16.95 | Fielding's Mexico | $18.95 |
| Fielding's Bahamas | $16.95 | Fielding's New Orleans Agenda | $16.95 |
| Fielding's Baja | $18.95 | Fielding's New York Agenda | $16.95 |
| Fielding's Bermuda | $16.95 | Fielding's New Zealand | $16.95 |
| Fielding's Borneo | $18.95 | Fielding's Paris Agenda | $14.95 |
| Fielding's Budget Europe | $17.95 | Fielding's Portugal | $16.95 |
| Fielding's Caribbean | $18.95 | Fielding's Paradors, Pousadas and Charming Villages | $18.95 |
| Fielding's Caribbean Cruises | $18.95 | Fielding's Rome Agenda | $14.95 |
| Fielding's Disney World and Orlando | $18.95 | Fielding's San Diego Agenda | $14.95 |
| Fielding's Diving Indonesia | $19.95 | Fielding's Southeast Asia | $18.95 |
| Fielding's Eastern Caribbean | $17.95 | Fielding's Southern Vietnam on 2 Wheels | $15.95 |
| Fielding's England | $17.95 | Fielding's Spain | $18.95 |
| Fielding's Europe | $18.95 | Fielding's Surfing Indonesia | $19.95 |
| Fielding's European Cruises | $18.95 | Fielding's Sydney Agenda | $16.95 |
| Fielding's Far East | $18.95 | Fielding's Thailand, Cambodia, Laos and Myanmar | $18.95 |
| Fielding's France | $18.95 | Fielding's Vacation Places Rated | $19.95 |
| Fielding's Freewheelin' USA | $18.95 | Fielding's Vietnam | $17.95 |
| Fielding's Hawaii | $18.95 | Fielding's Western Caribbean | $18.95 |
| Fielding's Italy | $18.95 | Fielding's The World's Most Dangerous Places | $19.95 |
| Fielding's Kenya | $16.95 | Fielding's Worldwide Cruises | $19.95 |
| Fielding's Las Vegas Agenda | $14.95 | | |

To place an order: call toll-free 1-800-FW-2-GUIDE
(VISA, MasterCard and American Express accepted)
or send your check or money order to:
Fielding Worldwide, Inc., 308 S. Catalina Avenue, Redondo Beach, CA 90277
http://www.fieldingtravel.com
Add $2.00 per book for shipping & handling (sorry, no COD's),
allow 2–6 weeks for delivery

# Favorite People, Places
# & Experiences

| ADDRESS: | NOTES: |
|---|---|

**Name**

**Address**


**Telephone**

**Name**

**Address**


**Telephone**

**Name**

**Address**


**Telephone**

**Name**

**Address**


**Telephone**

**Name**

**Address**


**Telephone**

**Name**

**Address**


**Telephone**

**Name**

**Address**


**Telephone**

# NEW FIELDING WEAR!

Now that you own a Fielding travel guide, you have graduated from being a tourist to full-fledged traveler! Celebrate your elevated position by proudly wearing one of these heavy-duty, all-cotton shirts, selected by our authors for their comfort and durability (and their ability to hide dirt). Choose from three styles—radical "World Tour," politically correct "Do the World Right," and elegant "All-Access."

Important Note: Fielding authors have field-tested these shirts and have found that they can be swapped for much more than their purchase price in free drinks at some of the world's hottest clubs and in-spots. They also make great gifts.

## WORLD TOUR

Hit the hard road with a travel fashion statement for out times. Visit all 35 of Mr. D.P.'s favorite nasty spots (listed on the back), or just look like you're going to. This is the real McCoy, worn by mujahadeen, mercenaries, UN peacekeepers and the authors of Fielding's The World's Most Dangerous Places. Black, XL, heavy-duty 100% cotton. Made in the USA. $18.00.

## DO THE WORLD RIGHT

Start your next adventure wearing Fielding's polically correct "Do the World Right" shirt, complete with freaked-out red globe and blasting white type. A shirt that tells the world that within that high-mileage, overly educated body beats the heart of a true party animal. Only for adrenline junkies, hard-core travelers and seekers of knowledge. Black, XL, heavy-duty 100% cotton. Made in the USA. $18.00.

## ALL ACCESS

Strike terror into the snootiest maitre'd, make concierges cringe, or just use this elegant shirt as the ultimate party invitation. The combination of the understated red Fielding logo embroidered on a jet-black golf shirt will get you into the snobiest embassy party or jumping night spot. An elegant casual shirt for those who travel in style and comfort. Black, XL or L, 100% pre-shrunk cotton, embroidered Fielding Travel Guide logo on front. Made in the U.S.A. $29.00.

Name:

Address:

City:

State:                    Zip:

Telephone:
Shirt Name:
Quantity:

For each shirt add $4 shipping and handling. California residents add $1.50 sales tax. Allow 2 to 4 weeks for delivery.
Send check or money order with your order form to:                    or

Fielding Worldwide, Inc.                    order your shirts by phone,:
308 South Catalina Ave.                    1-800-FW-2-GUIDE
Redondo Beach, CA 90277                    Visa, MC, AMex accepted

# International Conversions

## TEMPERATURE

To convert °F to °C, subtract 32 and divide by 1.8. To convert °C to °F, multiply by 1.8 and add 32.

## WEIGHTS & MEASURES

### LENGTH

| | | |
|---:|:---:|:---|
| 1 km | = | 0.62 miles |
| 1 mile | = | 1.609 km |
| 1 meter | = | 1.2936 yards |
| 1 meter | = | 3.28 feet |
| 1 yard | = | 0.9144 meters |
| 1 yard | = | 3 feet |
| 1 foot | = | 30.48 centimeters |
| 1 centimeter | = | 0.39 inch |
| 1 inch | = | 2.54 centimeters |

### AREA

| | | |
|---:|:---:|:---|
| 1 square km | = | 0.3861 square miles |
| 1 square mile | = | 2.590 square km |
| 1 hectare | = | 2.47 acres |
| 1 acre | = | 0.405 hectare |

### VOLUME

| | | |
|---:|:---:|:---|
| 1 cubic meter | = | 1.307 cubic yards |
| 1 cubic yard | = | 0.765 cubic meter |
| 1 cubic yard | = | 27 cubic feet |
| 1 cubic foot | = | 0.028 cubic meter |
| 1 cubic centi- meter | = | 0.061 cubic inch |
| 1 cubic inch | = | 16.387 cubic centimeters |

### CAPACITY

| | | |
|---:|:---:|:---|
| 1 gallon | = | 3.785 liters |
| 1 quart | = | 0.94635 liters |
| 1 liter | = | 1.057 quarts |
| 1 pint | = | 473 milliliters |
| 1 fluid ounce | = | 29.573 milliliters |

### MASS and WEIGHT

| | | |
|---:|:---:|:---|
| 1 metric ton | = | 1.102 short tons |
| 1 metric ton | = | 1000 kilograms |
| 1 short ton | = | .90718 metric ton |
| 1 long ton | = | 1.016 metric tons |
| 1 long ton | = | 2240 pounds |
| 1 pound | = | 0.4536 kilograms |
| 1 kilogram | = | 2.2046 pounds |
| 1 ounce | = | 28.35 grams |
| 1 gram | = | 0.035 ounce |
| 1 milligram | = | 0.015 grain |

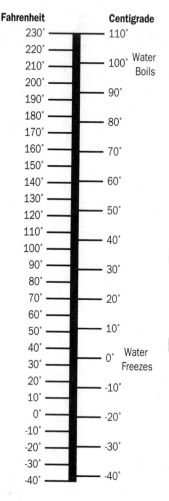

Fahrenheit / Centigrade

- 230° / 110°
- 220°
- 210° / 100° — Water Boils
- 200° / 90°
- 190°
- 180° / 80°
- 170°
- 160° / 70°
- 150°
- 140° / 60°
- 130°
- 120° / 50°
- 110°
- 100° / 40°
- 90° / 30°
- 80°
- 70° / 20°
- 60°
- 50° / 10°
- 40°
- 30° / 0° — Water Freezes
- 20°
- 10° / -10°
- 0°
- -10° / -20°
- -20° / -30°
- -30°
- -40° / -40°